THE NEW CAMBRIDGE HISTORY
OF INDIA

Socio-religious reform movements
in British India

T0312118

THE NEW CAMBRIDGE HISTORY OF INDIA

General editor GORDON JOHNSON

President of Wolfson College, and Director, Centre of South Asian Studies,
University of Cambridge

Associate editors C. A. BAYLY

Vere Harmsworth Professor of Imperial and Naval History,
University of Cambridge, and Fellow of St Catharine's College

and JOHN F. RICHARDS

Professor of History, Duke University

Although the original *Cambridge History of India*, published between 1922 and 1937, did much to formulate a chronology for Indian history and describe the administrative structures of government in India, it has inevitably been overtaken by the mass of new research published over the last fifty years.

Designed to take full account of recent scholarship and changing conceptions of South Asia's historical development, *The New Cambridge History of India* will be published as a series of short, self-contained volumes, each dealing with a separate theme and written by a single person, within an overall four-part structure. Most volumes conclude with a substantial bibliographical essay designed to lead non-specialists further into the literature.

The four parts are as follows:

I The Mughals and their contemporaries

II Indian states and the transition to colonialism

III The Indian Empire and the beginnings of modern society

IV The evolution of contemporary South Asia

A list of individual titles already published and in preparation will be found at the end of the volume.

THE NEW CAMBRIDGE HISTORY OF INDIA

III · 1

Socio-religious reform movements in British India

KENNETH W. JONES

DEPARTMENT OF HISTORY,
KANSAS STATE UNIVERSITY

CAMBRIDGE
UNIVERSITY PRESS

CAMBRIDGE UNIVERSITY PRESS
Cambridge, New York, Melbourne, Madrid, Cape Town, Singapore, São Paulo

Cambridge University Press
The Edinburgh Building, Cambridge CB2 2RU, UK

Published in the United States of America by Cambridge University Press, New York

www.cambridge.org
Information on this title: www.cambridge.org/9780521249867

First published 1989
Reprinted 1997, 2003
This digitally printed first paperback version 2006

A catalogue record for this publication is available from the British Library

Library of Congress Cataloguing in Publication data
Jones, Kenneth W.
Socio-religious reform movements in British India.
(The New Cambridge history of India; III. 1).
Bibliography.
Includes index.
1. India – Religion. 2. Religion and sociology –
India. I. Title. II. Series.
BL2007.5.J65 1989 306′.6′0954 88–30433

ISBN-13 978-0-521-24986-7 hardback
ISBN-10 0-521-24986-4 hardback

ISBN-13 978-0-521-03105-9 paperback
ISBN-10 0-521-03105-2 paperback

To
PROFESSOR WOLFRAM EBERHARD
who introduced me to
the relations between society
and religion

CONTENTS

MAPS

PREFACE

In keeping with the general intent of *The New Cambridge History of India*, this volume explores a single historical subject, that of social and cultural change in the British–Indian Empire as expressed in numerous religious movements. Because of the breadth of this study, which examines investigated religious developments among Christians, Hindus, Muslims, Sikhs, and Zoroastrians, a diverse body of nineteenth and twentieth-century literature in the social sciences and humanities was consulted as well as government reports and unpublished manuscripts. These included sources in English, Hindi, and Urdu. The volume that resulted begins with a chapter that presents a conceptual framework for socio-religious movements. It then examines traditions of religious dissent within western, Perso-Arabic, and Hindu–Buddhist civilizations, traditions that interacted within the South Asian subcontinent and created the basic forms of socio-religious movements in the nineteenth and twentieth centuries. Four regionally defined chapters follow that investigate these movements in the context of place, time, and culture. Next, a single chapter discusses five successful movements in the twentieth century and their role within the context of increasing politicization and competing nationalisms. A final chapter analyses the interaction between the dynamic civilizations of South Asia and the imported British version of western civilization. This volume should provide a basic reference for those who seek to explore social and religious change in modern South Asia. It also contains a new vision of this change and a method of differentiating between what was new in the nineteenth century and what was a modification of long-standing cultural patterns.

Such an approach entails certain sacrifices particularly given the necessity of covering a vast scope within the limits of a single volume. Consequently, this meant that not every socio-religious movement nor every historical event could be included. The decision on what to include or exclude rested on several factors: the existence of information, the relative importance of a given group, and the value in illustrating examples of different forms of dissent. Scholars have just begun to explore the social and religious history of modern South Asia. Yet even today a complete and comprehensive picture would require several volumes rather than just one. This book has two levels of approach: first, it contains a wide-ranging examination of the period and of scholarship as it now exists; secondly, it presents one vision, one set of concepts that provide a manner of viewing socio-religious change. It is, consequently, a source from which students and scholars can initiate further reading or research.

Several individuals and one institution aided in the preparation of this volume. I would like to give particularly warm thanks to Kansas State University, the sole provider of financial support for the research and writing. They made possible several trips to Chicago, a semester sabbatical leave, and yearly research expenses. I also received invaluable assistance from Maureen Patterson and her staff at the University of Chicago Library. She graciously made available to me the card files used in preparation for her monumental bibliography, thus saving me hours of tedious work. I would also like to thank Mark Juergensmeyer and Elleanor Zelliot, who sent me their unpublished manuscripts, and Sheikh Mubarak Ahmad of the American Fazl Mosque in Washington DC, who supplied me with crucial literature on the Ahmadīyah movement. I wish to express my appreciation to the editors of *The New Cambridge History of India*, whose comments and criticism proved extremely useful, and my wife, Marguerite, for a great deal of support, patience, and helpful criticisms. The final results are, of course, my own and so responsibility rests solely with me and not with those who kindly aided in the completion of this study.

NOTE ON TRANSLITERATION

The policy of transliteration in this volume is one of compromise since words rendered into the Roman alphabet are derived from one Semitic language, Arabic, a number of Indo-European languages of north and central South Asia, as well as from the Dravidian languages of the South. No standard transliteration system for such a diverse group of languages exists, nor in most cases is there agreement among linguists as to a single system for a given language. In addition, transliterations in the sources for this volume are often inconsistent and without relation to any linguistic principle. Consequently transliterations are founded on several basic principles. First, diacriticals have been kept to a minimum, with long vowels demarcated as much as possible according to the original language by tracing the word back to the script in which it was written. For languages using the Arabic script or a version of it, such as Persian and Urdu, the *hamza* is indicated with a ' and the letter *'ain* with a '. Some variations in regional languages are not shown in favour of an overall standardization: for example, the common spelling of *guru* in Hindi versus the spelling of *gurū* in Punjabi. In the case of names, which are spelt differently depending on the regional sources, preference is given to the spellings that appear in their place of origin and/or in common use. The same policy is followed in nouns; for example, *ryotwarī* rather than the more accurate *ra'yotwarī*.

At times the transliteration of words into different languages presents almost hopeless difficulties, since the present research is largely based on secondary sources. An excellent example of this problem can be seen in terms from Parsi, terms that originated in ancient Persian, then were written in Gujarati, and finally were put into the Roman script. It is hoped that the present transliterations will enable those who know various languages to recognize the words that appear here, and that those who do not know a South Asian language will be able to gain a more accurate idea of the spelling and pronunciation of these terms.

CHAPTER ONE

CONCEPTS AND CONTEXT

Street preaching is very much in vogue here now-a-days. All along Anarkali, Hindu, Mohamedan, Christian, Arya and Brahmo preachers may be seen earnestly expatiating on the excellences of their respective creeds, surrounded by crowds of apparently attentive listeners.

Lahore *Tribune*, 30 March 1889

THE CONCEPTUAL FRAMEWORK

Professional missionaries, polemical tracts, and new rituals of conversion, were only three of the components of religious innovation in South Asia during the nineteenth and twentieth centuries. Aggressive proselytism became the norm among sects and religions with new and refurbished forms of action, ranging from public debates on the meaning of scriptural sources to the use of printing to produce books, journals, and a multitude of pamphlets. Religious conflict was implicit in the competition for converts, and explicit in assassinations and riots. Sustaining religious pursuits were new organizations fashioned from the traditions of the subcontinent and modified by British culture. South Asians constructed religious societies fully equipped with elected officials, weekly meetings, annual published reports, bank accounts, sophisticated systems of fundraising, annual meetings, executive committees, subcommittees, bye-laws, and constitutions. Religious societies founded and successfully managed a number of organizations including hospitals, schools, orphanages, and relief programmes. Conflict, competition, and institution-building emerged from, and rested on, adherents to diverse ideologies made explicit in speech and writing. For many, religion became a matter of creeds that were explained, defined, and elaborated. It was an age of definition and redefinition initiated by socio-religious movements that swept the subcontinent during the years of British colonial rule.

Before turning to a discussion of the past, it is necessary to consider the concept of 'socio-religious movements' as used here, and its three crucial dimensions. The term 'socio' implies an attempt to reorder

I

society in the areas of social behaviour, custom, structure or control. A movement may have sought to reshape any one of these components or a combination of them. All socio-religious movements demanded changes, ranging from the relatively limited approach of defensive and self-consciously orthodox groups to radicals who articulated a sweeping condemnation of the status quo. The term 'religious' refers to the type of authority used to legitimize a given ideology and its accompanying programme. This authority was based on scriptures that were no longer considered to be properly observed, on a reinterpretation of doctrines, or on scriptural sources arising from the codification of a new religious leader's message. At times different types of authority were combined to legitimize a particular programme. The teachings of an individual, once adopted by his disciples, were standardized, codified and transformed into an ideology, that is, a structured explanation of the present in terms of past events. Such formulae also outlined a path towards the purified future, either for an individual or for society at large. The leader initially, and later the ideology, furnished the vehicle for an individual's participation in a particular movement. Here the term 'movement' refers to an aggregate of individuals united by the message of a charismatic leader or the ideology derived from that message. Such a movement might be loosely organized, especially during the lifetime of its founder, but if it was to last beyond his death, his disciples needed to create and sustain a formal organizational structure. In short, a socio-religious movement advocated modifications in social behaviour, justified such advocacy by one or another form of religious authority, and then built an organizational structure it maintained over time.

This study will focus on socio-religious movements active during the period of British military and political domination. Beginning in 1757 they gradually expanded their hold and by 1849, either directly or indirectly, ruled the entire subcontinent. The experience of those who were conquered and then administered by the English varied sharply, depending on the time and the circumstances that saw them incorporated into the new colonial world. Their reactions were also shaped by the regional culture in which they lived, by their place in the social hierarchy, and by their membership in a particular religious community. The British themselves changed in their attitudes and in their own culture as the eighteenth century gave way to the nineteenth, and the nineteenth to the twentieth. This study will employ the term 'colonial milieu' to indicate areas of time and place where the indigenous civilizations of South Asia came into active contact with British culture. A sphere of military and political control was established first, while the zone of cultural interaction evolved slowly from within the conquered territories. Conquest did not necessarily create the colonial milieu for all individuals or for a given region; that was determined by human interaction, by those who found it expedient or necessary to become part of the new colonial world and the culture which it contained.

The uneven development of a colonial milieu and the persistence of indigenous forms of socio-religious dissent produced two distinct types of movement within the period of British rule, the one 'transitional' and the other 'acculturative'. Transitional movements had their origins in the pre-colonial world and arose from indigenous forms of socio-religious dissent, with little or no influence from the colonial milieu, either because it was not yet established or because it had failed to affect the individuals involved in a particular movement. The clearest determinant of a transitional movement was an absence of anglicized individuals among its leaders and a lack of concern with adjusting its concepts and programmes to the colonial world. Transitional movements linked the pre-colonial period with the era of English political domination and, if successful, over time with the colonial milieu. Once in contact with it, transitional movements made limited adjustments to that environment.

The second of the two types of socio-religious movement, termed 'acculturative', originated within the colonial milieu and was led by individuals who were products of cultural interaction. The founder of such a movement may or may not have been drawn into the world of British culture, but his followers and those who moved into positions of leadership were largely English-educated South Asians influenced by the specific culture of England. Acculturative movements sought an accommodation to the fact of British supremacy, to the colonial milieu that such supremacy had created, and to the personal position of its members within the colonial world. The basis of such movements and many of their declared aims rested on the indigenous heritage of social and religious protest. In no way were acculturative movements totally new or without roots in the general high cultures of South Asia and the specific subcultures of a given region. Thus the difference between the transitional and acculturative movements was primarily at their point of origin.

Because of the importance of regional cultures on socio-religious movements as well as the differing role of the English within the geography of the subcontinent, this study will focus on five geographic areas. The socio-religious movements of a given area must be examined in relation to British influence and political dominance, in terms of the local and regional culture, and according to patterns of interaction between different religious communities. The historic role of socio-religious movements can only be understood within the context in which they originated and functioned.

South Asia has been the scene of an extremely complex pattern of cultural interaction. The indigenous Hindu–Buddhist civilization evolved in semi-isolation. Different cultural groups entered the subcontinent from the North-West and were incorporated into the expanding civilization of South Asia. At the close of the twelfth century and the beginning of the thirteenth, Muslim conquerors swept across north India and by the mid-fourteenth century gained political control of nearly two-thirds of the subcontinent. They carried a new civilization, the Perso-Arabic, that retained its identity in spite of numerous cultural adjustments. Next the British introduced their own version of western civilization as they gained control of South Asia in the eighteenth and nineteenth centuries. By the nineteenth century, three layers of civilization interacted and moulded the socio-religious movements of that century. Each civilization contained its own tradition of protest and dissent that provided the basic past framework for socio-religious movements of the British period.

TRADITIONS OF PROTEST

Within the Eurasian land mass and the islands associated with it, four civilizations evolved, three of which were directly relevant to South Asia.[1] As each civilization matured, patterns of dissent emerged as individuals and groups challenged the established order. Religion

[1] The fourth civilization of the Eurasian land mass, the Sinitic civilization of East Asia, does not fall within the scope of this volume, since it did not have a direct impact on South Asia. It did, however, exhibit a similar pattern of protest, legitimized by religion throughout the 2,000 years of Chinese dynastic history.

played a dual role within each of these three civilizations. In its orthodox forms, it supplied much of the legitimization for the status quo, but
as heterodox sects, foreign religions or orthodox ideals were carried to a
logical extreme, religion furnished sources of authority available to
dissenters. Within the three civilizations were socio-religious movements of protest and dissent. Yet each had its own unique pattern of
relationships between the spheres of religion, politics, society, and
economics that shaped the nature of protest.

Western civilization evolved from a rich heritage of diverse religions
that lay within the Mediterranean and Near Eastern regions. From the
Iranian plateau came Mazdaism with its dualistic struggle between
good and evil; the heretical monotheism of Zurvan and the teachings of
Mani (AD 216–76), whose ideas, in the form of Manichaeism, influenced
both the Roman and post-Roman worlds. A variety of mystery cults
that existed, at times openly and at other times as suppressed under-
ground associations, supplied additional forms of religion. To this
religious complexity Judaism contributed a line of prophets and an
apocalyptic tradition with its millennial promises of a final stage of
human existence when injustice and oppression would be replaced by
an ideal world of peace and divine justice. As Christianity grew from its
Judaic heritage, it elaborated its own messianic concepts and interacted
with the religious heritage of the Mediterranean cultures. Initially,
Christianity was a socio-religious movement of dissent, which attracted those who wished to challenge the norms of society.

During the process of defining Christianity and codifying acceptable
texts as well as doctrine, prophets arose repeatedly with their own
visions of a new world, and were rejected as heretical, as were various
'false' scriptures. As Christianity achieved dominance in the late
Roman world and was brought under control of a single religious
institution, the Roman Catholic Church, dissent continued. Jeffrey B.
Russell noted that prior to AD 700 it remained largely theological and
was led by members of the clergy. This pattern shifted afterwards to
movements of reform and change led by laity and based on moral
themes.[2] These movements were legitimized by one or another religious authority. After the eleventh century, religious dissent and
protest took a violent turn both by those who engaged in it and by the

---

[2] See Jeffrey B. Russell, *Dissent and Reform in the Early Middle Ages* (Berkeley, University
of California Press, 1965), p. 4. Also a useful reference is Norman Cohn, *The Pursuit of the
Millennium* (Fairlawn, New Jersey, Essential Books, 1957).

authorities who used force to suppress them. Religious dissent often attracted dissatisfied and suppressed elements of society who, in the process, challenged the Church with its wealth and power as well as governments to which it was closely allied. From the communal uprising at Cambrai in the eleventh century that responded to the teachings of Ramihrd, to the Bundschuh of the sixteenth century with its vision of an egalitarian future, socio-religious movements appeared, took violent form, and were suppressed. Orthodox Christianity as with other religions, faced challenges from mystics who found authority in their own direct experiencing of God and then developed an ideology to explain and elaborate on their achievements. Tanchelm and his ideological descendants, the Brethren of the Free Spirit, found God within them and so rejected the Church as a hindrance to their search for salvation as they mobilized individuals to reject all religious authority except for their own. The concept of a 'spirit within' remained a permanent part of western civilization and the basis of protest movements.

Concepts and symbols for the opponents of orthodoxy were also available from pre-Christian religions. As Christianity spread northwards through Europe, elements of existing religions were either adopted and included within Christianity or defined as 'Satanic' and forbidden. They did not totally disappear, however, but remained below the surface as vehicles of dissent. From outside the expanding Christian sphere, both ancient and existing religions provided Europeans with sources of symbols and possible legitimization for socio-religious movements. The rise of Freemasonry in the fourteenth century, with its legendary beginning in pre-Islamic Egypt, and its use of Islamic symbols fused with Christian doctrines, exemplifies the pattern of adapting elements from non-Christian religions to give form to protest within western civilization.

The nature of dissent in western civilization was fundamentally changed by the Protestant Reformation, which destroyed the idea of a single religious authority and taught that each individual could make his judgment of religious truth through a study of the scriptures. This ideological position was made feasible through three interrelated developments: the technology of printing, translations of the scriptures into regional languages, and rising rates of literacy. Gutenberg's printing of the Bible in movable type by 1456, and Martin Luther's translation of it into German in 1522, marked the beginning of this

6

revolution. Religiously expressed dissent continued as part of western civilization. There was, however, another crucial development, namely the rise of secular systems of thought in the seventeenth and eighteenth centuries, which supplied non-religious legitimization for protest. By the eighteenth century, Europe exported religious and secular concepts that justified social orthodoxy and social change. The Perso-Arabic civilization, by contrast, based social and political behaviour solely on religious authority.

Perso-Arabic civilization shared many of the same religious roots as western civilization. This similarity was clearly demonstrated with the emergence of Islam. The Prophet Muhammad drew on the Judeo-Christian heritage as well as other religions in the Middle East. In the seventh and eighth centuries, Islam swept over the existing religions and cultures from northern Africa and the Iberian Peninsula in the West, to the edge of Central Asia and India in the East. Islam evolved from the prophetic message of Muhammad as codified in the sacred scriptures, the Qur'an, and the record of Muhammad's words and deeds, the *hadīth*. For the majority of Muslims – the Sunnis – religious authority originated with Muhammad and after his death rested with the Qur'an, the *sunnah* (established practices), *hadīth*, *ijmā* (the consensus of the Muslim community), and *fiqh* (Islamic law as interpreted by generations of legal scholars). Muslims were to follow the *sunnah* until the arrival of the *madhī* (the rightly guided one), who would descend to earth, destroy those who held erroneous beliefs, and establish a period of religious perfection. Thus Islam contained a form of both the messianic vision of an ideal future and prophetic tradition, on the line of prophets from Abraham to Muhammad. Not all Muslims, however, considered Muhammad as the final figure of religious authority.

Those who accepted Shi'ah Islam maintained that special knowledge and power passed from Muhammad to his son-in-law, 'Ali, and to 'Ali's descendants. This concept resulted in a line of *imāms* (living religious leaders), who possessed authority as successors to the Prophet Muhammad. The Shi'ah system of religious leadership led to numerous controversies over who was or was not the proper and legitimate *imām*. More than one line of *imāms* emerged. The Itna 'Ashariyas, a major subdivision of the Shi'ahs, followed a progression of twelve *imāms*, the last of whom disappeared and would reappear some time in the future. By contrast, the Isma'ilis claimed only seven *imāms*.

Sufis or islamic mystics existed both in Sunni and Shi'ite Islam. They contained a rich heritage of asceticism, of religious discipline and theological speculation, centred on religious teachers, *pīrs* and *shaikhs*, and organized into orders, *silsilahs*, or *tarīqahs*, that is paths to truth. As with other forms of mysticism, Sufis sought to experience God directly and in doing so became divided into orthodox and heterodox Muslims, under the leadership of a *pīr* or *shaikh*. *Pīrs* taught a wide variety of religious concepts and practices. When alive they built reputations for sanctity and wisdom, initiated their disciples through *bai'at*, and provided counsel for their followers. After their deaths a *pīr's* tomb often became a place of pilgrimage and worship. The Sufis provided an extensive pool of symbols, organizational structures, and rituals utilized by Islamic movements of return.

The belief in a *madhī* or an *imām* and the practices of the Sufi mendicants created a reservoir of symbols, myths, institutions, and ideas that legitimized protest in terms of religion. Since Islam was a fusion of religion and polity, religious dissent contained a political dimension, as illustrated by the Khawarijites. The earliest of the sectarian Islamic movements was sparked by the controversy that surrounded 'Ali and his claim to be the rightful successor to Muhammad. The puritanical sect, the Khawarijite sect, opposed 'Ali and later the Umayyad state. Expressing an extreme egalitarianism and strict adherence to Islamic principles, they represented a reassertion of nomadic attitudes against what they saw as 'sedentary conformists' who had been unfaithful to Islamic teachings.[3] The Khawarijites were the first of a long line of 'movements of return' that sought to rediscover the period of righteousness and purity that existed during the life of Muhammad and his immediate followers. As in all religions that have at their base a prophetic message, debates continued within Islam as to what constituted proper belief and practice. In the eighteenth century, Muhammad ibn 'Abd al-Wahhab founded a puritanical movement aimed at removing all erroneous innovations within Islam, including the worship of saints, the use of a rosary, and the veneration of shrines. This socio-religious movement was reminiscent of the Khawarijites. Though suppressed by the Ottoman Empire, the Wahhabi movement survived and continued to be influential in the Islamic world.

Not all Islamic sects remained within the limits of their parent

[3] Fazlur Rahman, *Islam*, 2nd edn. (University of Chicago Press, 1979), p. 167.

religion. In the nineteenth century a Persian, 'Ali Muhammad, came into contact with the ultra-Shi'ite doctrines of Shaikh Ahmad ibn Zayn al-Din al-Ahsai. As a result, 'Ali Muhammad declared himself the *madhi* and took the title *Bāb* (the gate). He taught a messianic, egalitarian Islam that rejected the use of a veil for women, circumcision for men, and ritual ablution before prayer. He ordered a variety of other changes and legitimized them by allegorical interpretations of the Qur'an. This new prophet attracted followers from among the disenchanted in Persian society[4] and acquired othodox opponents with the result that 'Ali Muhammad was executed in 1850. After his death his disciple, Baha-Allah, stepped forward as his successor. Baha-Allah and his son, Abbas Effendi 'Abd al-Baha, moved beyond Islam and launched a new religion, Bahaism.

Within the South Asian subcontinent the two imported civilizations interacted with the indigenous Hindu–Buddhist civilization that evolved from an interaction between three cultures: the agricultural and urbanized civilization of the Indus Valley, the nomadic Aryans, who became militarily dominant over the Indus civilization around 1700 to 1500 BC, and the Adivasis, indigenous inhabitants of the subcontinent, many of whom lived at pre-agricultural stages of development. The Aryans contributed their language, Sanskrit, the sacred literature of the Vedas, plus their own deities and rituals. Remnants of the Indus Valley people provided many elements of the later civilization, particularly as the nomadic Aryans began to settle into an agricultural existence. The Adivasis were either incorporated into the expanding civilization or pushed back into the hills and jungles. By 1000 BC, urban life began to re-emerge after the fall of the Indus cities and with them came a rise of small city states. The process of political consolidation gained speed in the next few centuries. Small kingdoms became larger until the establishment of a subcontinental state, the Mauryan Empire, *c.* 322–183 BC. During these years of rapid social, economic, and political change the older ways of life and much of religion as it then existed were no longer compatible with the reality of urbanization and political growth.

In the texts of the Upanishads, eighth to fourth centuries BC, there appeared a trend toward indirect criticism of the existing sacrificial religion with its expensive and elaborate rituals conducted by Brahman

[4] Philip K. Hitti, *The Near East in History: A 5000 Year Story* (Princeton, New Jersey, D. Van Nostrand Co., 1961), p. 404.

priests. The Upanishadic thinkers, Brahmans, who had left the ordinary world of religious practice, pursued immortality as a final answer to the problems of life, death, and rebirth. For them sacrificial rituals produced only transitory gains, and were thus useless. They did not directly attack orthodoxy, but brushed it aside in a search for more lasting solutions to life's problems. These renegade Brahmans did not found socio-religious movements. Theirs was an elite doctrine for the chosen few. The Upanishads, however, marked the beginning of a long tradition of criticism and religious dissent, through which those who rejected established norms of society could find expression.

In the sixth and fifth centuries BC a number of socio-religious movements appeared; two of these, Jainism and Buddhism, began as Hindu cults, and eventually became separate religions. Both disagreed sharply with existing orthodoxy. They rejected the authority of the Vedas, the use of sacrifices, and the role of Brahman priests. As movements preaching new doctrines, they used the vernaculars rather than Sanskrit, were open to all social classes, including women as well as men, and discarded the current social distinctions. Both of these religious movements found support among a variety of classes: the ruling elite, merchants, artisans, and those at the bottom of the social structure. Buddhism and Jainism spread first throughout the Gangetic Plain, then southwards, finally to the peninsular world of the Dravidians.

The four centuries, from roughly the second century BC to the second century AD, remain unclear as to the pattern of historical developments, especially in northern India. By the sixth to seventh centuries AD, however, a new type of Hinduism appeared with the rise of *bhakti* (devotionalism), with a highly emotional and personal focus on a single deity. There is considerable scholarly debate as to whether the roots of *bhakti* were in the northern cults of Pancharatras, Bhagavatas, and Pashupatas, or in the Dravidian South. Not open to question, however, was the beginning of a wave of *bhakti* movements in the Tamil area of peninsular India during the sixth to seventh centuries AD.

For centuries south India had been penetrated by northern culture with its emphasis on Brahmanical rituals, priestly superiority, the sanctity of the Vedas, and the use of Sanskrit in ceremonies and rituals. This influence, however, did not extinguish Dravidian culture, which reasserted itself with the rise of the new devotionalism. Poet-saints flourished who expressed themselves in Tamil and later in other languages of the South. They came from all social classes including the lowest and most disadvantaged. For the exponents of *bhakti*, devotion and faith were all that truly mattered. God, in his mercy, would release them from rebirth and the misery of life, if only the devotees were true to their faith. Caste, rituals, and priests were all irrelevant. The devotees could, and occasionally did, leave their normal social roles and responsibilities to concentrate on worship. In the process social control was lost and dissent made a reality.

The early radicalism of *bhakti* slowly declined. Devotional hymns were collected, standardized, and brought within the sphere of orthodoxy. The Hindu saint, Ramanuja (d. AD 1137?), argued successfully that *bhakti* could be considered one more path to release from rebirth. He accepted both the caste system and the authority of orthodoxy. As a Tamil Brahman, Ramanuja incorporated *bhakti* into orthodox Hinduism and brought non-Brahmans into greater prominence within that orthodoxy. His compromise also muted the earlier radical dissent of the Vaishnavite devotees. A similar process took place among the poet-saints of Lord Shiva. In time the Shaivite *bhakti* hymns were codified and given a sophisticated system of philosophy to create the Shaiva Siddhanta form of orthodox Hinduism. Two schools of thought emerged in Shaiva Siddhanta, one based on Sanskritic literature as interpreted by Brahmans and the other, using Tamil texts, expounded largely by upper-caste non-Brahmans. Thus the social and cultural radicalism of southern *bhakti* was drawn into a broadened orthodox Hinduism becoming one more acceptable path to release from the cycle of rebirth.

One socio-religious movement in southern India, Virashaivism, stands out for its radical ideas and its institutional success. Founded by Basava (?1125–70), this movement centred on the worship of Shiva. It was an aggressive, proselytizing, and uncompromising sect that rejected Vedic authority, the role of priests, caste distinctions, and the rite of cremation, favouring burial instead. The Virashaivas also attempted to restructure the place of women in society. They considered men and women equal; allowed widows to remarry; condemned child marriage and arranged marriage, and no longer classed women as polluted during their menses. Their strict moral code included vegetarianism and a ban on the use of liquor and drugs. The Virashaivas entered into competition with the Jains, Buddhists, and orthodox Hindus. In order to maintain their separate communal identity and to replace the Brahmans, they created their own priests, and founded a number of monasteries as focuses of religious authority. This system is still maintained today, as is a sense of separateness among the Virashaivas.

The wave of devotionalism moved northwards as poet-saints became active throughout the Deccan, then in the Gangetic plain, Bengal, and the North-West. *Bhakti* saints wrote in the vernacular languages and thus extended Hinduism to all levels of society. The arrival of devotional Hinduism in the North followed a fundamental change in the political–religious structure, as Islam, with the values and attitudes of the Perso-Arabic civilization, entered the subcontinent. The years AD 1192–1206 witnessed the conquest of the North from the borders of the Mid-East to Bengal with pockets of Hindu resistance in Rajasthan and the Himalayan foothills. During the fourteenth century the Muslim ruling elite pushed south into the Deccan, gaining control over roughly two-thirds of the subcontinent.

Islam arrived in its various forms: Sunni, Shi'ah, and Sufi. At the orthodox level, Islam and Hinduism clashed, since they expounded almost diametrically opposed doctrines. At the popular and mystical levels, however, it was possible for the two religions to interact. The popular Islamic reverence for saints, miracles, and religious healing, as well as the institution of wandering Sufi mendicants, were compatible with Hindu practices. Also, the more fundamental concepts of monotheism, egalitarianism, and the rejection of idolatry, paralleled many of the teachings found among Hindu followers of *bhakti*. Devotionalism and the movements of protest that it often sustained coexisted within the context of the indigenous and the new-conquest civilization with its own tradition of dissent.

A powerful mixture of social criticism and devotion grew from the teachings of Ramananda (1360–1470). He was a Sri Vaishnava leader, fifth in the line of succession after Ramanuja. Ramananda taught an egalitarian devotionalism focused on Rama, used simple Hindi as his language, and accepted disciples from all segments of society. Ramananda's teachings spread throughout the northern plains and were carried forward by his disciples, often in more radical forms than his own. Kabir (1440–1518), a weaver, possibly a Muslim by birth, became a disciple of Ramananda. Kabir taught a strict monotheism, arguing that each devotee should seek God directly and that he could do so without becoming a mendicant and abandoning his family. Kabir rejected both orthodoxies, Hindu and Islamic, as well as all forms of caste. His doctrines enjoyed broad appeal among peasants, artisans, and untouchables. This was a sustained attack on the established order; one that envisioned a new egalitarian society.

A similar message was proclaimed by Guru Nanak (1469–1539), a householder and a clerk for the provincial Punjab government. Guru Nanak created a quietist movement that rejected priestly Hinduism, its rituals, idols, and basic authority. He also taught equality. Nanak was followed by a succession of nine *gurus*. The Sikhs, as his followers came to be known, created their own scripture, the Granth Sāhib written in Punjabi, using the Gurmukhi script. They developed new life-cycle ceremonies conducted by their own members, thus gradually cutting their ties with Hinduism. Beginning as a quietist sect, the Sikhs evolved into a structured socio-religious movement and finally a separate religion.

The tradition of dissenting *bhakti* initiated by Ramananda persisted throughout the North. Dadu (1544–1603), a disciple of Kabir, marked the emergence of the next generation in this line of *bhakti*. He was a mystic who preached egalitarian ideas, rejected rituals, priests, pilgrimages, and temples, calling for all to worship Brahma as a deity without form (*nirguna*). His adherents, the Dadupanthis, were strongest among the lower castes of Rajasthan. Malukdas (1574–1682) continued Ramanandi devotionalism as did Charan Das of Delhi (1703–82). Some *bhakti* leaders attempted to draw upon both religions thus creating a bridge between them. The Damis, founded by Pran Nath in the seventeenth century, used excerpts from the Qur'an and the Vedas to express their ideas. Similarly Bab Lal, also of the seventeenth century, turned to the Vedanta of the Hindus and to Sufi writings from Islam as inspiration for his own ideology.

By contrast, two very successful *bhakti* movements demonstrate that devotionalism was not inevitably associated with dissent. In Bengal, Chaitanya (1486–1533) taught an intensely passionate worship of Lord Krishna, which utilized music, singing and dancing as its major modes of expression. As with many devotional sects, it was open to all, even Muslims. Chaitanya prohibited animal sacrifice, permitted widow remarriage, and preached a strict moral code, but his main approach to orthodoxy was to ignore it. Devotion to Krishna was all that mattered. His disciples used both Bengali and Sanskrit in their literature, a compromise position to begin with and one that saw them soon incorporated into Hindu orthodoxy. Similar to and contemporaneous with Chaitanya's movement was the one founded by Vallabhacharya (1479–

1531). It soon became popular in Gujarat and the surrounding areas. Vallabhacharya focused on Krishna and the erotic interaction between Krishna and the *gopīs* (milk maids). This was a devotional movement of passion, joy, and religious exaltation. It raised no issues of social or religious revolt and was orthodox from the beginning. *Bhakti*, then, cannot be equated with dissent and protest; it was instead a source of ideas and institutions that could legitimize the condemnation or the maintenance of established society.

With the evolution of Hindu–Buddhist civilization, the introduction of Perso-Arabic and western civilizations, religion played a dual role. It sustained and justified the established social order while also providing an instrument for challenges to that order. Repeatedly socio-religious movements arose which called for the creation of an egalitarian society, rejected the role of priests and the rituals they conducted, turned against the worship of idols, and promoted the concept of monotheism. Such movements often attempted to redefine the role of women, granting them equality that included marriage customs, the right to education and, at times, relief from the restrictions of ritual pollution. It is against this background that we must attempt to understand the socio-religious movements that flourished during the years of British political rule and within the context of three interacting civilizations.

CHAPTER TWO

BENGAL AND NORTH-EASTERN INDIA

THE SETTING

The first region under consideration is Bengal and its adjoining territory of Assam in the North-East. Bengal proper is a huge delta built up
by the combined river systems of the Ganges and the Brahmaputra.
Bengal and its environs are ringed by mountains in the North and East,
by the bay to the South, the hills of Orissa and Chota Nagpur to the
South-West, and Bihar to the West. Divided by numerous rivers and
consisting of swampy land with abundant rainfall, Bengal was developed late in the history of South Asia and remained at the edge of
Hindu–Buddhist civilization. Eastern Bengal, Assam, and the hill tracts
bordering Burma marked the end of one major civilization and the
beginning of the South-East Asia cultural sphere.

The incorporation of Bengal into the expanding culture of north
India brought with it Sanskrit, Hinduism, and the caste structure.
Brahman priests ascended to the foremost position in society, but never
with the same degree of dominance as in the central Gangetic Plain or in
south India. The Kshatriya (warrior) and Vaishya (merchant) castes
were absent. Instead two smaller groups, the Kayasthas, a writer-clerk
caste, and the Baidyas, once physicians and later landlords, marked the
next levels below the Brahmans. Thus the mass of Bengalis were classed
as Sudras or peasants; beneath them were the untouchables. Within this
region Buddhism and, to a lesser degree, Jainism provided a long-
standing challenge to Hinduism. In the surrounding hill tracts, the high
civilization of the valleys and the delta faded away. Many of the tribes
within the jungles and highlands had their own languages, deities, social
structures, and tribal culture.

In the first decade of the thirteenth century, the Hindu–Buddhist
world of Bengal was significantly altered by Islamic conquerors. The
establishment of Muslim rule cut ties of political influence and economic support between Hinduism and the state. Over the centuries
Islam also changed the socio–religious composition of Bengal through
conversion. Eastern Bengal became heavily Muslim, so much so that by

1 Bengal and north-eastern India

the nineteenth century they constituted a majority of the population. Hindus resided throughout Bengal in smaller percentages to the East and larger in the West. The creation of a Bengali Muslim population was concentrated at two ends of the socio-economic spectrum, a small elite, urban-based, and composed mostly of a ruling class who conquered and then governed this region and, through conversion, a peasant–untouchable class, illiterate, uneducated, rural and poor. A middle section was missing. Consequently, between the ruling elite and the mass existed numerous Hindu groups who staffed the governmental administration and conducted most of the economic functions of the province.

Changes in society brought about by Islamic conquest were mirrored by a new linguistic complexity. Sanskrit remained the sacred language of Hinduism, but lost its association with government. Persian and Urdu became languages of administration, while Arabic was limited to Islamic scholars, and Sanskrit to the Hindu priests. Bengali, in one or another dialectical form, constituted the language of the peasants, both Hindu and Muslim. Its popularity increased with devotional movements, since the elite languages were useless in communicating with the wider Bengali community regardless of religious affiliation.

The arrival of the British as merchants of the East India Company had a restricted impact, but after the battles of Plassy (1757) and Buxar (1764), the English gained military control and formed a new government. The Muslim ruling elite was pushed aside and replaced by Englishmen. This process took time, but with the establishment of the Indian Civil Service by Lord Cornwallis (1786–93), all senior administrative positions were restricted to Englishmen. Ascendancy of British law and later the English language accompanied the creation of a new administration. At a stage when their administration was still relatively crude, the British reordered Bengal's socio-economic system. In 1793, they announced the Permanent Settlement, regulations that defined a diverse group of individuals ranging from petty chiefs to hereditary tax-collectors as absolute owners of land. Private property as known in the West had not existed in South Asia where the major issue was over shares in the productivity of land, not to land itself. Traditional landed rights disappeared as peasants became tenants in the western sense of the word. The government restricted its interest in landowners to the collection of an annual tax. Thus by the end of the eighteenth century

and the beginning of the nineteenth, British administration had redefined landed wealth and its ownership. They also excluded all 'natives'
from senior governmental positions, were they Hindu or Muslim. This
latter step affected the Muslim elite and, in time, a new Hindu group,
but for the majority of Bengalis it was issues relating to land and
productivity that remained the most relevant.

A TRANSITIONAL MOVEMENT AMONG
BENGALI MUSLIMS

The Fara'izis

Socio-religious movements among Bengali Muslims drew upon the
dynamics of that society for their motivation, but the concepts, symbols, and intellectual framework for such movements came from Indian
Islamic thought as centred on Delhi and from the Sa'udi Arabian cities
of Mecca and Medina. These were the two main sources, although ideas
might occasionally reach Bengal from other centres of Islam. The
Mughal Emperor, Akbar (1556–1605), adopted a policy of accommodation with the Hindu nobility. This approach was successful in establishing the Empire, but alienated many orthodox Islamic leaders.
Under Akbar, the state could no longer be depended on to enforce
Islamic law and practice. Akbar's actions stimulated a counter trend of
protest and movements of return. One of the ablest exponents of
Islamic fundamentalism, Shaikh Ahmad Sirhindi (1564–1624), called
for a strict adherence to the *shari'at*, the Islamic code of behaviour, and
opposed popular customs that appeared to be heresies adopted from
the surrounding sea of Hinduism. Sirhindi's teachings gained acceptance as the Mughal Empire moved away from the policies of Akbar and
towards the official orthodoxy of the Emperor Aurangzeb (1659–1707).

With the disintegration of the Mughal Empire in the eighteenth
century, a new and more severe crisis struck Indian Muslims. Shah Wali
'Ullah of Delhi (1703–63) linked the decline of Muslim power and
morality to ignorance that resulted in an inability to comprehend the
true nature of Islam. He advocated an education focused on the
Qur'an and *hadith* that would enable Muslims to regain their past
status, to bring an end to the internal struggles between differing
Muslim groups, and purge their faith of non-Muslim customs. Thus he
shared many of the same aims and goals of al-Wahhab, but was less

radical and less uncompromising in his approach. Wali 'Ullah wanted
to extinguish conflict among Indian Muslims, since communal unity
was needed to restore Islam politically and spiritually to its proper
pre-eminence. To this end, Shah Wali 'Ullah translated the Qur'an
into Persian, a language more widely known than Arabic among his
fellow Muslims. This act was bitterly opposed by orthodox leaders, but
one of his sons, Shah 'Abdul Qadir, went one step further by trans-
lating the Qur'an into idiomatic Urdu. The teachings of Shah Wali
'Ullah and the Delhi School of Islamic thought plus the doctrines of
al-Wahhab of Sa'udi Arabia constituted a basic frame of reference for
socio-religious movements among South Asian Muslims, as exemplified by the Fara'izis of Bengal.

Shari'at 'Ullah, the founder of the Fara'izis, was born in 1781 in
the village of Shmail in eastern Bengal. He received his elementary
education in Calcutta and Hughly. In 1799, at the age of eighteen,
Shari'at 'Ullah left for Mecca. The first two years he studied under an
emigrant Bengali, Maulana Murad, and for the next fourteen years
became the student of the Hanafi scholar, Tahir Sombal. Shari'at
'Ullah was also initiated into the Qadiriyah order of Sufism during
this period. In addition he spent two years at al-Azhar University in
Cairo. When he returned to Bengal in 1818 as a scholar of Islamic law
and philosophy,[1] he began preaching, but soon returned to Mecca,
where he obtained the formal permission of his teacher to initiate his
own religious campaign. After returning to Bengal, probably in 1820 or
early 1821, he quickly attracted adherents among the peasants of eastern Bengal.

Shari'at 'Ullah's message was one of religious purification. He was
deeply shocked by improper beliefs and behaviour popular among
Bengali Muslims. He called for a return to *fara'iz* (the obligatory
duties of Islam), specifically the 'profession of faith (*kalimah*), attending daily prayers (salat or namaz), fasting in Ramadan (*sawm* or *rozah*),
paying the poor tax (*zakat*) and pilgrimage to Mecca (*hajj*)'. Along with
these rites Shari'at 'Ullah stressed the principle of *tawhīd* (monotheism). Deviations from the original message of Muhammad were the
products of either *bid'ah* (sinful innovations), or *shirk* (polytheistic
religious beliefs). In practical terms Shari 'at 'Ullah condemned the

[1] Mu'in-ud-din Ahmad Khan, *History of the Fara'idi Movement in Bengal, 1818–1906*
(Karachi, Asiatic Society of Pakistan, 1965), pp. 2–3. This is the most authoritative study of
the Fara'izis available today and will be used here extensively. If other sources are utilized,
they will be indicated by a footnote.

worship conducted at the shrines of various Islamic saints, rituals connected with the birth of a child or with circumcision, and the intense wailing at ceremonies to honour the Shi'ah heroes, al-Hasan and al-Husain. Some of these rituals were blamed on Hindu influence either retained by converts to Islam, or simply accepted by uneducated Muslims copying customs from the non-Muslim community.

The scripturalist fundamentalism of Shari'at 'Ullah won acceptance primarily among peasants in eastern Bengal. In order to effectively reach this audience the Fara'izi leaders preached in Bengali and used that language in their initiation ceremony rather than Persian, Arabic or Urdu. They introduced a distinct pattern of dress that distinguished members of their movement from the rest of their community. Militant, united, and composed mainly of illiterate peasants and artisans, the Fara'izis soon faced opponents as they penetrated the eastern Bengali districts of Dacca, Faridpur, Jessore, and Badkarganj.

To begin with, Fara'izis directly challenged the orthodox or Sadiqi Muslims who wished to maintain the practice of Islam as it was then. The Sadiqis were mainly descendants of the Muslims who had entered Bengal after the conquest. Many of them were members of the landlord class, a group seen by the Fara'izis as economic, as well as ideological enemies. Hinduism was also an opponent, a fountain of polytheism and evil innovations. Once more economics heightened religious tensions, since the majority of landlords in eastern Bengal were Hindus. As early as 1831, Barasat had become the centre of Fara'izi-led disturbances against the power of local landlords. Indigo factories were burnt and peasants refused to pay rents to Hindu landlords because they often demanded illegal payments.[2] Muslim peasants resisted for religious as well as economic reasons. Hindu landlords collected money for ceremonies such as Durga Puja, the annual celebration of a Hindu goddess. Shari'at 'Ullah urged his followers to reject such demands and they did. Throughout the 1830s conflict flared between the Fara'izis and their landlords with each side blaming the other, as the religious movement slowly became enmeshed in economic and political issues. This trend toward rural conflict continued after the death of Shari'at 'Ullah in 1840 when his son, Dudu Miyan, succeeded him as head of the community.

Born in 1819 under the name Mushin al-Din Ahmad, but known as

---

[2] Blair B. Kling, *The Blue Mutiny: Indigo Disturbances of 1859–1862* (Philadelphia, University of Pennsylvania Press, 1966), p. 68.

Dudu Miyan, he was the only son of Shari'at 'Ullah. Dudu Miyan was educated by his father and then at the age of twelve was sent to Mecca for further studies. He never achieved the levels of scholarship attained by his father, but Dudu Miyan quickly proved himself an energetic leader; able to create an effective organizational structure for the Fara'izis in their struggles with opposing movements and the landlord–planter class of Bengal. At first he organized his followers along two lines of authority: the *siyāsī*, which focused on political issues, and the *dīnī* concerned with religion. He later fused them into a single hierarchy. Dudu Miyan held the position as supreme leader or *ustād*. Under him served three levels of officials: the *uparast khalifāh*, the superintendent *khalifāh*, and a *goān khalifāh* or village-level leader. Each official was in charge of a circle of decreasing size, with the village officials responsible for a cluster of 300 to 500 families. These officers were charged with organizing village courts to replace the governmental legal system and raising volunteer fighters to defend their community when needed.

Unlike his father, Dudu Miyan entered the world of politics and economics with a direct challenge to the status quo. He proclaimed that all land belonged to God and that the land tax was thus both illegal and immoral.[3] This declaration was extremely popular among Muslim peasants, but completely unacceptable to landlords, indigo planters, and the police. Serious clashes took place in 1841 and 1842, and as a result Dudu Miyan and forty-eight of his followers were arrested, tried, and convicted. The case proceeded slowly through various stages of appeal and finally in 1847 the conviction was set aside by the High Court in Calcutta. This was a dramatic victory for the Fara'izis, one that greatly increased their prestige and also brought about a decade of peace between them and the landlords. The outbreak of fighting in 1857 prompted the British to arrest and imprison Dudu Miyan. He was released in 1859, rearrested, and finally freed in 1860. By this time he was seriously ill and died while staying in Dacca in 1862. The death of Dudu Miyan created a void which was not quickly filled. His eldest son, Ghiyath al-Din, was chosen to replace him in 1864, but died later that same year. The second son, 'Abd al-Ghafur, known as Naya Miyan, followed his elder brother; however, since he was still too young for effective control, three lieutenants became his guardians and

[3] Tauriq Ahmad Nizami, *Muslim Political Thought and Activity in India During the First Half of the 19th Century* (Aligarh, Three Mens Publications, 1969), pp. 83–4.

supervised the movement until sometime in the 1870s when Naya Miyan assumed active leadership of the community.

Naya Miyan was born in 1852. Educated at first by his father, after the arrest of Dudu Miyan he studied under a tutor. The picture of Naya Miyan's youth is sketchy. Apparently he did not travel to Arabia but received his entire education in Bengal. In 1874, under his leadership, struggles with the landlords reached a crucial turning point. Tenant farmers demanded written leases that would legalize their occupancy rights to the land. The landlords refused to issue such leases and also demanded the payment of a cess, considered illegal by the tenants. The Fara'izis were deeply involved in this struggle. They furnished much of the leadership and manpower behind peasant resistance. Open conflict lasted until 1879 when the peasants won with the aid of a sympathetic British official, thus beginning a period of cooperation with the government that lasted into the twentieth century.[4]

After his death, in 1884, Naya Miyan was replaced by his youngest brother, Sa'id al-Din Ahmad (1855–1906). Under his leadership the Fara'izis survived primarily as a religious movement without significant economic and political goals. Their amiable relations with the British were recognized in 1899 when the government granted Sa'id al-Din the title of Khān Bahādur. A group of Fara'izis separated from the parent organization as a protest against closer ties with the British, thus generating the first schism within this extremely stable movement. Nonetheless the Fara'izis had succeeded in redefining Islamic belief and practice among many of the Muslim peasants of eastern Bengal. Its overall impact, however, must be seen in terms of competitive and complementary groups active within the same area and with the same constituency.

An Islamic leader, Sayyid Ahmad Barelwi, launched a revivalist movement, the Tariqah-i-Muhammadiyah, that preached both a return to past purity and an open struggle, a *jihād*, with non-Muslims. He had interpreted the *fatwa* of 'Abdul 'Aziz as declaring British India *dār ul-harb* (the house of war), that is a territory ruled by non-Muslims, and one that pious Muslims must oppose as a sacred duty.[5] By the late 1820s one of Sayyid Ahmad Barelwi's disciples, Titu Mir (1782–1831),

[4] Kalyan Kumar Sengupta, 'Agrarian disturbances in 19th century rural Bengal', *Indian Economic and Social History Review*, 8, no. 2 (June 1971), pp. 201–2, 204–5.
[5] For a more detailed examination of the career of Sayyid Ahmad of Barelwi and the Tariqah-i-Muhammadiyah, see chapter 4.

began preaching in rural western Bengal. He expounded a fundamentalist doctrine that condemned elements of popular Islam as errors, called upon his followers to practise equality among their coreligionists, and to adopt a unique form of dress as an outward sign of their religious commitment. He opposed Hinduism and the landlord class. Titu Mir quickly won supporters among the peasants. His movement, however, ended in 1831 when he and his followers rose against the government. They briefly controlled three districts, but were subdued by British troops. In 1832, another disciple of Sayyid Ahmad, 'Inayat 'Ali, arrived in Bengal. He began touring the rural areas and expounded to the Muslim peasants a purified Islamic creed. 'Inayat 'Ali travelled until 1840 and settled in the district of Jessore. Within four years another disciple reached Bengal.

In 1835 Mawlana Karamat 'Ali moved to Bengal, where he remained an effective proponent of Islam until his death in 1873. Karamat 'Ali sailed the rivers of Bengal and Assam for nearly forty years in a flotilla 'which constituted a travelling-cum-residential college'.[6] His Ta'aiyuni movement taught a purified Islam shared by the Tariqah-i-Muhammadiyah and other nineteenth-century Islamic movements. There were, however, deep and at times bitter points of divergence between Karamat 'Ali and the Fara'izis. This was first demonstrated when he met with Shari'at 'Ullah in 1836–7. Differences between the two became public in 1839 at Barisal, the scene of a debate between Karamat 'Ali and the Fara'izis. The primary point of disagreement lay over whether or not congregational prayers could be legally held on Fridays and on the annual 'Id festivals. Below this rested the question of whether British India should be classed as *dār ul-harb* or *dār ul-Islām* (the house of Islam), where Muslims could and should practise their religious rituals. Both the Tariqah-i-Muhammadiyah and the Fara'izis adopted the former interpretation, and based it on the *fatwa* of 'Abdul-'Aziz. Karamat 'Ali, however, rejected this view. Thus for the Ta'aiyunis these prayers were proper and even required. Although the two movements shared basic points of theology, such as an acceptance of the Hanafi school of law, a rejection of polytheism and erroneous innovations, and an emphasis on puritanical Islam, the question of prayers remained an acrimonious point of difference between them.

  [6] Abdus Subhan, 'Social and religious reform movements in the nineteenth century among the Muslims – a Bengali reaction to the Wahhabi movement' in S. P. Sen (ed.), *Social and Religious Reform Movements* (Calcutta, Institute of Historical Studies, 1979), p. 487.

These two movements clashed repeatedly. Tracts defending each position were published as this controversy came to symbolize respective dogmas. In general, the Ta'aiyunis were more moderate than the Fara'izis or the Tariqah-i-Muhammadiyah. Karamat 'Ali, himself a Shi'ah, accepted the *pir-muridi* system of religious teachers and their disciples rejected by other movements, although he labelled as illegitimate the *'urs* or annual death anniversary rites of famous *pirs*. During the second half of the nineteenth century, public disputes between sectarian movements became commonplace among Bengali Muslims. Not all Islamic movements publicly disagreed. The Ahl-i-Hadith, another descendant of the Tariqah-i-Muhammadiyah, entered Bengal. It too practised Jum'ah and 'Id prayers, but there is little indication of conflict between it and the Fara'izis. Internal Muslim discord was moderated in the twentieth century by a strengthened sense of communal unity.

The proponents of a purified Islam and the socio-religious movements they created produced serious changes among Bengali Muslims, particularly in the rural areas. The sense of communal identity, of being a Muslim, was clarified and made explicit. All aspects of Muslim belief and life were discussed by popular tracts, *nasihat namahs*, written in Bengali. This literature was intended to instruct ordinary Muslims in the basic tenets of Islam. It also described the proper life for all Muslims. The creation of widespread religious literature in Bengali inspired Muhammad Naimuddin's translation of the Qur'an into that language completed in the years 1892–1908. Public religious debates popularized the basic concepts of Islam and became occasions of social mobilization and social integration as well.[7]

The Fara'izis, Ta'aiyunis, Ahl-i-Hadith, and Tariqah-i-Muhammadiyah were all transitional movements of return led by members of the *'ulama* (theologians) who drew their followers primarily from the peasant classes, expressed their ideas through the vehicle of Bengali, and their inspiration from both Delhi and Sa'udi Arabia. In their search for a purified religion the Fara'izis and allied movements attempted to purge Islam of what they considered errors that stemmed from ignorance, superstition or implied borrowing from Hinduism. This search led them into opposition with the established orthodoxy of

---

[7] Rafiuddin Ahmed, 'Islamization in nineteenth century Bengal' in Gopal Krishna (ed.), *Contributions to South Asian Studies*, no. 1 (Delhi, Oxford University Press, 1979), p. 105.

the Sadiqi Muslims. In the case of the Fara'izis and the followers of Titu Mir, they linked religious issues with economics with the result that both groups clashed with Hindu landlords and the British government. Titu Mir's followers were suppressed, but the Fara'izis accepted the presence of the British and were accepted by them. These movements mobilized and Islamized Bengali Muslims, thus strengthening their communal identity and their separation from Bengali Hindus. The socio-religious movements of the Bengali Hindus by contrast emerged from the colonial milieu after it was established in Bengal.

THE CREATION OF THE COLONIAL MILIEU

From the early seventeenth through the mid-eighteenth centuries, extremely limited forms of cultural interaction had existed between the English merchants and South Asian society. During this period power rested with Indian governments and consequently there was little incentive to learn from an alien western civilization. Initially the British found themselves one state among many, but by 1818 they had become militarily dominant throughout the subcontinent. During this process of conquest Indians sank from undisputed rulers to the status of 'natives', a conquered and subjugated people. This reordering of relationships created one of the most important dimensions to the overall context within which all social, religious, and cultural change took place; another was the fundamental needs of government perceived by the English as they themselves were transformed from merchants into bureaucrats and administrators.

During the governorship of Warren Hastings (1772–85), as the British began to accept their new role as rulers, policies and attitudes became apparent that dictated the outlines of cultural interaction within the emerging colonial milieu. The English of this period did not exhibit the sense of racial and cultural superiority so characteristic of the nineteenth century. For many, particularly Hastings and those senior officials who surrounded him, it was an era of excitement and discovery as they examined the civilization now under their control. With minds influenced by European classicism, the British turned to a study of Indian languages, literature, religion, and social structure. Underlying this scholarship was the assumption that English rule would be transitory, lasting only until the indigenous culture had reclaimed its former pinnacle of achievement. English scholar-officials spoke of a 'golden age' of antiquity and contrasted this with contemporary decay. British scholarship and governance had as its task and justification the restoration of Indian civilization to its past purity. Thus the 'Orientalist' was born, a non-Indian scholar who explained and ordered the culture of South Asia.

Hastings supported 'Orientalism' personally and through governmental policy. As the new rulers established an administrative structure, they needed an expanding number of trained officials, both English and Indian. Under Hastings senior appointments were reserved for Englishmen who 'demonstrated linguistic proficiency, a deep understanding of India and a sense of benevolent responsibility in regard to the Indian people'.[8] In 1781, he founded the Calcutta Madrassah as a school for Muslim officials of the East India Company. The language of instruction at this school was Persian, the court language of the Bengal government and the Mughal Empire. Thus the British attempted to rule through the languages already in use by government and through their own version of European classicism, but they could not ignore the regional language. By the 1770s, it became necessary to reproduce government documents in Bengali, which was achieved after Robert B. Wray succeeded in casting Bengali type in 1778.

In 1800, the Orientalist dream of an acculturated and linguistically proficient administrator found its concrete expression with the establishment of Ft. William College. Lord Wellesley (1798–1805) created this 'Oxford of the East' to train civil servants. Scholars at the College translated ancient texts, wrote grammars, compiled dictionaries, and collected a library of manuscripts. With the expansion of British territory, the vernacular languages became increasingly important. A knowledge of Sanskrit or Persian was of little use to a district official who had to communicate with the society around him. This need for command of the vernaculars led the government to seek aid from missionaries resident in the Danish enclave of Serampore. East India Company policy had forbidden missionaries from residing within Company territory. Because of this ban three Englishmen, W. Carey, J. Marshman and W. Ward, lived at Serampore. As Baptist missionaries they focused their attention on the vernaculars in order to reach, and

---

[8] David Kopf, *Orientalism and the Bengal Renaissance: The Dynamics of Indian Modernization, 1773–1835* (Berkeley, University of California Press, 1969), p. 222.

possibly convert, the ordinary Indian. By 1805 they could print works in Bengali, Urdu, Oriya, Tamil, Telugu, Kanarese, and Marathi. In this first decade of the nineteenth century various individuals and organizations produced literature in both classical and vernacular languages. The shift of emphasis from classical to vernacular languages was followed by an increasing demand for the use of English as the language of administration and education.

The question of which language should become the instrument of government and education was debated during the first three decades of the nineteenth century between the Orientalists and the 'Anglicists', who maintained that English was preferable to a revival of the classical languages and to the use of the vernaculars at the higher levels of education and administration. This debate was concluded in the 1830s under dramatically different circumstances from those of the later eighteenth century. By 1818–19, the British had annexed vast tracts of land with a variety of vernacular languages. Administration of this enlarged Empire could not be conducted solely in the vernaculars, but needed a single-link language understood by the ruling elite. The decision was already made by Lord Cornwallis when he created the Indian Civil Service and restricted it to Englishmen. His action produced a uniform governing elite that used its own language. With the growth of bureaucracy the area of English language usage also expanded. Thus the British in India followed a pattern similar to other colonial powers who ruled through their own language.

In 1813, with the twenty-year renewal of the East India Company Charter, two decisions were taken which affected both language and culture. The long-standing ban on missionaries was removed, allowing for a rapid penetration of Christian missionary organizations into Company territory. Also imbedded within the new Charter was an annual £10,000 expenditure of government funds for education. As a result, the different aims of the Orientalists and Anglicizers sparked a formal debate as to what kind of education, English or classical Indian, should be funded. During the governor-generalship of Lord William Bentinck (1828–35) this controversy was formally settled. In 1835, Thomas Babington Macaulay's Minute on Education deprecated the use of South Asian languages and the study of Indian knowledge as useless. It was the duty of the British-Indian government to finance an education that was English in content and language. Macaulay envisioned the creation of a class that would act as a link between rulers and ruled, as well as be a source of inexpensive manpower for the lower levels of the administration. Even before this debate was concluded, the transfer to English was well under way. In 1826 the government gave preference in junior law appointments to Indians with 'suitable English certificates'.[9] Consequently a knowledge of English became the key to government service and to careers in a number of allied fields, such as law, medicine, teaching, business, and journalism – all forms of employment that brought individuals into regular contact with the new rulers.

Indian response to new opportunities created by the British was determined largely by their place in pre-British society. At the height of the Orientalist period, scholars of Sanskrit, Arabic, Persian, and of South Asian learning were hired by such institutions as Ft. William College. With the shift to English education those castes that were already literate supplied the students of this new language; in practice this meant primarily Bengali Hindus of the Brahman, Baidya, and Kayastha castes. In previous generations individuals from these groups mastered Persian to gain employment under the Mughal and post-Empire Muslim rulers. Now they learned English.

By the second decade of the nineteenth century, a new anglicized elite began to create institutions to serve its own interests. In 1816, they founded the Hindu College. Instruction in this school included elements of both the Orientalist concern for classical languages and the Anglicizers' desire to impart English education. Nearly half the student body studied western subjects and the English language even though they were not required to do so. In the following year, through the joint efforts of Indians and Englishmen, the Calcutta Book Society was established to provide inexpensive textbooks for elementary schools. The society also encouraged the creation of new elementary schools. The sole aim of the Calcutta School Society founded in 1818 was to promote education beyond that initiated by the government. In 1824 they launched the Sanskrit College, an institution that also taught English and western science. Expansion of educational facilities proceeded at a steady pace. In 1829, Gour Mohan Addy opened the Oriental Seminary, a Hindu-supported school that taught English language and literature, western mathematics, and sciences. Unlike

[9] Sufia Ahmed, *Muslim Community in Bengal, 1884–1912* (Dacca, Oxford University Press, 1974), p. 7.

some of the earlier schools, the Oriental Seminary was open to all castes. A third source of English education sponsored by the missionaries reached a new degree of effectiveness and notoriety when Alexander Duff inaugurated his school in Calcutta. Duff offered a free English education for anyone who wished to attend.

Acceptance of English education lay primarily among a small group of Indians clustered in Calcutta. They exhibited a variety of responses to English ideas, customs, and the implications of western civilization. Conservatives such as Radhakanta Deb, Rasamoy Dutta, and Ramkanal Sen, who were all leaders in the Hindu Dharma Sabha, accepted the necessity of learning English, but attempted to limit the incorporation of foreign culture within Hindu society.[10] Opposed to them were cultural radicals who rejected Hindu social norms in favour of English culture and the secular rationalism imported from Europe. These young radicals were led by a Eurasian, Henry Louis Vivian Derozio (1809–31). Brilliant, an impressive speaker, a poet and teacher, Derozio was appointed instructor of English literature at the Hindu College in 1826. Within two years his ardent disciples had begun publishing an English-language weekly, the *Parthenon*, which viciously attacked Hindu religion and society. An intense clash ensued between radical and conservative Hindus who, in the spring of 1831, succeeded in forcing Derozio to resign his post at the Hindu College. He retained his influence among students after his resignation, but died later that year at the age of twenty-two.

The distance between Radhakanta Deb and Henry Derozio marked the differences between a minimal acceptance of the new culture and a maximal one. The radicals enthusiastically embraced all that was English – language, ideas, and customs such as beef-eating and hairstyles. Hindu conservatives, by contrast, wanted the practical advantages afforded by a command of English, but were willing to make only those changes in customary behaviour needed to work with the new rulers. They defended the status quo from the external criticisms of the Christian missionaries and the internal attacks of Hindu radicals. For those who lived and worked within the sphere of this new power and its accompanying culture, that is, within the colonial milieu, they had no choice but to examine a set of questions that affected their lives.

[10] Salahuddin A. F. Ahmed, *Social Ideas and Social Change in Bengal, 1818–1835* (Leiden, E. J. Brill, 1965), p. 166.

These queries ranged from the fundamentals of religious belief to the practical aspects of daily living as was shown by the first socio-religious movement that arose within the colonial milieu of Bengal.

ACCULTURATIVE MOVEMENTS AMONG BENGALI HINDUS

The Brahmo Samaj

The unfolding of Hindu acculturative movements began with the career of a Bengali Brahman, Rammohun Roy (1772–1833). He was born into a world of diverse cultural influences. His father's family followed Chaitanya, and his mother was a worshipper of divine female power. Professionally the Roys had served under Muslim rulers and so were among the Persianized members of the Hindu elite. This tie to non-Hindu government gave them a somewhat lowered status, as they were not counted among the purest of the Brahmanical community. Roy learned Bengali as his mother tongue, but also studied Persian in preparation for future employment and Sanskrit as befitted his priestly rank.[11] Young Roy questioned orthodox beliefs, and consequently came into conflict with his parents. The year after his father's death in 1803, Roy published his religious views in a Persian tract, *Tohfat al-Muwahhiddīn* (A Gift to Deists, 1804), making public his criticisms of idolatry and polytheism. Roy had already entered the world of private banking and from there he was drawn into the colonial milieu, for his clients included several English officers. He began to learn English and spent nine years working for the East India Company. He retired in 1814 and afterwards turned his energies to issues of social custom and religious belief.

The most dramatic question of Roy's varied career, and one that concerned him for the remainder of his life, was the rite of *satī*, the immolation of Hindu widows on their husbands' funeral pyre. *Satī* was not practised widely throughout the Hindu community, but it was strong among the higher castes in Bengal. Roy had been deeply upset, when one of his female relatives committed *satī*. In 1818, he published *A Conference Between an Advocate for and an Opponent Of the*

---

[11] Several accounts state that Rammohun Roy was sent to Patna for training in Arabic and Persian, and then to Benares for study in Sanskrit. There is, however, no conclusive evidence on these points. See *ibid.*, pp. 33–4.

Practice of Burning Widows Alive. Roy cited scriptural sources to justify his contention that *satī* was not required by Hindu law and was instead an erroneous accretion; an example of degenerate Hinduism. Orthodox Hindus were appalled by his condemnation of what they considered a proper and necessary ritual. Englishmen, particularly Christian missionaries, joined in this debate calling for a government ban on *satī*. Finally in 1829, after much hesitation, the British-Indian government outlawed *satī*. The law was challenged by orthodox Hindus and placed before the Privy Council for final decision. Roy travelled to England to give evidence in this case and also before Parliamentary hearings on the proposed Reform Act. It was on this trip that he died and was buried in England. *Satī* as an issue led Roy into the general question of women's rights, particularly the need for women's education. The other major role of his thinking revolved around the delineation of proper Hindu belief.

Roy's adherence to theism and his rejection of idolatry, Brahman priests, and their rituals, sketched the basic outlines of his reconstructed Hinduism; for, to him, God and his existence were proven by the complexity of reality. Rather like European rationalists, Roy envisioned God as the 'almighty superintendent of the universe'.[12] This rational and highly ethical vision of Hinduism had been lost over the centuries through the unfortunate influence of Brahman priests. Roy would return Hinduism to its past purity. Once proper belief was re-established, erroneous customs such as *satī*, the debarring of women from education, elaborate and useless rituals, idolatry and polytheism would disappear. Roy based his vision of interpretation of Hinduism on the Vedas, Upanishads, and the Vedanta-Sutra. His own writings elaborated on the validity of these texts and the revised Hinduism they justified. With this approach he transformed the 'sins' of Hinduism into mere errors caused by ignorance.[13] He also attempted to legitimize his arguments on the basis of reason and social utility. For Roy, religion could not be judged solely on its own internal scriptural evidence, but it

---

[12] D. H. Killingley, 'Vedant and modernity' in C. H. Philips and Mary D. Wainwright (eds.), *Indian Society and the Beginnings of Modernization c. 1830–1850* (London, School of Oriental and African Studies, 1976), p. 132.

[13] John Morearty, 'The two-edged word: the treacherousness of symbolic transformation: Rammohun Roy, Debendranath, Vivekananda and "The Indian Golden Age" in Warren Gunderson (ed.), *Studies on Bengal* (East Lansing, Michigan, Asian Studies Center, Michigan State University, 1976), p. 89.

must also be measured by reason and shown to be free of contradiction and functioning to uphold a beneficial social order.[14]

Rammohun Roy substituted scriptures for priests as the sources of proper knowledge. This doctrine stimulated the translations of the Upanishads and of the Vedanta-Sutras into the vernacular languages as well as into English. It also meant an increased use of printing to make these texts and his own writings available to all who might wish to read them. This ended the prohibition against any but the first three *varnas* from reading the most sacred of Hindu literature. Now women, peasants, untouchables, and non-Hindus could read and study the sacred scriptures. In 1821, while struggling with the Serampore missionaries, Roy established his first journal, the bilingual *Brahmmunical Magazine*, to broadcast his opinions to a literate audience. Soon a number of individuals and associations had their own journals, tracts, and translations. Religious debates were conducted in public by anyone who wished to do so. Although orthodox leaders complained about Roy's arrogance in assuming he could define proper Hindu belief and custom, they had no alternative but to meet him in the new arena of public religious disputation.

Roy rejected missionary claims to superiority by pointing out that Christianity too was laced with superstition and error. If its absurdities were removed what remained was a 'simple code of religion and morality . . . so admirably calculated to elevate men's ideas to high and liberal notions of one God'.[15] He had the greatest respect for ethical Christianity; however, it was in no way superior to ethical Hinduism. Thus Roy pursued equivalence as the basic relationship between the two religions.

Hindu orthodoxy expressed its opposition to Roy's condemnation of contemporary religion through the Hindu Dharma Sabha founded in 1830. Yet this was not an organization of strictly orthodox pundits. Most of those involved in the Sabha were closely connected with the English government, and in order to achieve their goals they borrowed the organizational techniques of the West as well as the new technology of printing. The programme of the Dharma Sabha was aimed at limiting the intrusion of English culture. For them, Roy appeared as going too

[14] James N. Pankratz, 'Rammohun Roy' in Robert D. Baird (ed.), *Religion in Modern India* (New Delhi, Manohar, 1981), pp. 165–7, 172.
[15] J. N. Farquhar, *Modern Religious Movements in India* (New York, Macmillan Company, 1919), p. 32.

far in his willingness to change Hinduism and demonstrated too great an acceptance of Christian concepts.

Roy first attempted to establish an organizational base for his ideas when in 1815 he founded the Atmiya Sabha (Friendly Association). This was a private society that held weekly meetings at his residence. Members recited Hindu scriptures, sang hymns, and held discussions on religions and social issues.[16] The society ceased meeting sometime in 1819. Nine years later Roy organized the Brahmo Sabha that met for the first time on 20 August 1828. The Sabha gathered every Saturday evening from seven o'clock to nine o'clock. The service consisted of selections from the Upanishads first chanted in Sanskrit and then translated into Bengali, a sermon in Bengali and the singing of theistic hymns. Anyone who wished to could attend, but those who did were almost all Bengali Brahmans. At this time there was no membership, no creed, and no formal organization.

On 23 January 1830, the Sabha began its tenure in a new building erected by Roy and his supporters. A Trust Deed filed by Roy provided a sketchy statement of principles for the Sabha. It included a reaffirmation of egalitarianism, Roy's concept of the deity, 'the Eternal Unsearchable and Immutable Being who is the Author and Preserver of the Universe',[17] a prohibition of all forms of idolatry and sacrifice, and a ban on criticism of other religious beliefs and practices. Roy did not elaborate on these principles. In November 1830 he left for England, and after his death in 1833 the young Brahma Sabha faded almost to extinction.

Rammohun Roy's organization was revived by Debendranath Tagore (1817–1905), whose family were also Brahmans who had worked for the Muslim rulers of Bengal, and became associated with the British, and wealthy landowners as a result of the Permanent Settlement. Tagore experienced a religious crisis in 1838 and the following year formed the Tattvabodhini Sabha (Truth-Teaching Association), a society that held weekly religious discussions and monthly worship. He and his new organization accepted Vedanta, as had Roy, but in contrast emphasized the superiority of Hinduism. Tagore struggled with missionaries in general and Alexander Duff in particular.[18] In 1840, the

---

[16] *Ibid.*, p. 31; Ahmed, *Social Ideas and Social Change*, p. 35.
[17] Farquhar, *Modern Religious Movements*, p. 35.
[18] Warren M. Gunderson, 'The fate of religion in modern India: the cases of Rammohun Roy and Debendranath Tagore' in Gunderson, *Studies on Bengal*, p. 136.

Tattvabodhini School was established to counter Duff's own institution. Tagore began publication of the *Tattvabodhīnī Patrikā* in 1843, a newspaper that quickly became a forum for religious discussions and an outspoken critic of the missionaries. As a result Tagore gained a major voice in the propagation of theistic Hinduism. In spite of his success with the Tattvabodhini Sabha, he decided to revive the Brahmo Sabha.

Debendranath Tagore and a number of his friends joined the Brahmo Sabha in 1842, but it was a year later that he began to restore the Sabha by bringing to it a degree of structure and ideological coherence. He wrote the *Brahma Covenant*, a creedal statement that listed the basic obligations of membership and changed the name to the Brahmo Samaj. On 21 December 1843, he took an oath to accept the Covenant along with twenty of his friends. In 1850, he released a volume of scriptures, the *Brahma Dharma*, for use in public and private worship. Finally in 1861, Tagore revised the Hindu life-cycle rituals, giving them a particular Brahmo form; however, he did not deviate significantly from the Hindu sacraments already in existence.

Under Tagore's leadership and through the dynamism introduced by a new generation of Bengali youths, the Brahmo Samaj began to expand out of Calcutta into the cities of eastern Bengal. In 1846, a branch of the Samaj was opened in Dacca and during the next two decades the Brahmos continued to spread throughout the East. During the 1850s and 1860s young Bengalis were attracted to the Brahmo Samaj. They brought with them a restlessness, a sharp rejection of their parents' values, and a militancy not found among the older Brahmos. One man, Keshab Chandra Sen, stood out among these young disciples. Sen (1838–84) was born into a respectable Vaishnavite family of the Baidya caste. He received an English education and worked for the Bank of Bengal. By 1857, he had joined the Brahmo Samaj and by 1859 became an active worker. He was an impressive speaker who soon grew into an outstanding spokesman among the younger members of the Samaj and a close associate of Debendranath Tagore.

In 1860, Sen founded the Sangat Sabhas (Believer's Associations). These were small discussion groups that met weekly, but his energetic disciples soon showed a preference for action rather than talk. Their militancy led them to abandon caste and the sacred thread, to practise temperance, and work for the equality of women. Their desire to combine belief and action emerged from the study of Hindu and

Christian writings. Sen's disciples increased during the 1860s, bringing with them a drive for social radicalism and a growing missionary programme throughout Bengal. There was also a widening gulf between the younger and older members of the Samaj.

In 1862 Sen and his followers secretly celebrated an intercaste marriage, but in 1864 they sponsored an intercaste marriage that was also a widow remarriage, and did so publicly. The more conservative Brahmos were shocked and orthodoxy horrified.[19] Two years later Sen embarked on a grand tour of Madras and Bombay where he disseminated Brahmo ideology to members of the English-educated elite in these two major cities. His success as a dynamic leader brought the Samaj to new heights of expansion, and also to the edge of internal conflict. On 5 October 1864, the Samaj building was damaged by a cyclone and weekly meetings were shifted to the Tagore residence. Debendranath Tagore allowed those conducting the services to wear their sacred threads. Sen objected and in 1865 withdrew with his section of the Samaj. This division along generational and ideological lines was formalized on 15 November 1866, when Sen organized the Brahmo Samaj of India. Those loyal to Tagore grouped themselves into the Adi (original) Brahmo Samaj.[20]

The Adi Samaj depended on Tagore's leadership and reflected his own values. He saw the Samaj as strictly a religious organization defined by ritual and theology. He had little or no interest in social reform and devoted much of his attention to the defence of Hinduism from missionary criticisms. With its conservative orientation, the Adi Samaj objected to the proposed Brahmo Marriage Act of 1872, for it illustrated one of their constant fears, namely that they might be estranged from the community of Hindus. Concerned with defending Hinduism and remaining within it, the Adi Samaj drifted back towards contemporary Hinduism, becoming a small sect dependent on the person of Debendranath Tagore and comprised heavily of his close friends and relatives. With his death in 1905 the effective role of the Adi Brahmo Samaj came to an end.

Keshab Chandra Sen emerged from the break with Tagore as a dramatic leader who appealed to young Bengali Hindus in revolt

---

[19] Pradip Sinha, *Nineteenth Century Bengal, Aspects of Social History* (Calcutta, Firma K. L. Mukhopadhyay, 1965), p. 121.

[20] For a background on the split, see Sivanatha Sastri, *History of the Brahmo Samaj* (2 vols., Calcutta, R. Chatterjee, 1911), vol. 1, pp. 151–2, 158–60; also David Kopf, *The Brahmo Samaj and the Shaping of the Modern Indian Mind* (Princeton University Press, 1979), p. 229.

against contemporary religion. During the 1860s and 1870s a stream of recruits, often fleeing their families and their own excommunication, flowed towards Calcutta. Under Sen's tutelage, the Samaj won converts primarily from the villages and towns of eastern Bengal. The Brahmos also generated religious conflict between themselves and Hindu orthodoxy. By 1868, sixty-five Samaj branches were operating in the eastern section of the province; almost all of them allied to Keshab's movement. The Brahmo Samaj of India had by then twenty-four missionaries who were organized two years later into the Sri Durbar, an 'apostolic body of elders and teachers'.[21] They were effective in convincing villagers who had not been influenced by English education or urban values. As a group they followed the example of Bijoy Krishna Goswami, a Brahmo who stressed the religious nature of the Samaj and provided a dramatically different model of living from Sen with his love of ostentation and ceremony. As a result there gradually came into existence a division within the Samaj between religious ascetics and the majority who used their rationality and emancipation to live a more materially successful life. In 1870, Sen left for England where he toured, lectured, and met Queen Victoria. On his return, he demonstrated an increased interest in social action intended to restructure the society and customs of Bengal. He organized the Indian Reform Association with the intent of improving the life of the peasants and to reach them he published a journal, *Sulābh Samāchār*, written in simple Bengali prose. As a result a new faction coalesced around those members most enthusiastically dedicated to social action.

By 1872, Sen's organization had expanded throughout much of the subcontinent. Branches of the Samaj extended through Bihar, the United Provinces, and had reached as far as the Punjab. The Samaj also penetrated Assam, Orissa, Madhya Pradesh, and possessed limited influence in the South and West. Of the 101 Samajes that existed by 1872, the vast number were located in Bengal, and those founded elsewhere largely rested on communities of Bengalis who had travelled outside of their province to find employment.

In the early 1870s the Samaj was rocked by controversy over a legislative proposal, the Brahmo Marriage Act, passed in 1872. The law legalized Brahmo marriages, but did so by declaring that Brahmos were

---

[21] Kopf, *The Brahmo Samaj*, p. 229.

not Hindus and so were not subject to Hindu law. The social radicals had fought for this since it provided both a civil marriage freed from Hindu rituals, as well as a legalization of intercaste marriages. The controversy generated by the marriage bill was accompanied by other points of conflict, as radicals attempted to introduce further changes in the role of women. One such radical, Durga Mohun, proposed that women be allowed to sit with their relatives during services at the Brahmo temple. Sen argued against this and, following this debate, turned away from his advocacy of social change. After 1875 he demonstrated a new interest in strictly religious issues by organizing a seminar to study different religions and their prophets. Here he found Brahmos from the ascetic faction who gladly joined in this project.

By 1875–6, Keshab Chandra Sen had begun to focus on a new type of Brahmoism that contained elements of ecstatic religious experience and *shaktism* (the worship of female power). He met Ramakrishna Paramahansa, a Bengali mystic who may have furthered his involvement in devotional worship. So the rift deepened between Sen, who had drawn closer to the ascetics within the Samaj, and the social activists. This polarization led to a disagreement over the role of Sen as leader of the Samaj. His critics demanded the creation of a constitution and some degree of representation by members of the Samaj. Tensions erupted in February 1878 when he announced the marriage of his daughter to the Maharaja of Cuch Bihar. This marriage violated the Brahmo Marriage Act because of her youth and the proposed use of idolatrous ritual. On 15 May 1878, the Sadharan Brahmo Samaj was founded by Brahmos who rejected Sen's leadership.

Sen continued to move in the direction of *bhakti* and of a universalistic religious ideology. In February 1880, he called upon his supporters to create a religious revival and underscored his message by leading a procession through the streets of Calcutta. Equipped with flags, musical instruments and singing hymns, Sen and his disciples marched in the fashion of Chaitanya's devotional Vaishnavism. Sen's ideas moved towards an attempt to synthesize the world's religions, blending elements of different faiths into a single set of rituals and beliefs. In January 1881, he founded the Nava Vidhan (New Dispensation) symbolized by a red banner bearing the name of his church plus the Hindu trident, the Christian cross, and the Islamic crescent. Two months later he introduced the Christian Eucharist, substituting rice and water for bread and wine. As part of his efforts a newspaper, called the *New Dispensation*, appeared in March 1881, and in 1884 a new code, the *Nava Samhitā*, replaced the existing *Brahma Dharma*. Keshab Chandra Sen died later in 1884 and the movement quickly broke under the impact of factionalism. The future of the Brahmo Samaj rested instead with the Sadharan Samaj. It inherited the majority of branch *samājes* within and beyond Bengal. It also continued a programme of social action and rationalistic religion.

The Sadharan Samaj maintained its weekly Sunday services, the Brahmo Young Men's Union, the Sanghat Sabhas, and Sevak Mandala (Service Society). In 1891, it opened the Das Ashram, a welfare institution for untouchables, and the Brahmo Girls School of Calcutta. Throughout the last two decades of the nineteenth century, it founded small hospitals, orphanages, a leper asylum, offered legal aid to oppressed women, and began a mission movement among the Khasi hill tribes. The Sadharan Samaj allied with the movement of Verasalingam, a Telugu reformer, in Andhra, with groups in Bangalore, and also continued to expand in Bengal.[22] Protap Chandra Majumdar, a leader of the Brahmo Samaj, carried the ideas of the Sadharan Samaj to England and America in 1874, 1884, and again in 1893 at the Chicago World Parliament of Religions. In spite of its missionary efforts, the Sadharan Brahmo Samaj remained a relatively small elite organization.

The Brahmo Samaj, an acculturative movement among Bengali Hindus, was led by members of the English-educated elite and supported by them. It originated within the colonial environment of Calcutta and flowed out to other cities, then towns, following a line of Bengali emigrants north-west to the Punjab. It was carried to the South and West as well by Brahmos leaders. The acculturated ideology of Brahmoism with its reinterpreted Hinduism, western organizational forms of a voluntary religious association with congregational meetings, society officers, missionaries, a creed, printed literature and bank accounts, also reached to the far South and to the west coast through the travels of its leaders. There societies of the Samaj were founded or the Samaj was imitated by local members of the educated Anglicized elites. Thus the Brahmos provided a new Hinduism and a model of religious organization to others within the colonial milieu. Their own movement split into three different directions, the Adi Samaj back towards the parent religion, the New Dispensation towards a cult centred on the

[22] *Ibid.*, p. 330.

person of Keshab Chandra Sen and focusing on elements of the *bhakti* past, and the Sadharan Samaj that held to the original teachings of Rammohun Roy. Beginning in the 1880s, educated Bengalis moved away from Brahmo ideology and the social programme it attempted to implement. The Sadharan Brahmo Samaj continued to function in the twentieth century, but new trends of thought, both religious and secular, appealed to young men who were once attracted to Brahmoism.

Bijoy Krishna Goswami and the Vaishnavite revival

The religious career of Bijoy Krishna illustrates the interaction between pre-British culture and the new world of the colonial milieu. Bijoy was born on 2 August 1841 in Santipur, a village in eastern Bengal. His family worked as hereditary priests of the Chaitanya sect. They were deeply religious, orthodox, and unaffected by western culture or the new education. As a child Bijoy shared in this religiosity. He was devoted to the idol of Krishna and would fall into ecstatic trances. The young Brahman studied a traditional curriculum in the local elementary and high school. Yet there was a restlessness and questioning in the young Brahman. He felt uncomfortable in his expected role as a priest and *guru* with the result that he left home in 1859 to attend the Sanskrit College in Calcutta.[23] Here as a poor student he met Debendranath Tagore who gave him financial aid and drew him into the Brahmo Samaj. Tagore became his religious preceptor and also funded his study at the Calcutta Medical College.[24]

Exposed to western ideas and the Samaj, Bijoy intensified his questioning of Hindu institutions and beliefs. By 1860 he began attending the Brahmo services and enthusiastically entered this movement to the point of abandoning his sacred thread, an act that led to a break with his family and to his being excommunicated by his caste brotherhood. Bijoy participated in the Sangat Sabha in 1861 and its theological discussions. He accepted the leadership of Keshab Chandra Sen and became a successful Brahmo missionary. Bijoy, however, was uneasy in his Brahmoism. He clashed with Tagore in 1864 over the latter's attempt to reinstate the sacred thread and in 1866 he followed Sen into the newly founded Brahmo Samaj of India. Two years later Bijoy

[23] Alexander Lipski, 'Vijay Krsna Goswami: reformer and traditionalist', *Journal of Indian History*, 52, no. 1 (1974), pp. 209, 213; Kopf, *The Brahmo Samaj*, p. 220. Lipski's article is the standard source for this section; if others are used they will be cited.
[24] Kopf, *The Brahmo Samaj*, p. 219.

criticized Sen for 'avatarism', a concept that arose from Sen's insistence that he was the 'Saviour' of Hinduism.[25] Bijoy's partial disillusionment with the Samaj led him to study the *Chaitanya Caritāmrita*, a biography of the great *bhakti* saint, under the guidance of Harimohun Pramanil. Bijoy visited various Vaishnava *gurus* but did not break with the Samaj. Instead in 1869 he returned to his work as a Brahmo missionary, yet Bijoy increasingly blended devotional Vaishnavism as taught by Chaitanya with his own concept of Brahmoism.

Bijoy made eastern Bengal his own special sphere, winning new disciples from that area. In 1872 he organized the Bharat Ashram, where advanced devotees lived together while searching for spiritual enlightenment. Three years later he met Swami Ramakrishna Paramahansa whose influence stirred Bijoy to reconsider his view on monotheism, the role of *gurus*, and the worship of the goddess Kali. Still, he did not leave Brahmoism, although he did abandon Sen and join the newly founded Sadharan Samaj. Bijoy, however, remained unsatisfied with Brahmo ideology and with its leaders, particularly Sivanath Shastri and Ananda Mohan Bose. After searching for a *guru* able to satisfy his spiritual quest, Bijoy met Brahmananda Paramahansa, a Punjabi Brahman, who initiated him into *sanyās*, the formal stage of a renunciant, under the name of Swami Hariharananda Saraswati. Bijoy left his concern for social service for the study of yogas and *bhakti*, as he returned to worshipping the idols of Radha, Krishna, and Durga. He, too, became a *guru* and accepted his own disciples. His Brahmo colleagues reacted adversely to Bijoy's new religious style and launched an investigation of him on 17 May 1886. As a result Bijoy left the Sadharan Samaj and from 1888–97 he lived in Dacca at his own *āshram*. Bijoy became a minister in the east Bengal Brahmo Samaj, an organization that was independent of the other Brahmo Samajes, but in 1889 he finally broke completely with the Brahmo movement and began his career as a spokesman of revived Vaishnavism. In 1890, he visited Brindaban and Mathura and four years later travelled to Allahabad for the festival of Kumba Mela. In March 1897, he left Bengal for Puri where he died even as his religious hero, Chaitanya, had done centuries before.

Bijoy Krishna Goswami's life had been a circular pilgrimage from his orthodox Vaishnavism through the Brahmo Samajes of Tagore, Sen and

---

[25] *Ibid.*, p. 221.

the Sadharans, returning finally to the devotional Vaishnavism of Chaitanya. In the process he did not found a single structured movement, but he did inspire a revival of Vaishnavism through his disciples such as Bipan Chandra Pal and the religious literature they produced. Pal was an English-educated Brahman who joined the Brahmo Samaj, but after a visit to the United States became disillusioned with the West and the Samaj. In 1895, Bijoy Krishna initiated Pal as his own disciple.[26] This drift away from Brahmo ideals toward a revival of orthodox Vaishnava *bhakti* paralleled Keshab Chandra Sen's own path as well as the rise of nationalism and the emergence of another socio-religious movement that combined defence of Hinduism, social service, and a restructuring of ancient monasticism.

The Ramakrishna Math and Mission

The history of this acculturative socio-religious movement began with the birth of Gadadhar Chatterji on 18 February 1836, in the Hughli district of Bengal. He was born into an orthodox but poor Brahman family. During his youth, Gadadhar demonstrated both a restlessness and a fascination with religion. He received no formal education but found employment at the newly established Dakshineshwar Temple located just outside Calcutta. Gadadhar served as one of the priests who conducted the worship of Kali, the divine goddess. The young Gadadhar began to withdraw from his ritual duties, and devoted his time instead to meditation. He would sink into states of apparent unconsciousness and occasionally burst forth into extreme religious ecstasy. In 1859, Gadadhar's relatives attempted to turn him away from his preoccupation with personal religion by arranging his marriage. This strategy failed to change the young man's behaviour. Gadadhar abandoned his priestly duties and instead proceeded with his search for a direct, mystical union with God.

During the 1860s he studied with a Bhairavi Brahmani, a wandering female ascetic who instructed him in the Tantras, then with a north Indian Vaishnava mystic, and finally with Tota Puri, a devotee of Shankaracharya. Tota Puri initiated Gadadhar into *sanyās*, and gave him the name Ramakrishna. He next turned to an exploration of religions other than Hinduism. Ramakrishna studied Sufism and played the role of a Muslim in his dress, prayers, and total behaviour.

[26] Alexander Lipski, 'Bipanchandra Pal and reform Hinduism', *History of Religion*, 11, no. 2 (Nov. 1971), p. 229; also Farquhar, *Modern Religious Movements*, pp. 294–5.

Using similar techniques, he explored Christianity with the result that he had visions of both Christ and the Madonna. Ramakrishna acted out other roles such as Radha, the wife of Lord Krishna. In this instance he dressed and behaved as a Hindu woman. By 1871, Ramakrishna appears to have achieved a degree of inner peace. His young wife, Sarada Devi, joined him and in 1872 he worshipped her as the Divine Mother, transforming their marriage into a spiritual partnership.[27]

By the early 1870s, Ramakrishna was beginning to attract a small group of disciples, mainly young men, who found in him a nurturant, non-judgmental teacher. Many of them came from the growing number of English-educated. He provided a refuge from the strains, both cultural and psychological, generated from this educational experience. The disciples gathered, Ramakrishna talked, and occasionally they raised questions or spoke of their own doubts and needs. Ramakrishna did not teach a structured set of ideas. Two themes, however, ran through his discussions, the universality of all religions – all were true and led to God, and a corresponding logical conclusion that beliefs and rituals of Hinduism should be preserved. If all religions were true there existed no reason for criticism or conversion.[28] The teachings of Ramakrishna were popularized by Keshab Chandra Sen after 1875 when the two met for the first time. In 1882 one of the disciples, Mahendranath Gupta, began to record his teacher's conversations and continued to do this until Ramakrishna's death in 1886.

While Mahendranath prepared a written record of Ramakrishna's teachings, another disciple, Narendranath Datta, arrived. Narendranath was born on 12 January 1863. His father was a successful lawyer who saw to it that his son received an English education. The young Narendranath graduated from the Mission College in Calcutta and then began to study law. Like many of his generation, he was attracted to and joined the Sadharan Brahmo Samaj, but in 1882 Narendranath met Ramakrishna. The holy man was far more drawn to the student than vice versa, but after the deaths of Keshab Chandra Sen and of Narendranath's father in the early months of 1884, the bond between Ramakrishna and his new disciple grew much stronger. Narendranath's indecision as to whether to accept or reject this new *guru* finally

[27] Farquhar, *Modern Religious Movements*, pp. 188–94; Swami Gambhirananda, *History of the Ramakrishna Math and Mission* (Calcutta, Advaita Ashrama, 1957), pp. 8–12.
[28] Leo Schneiderman, 'Ramakrishna: personality and social factors in the growth of a religious movement', *Journal for the Scientific Study of Religion* 8 (Spring, 1969), 62–8.

ended in June 1885 when he participated in the annual festival of worship dedicated to the goddess Kali. In October 1885 Ramakrishna fell ill and was moved to Calcutta. His disciples went along to care for their *guru*. Narendranath organized his fellow devotees in their task and tried to bring a degree of order to their lives. When Ramakrishna lay near death he charged the young disciple to 'teach my boys' and 'keep them together'. On 16 August 1886 Ramakrishna died, leaving a vacuum in leadership and no central point of authority. Some of the disciples remained, lived together, and centred their attention on a search for release from the cycle of rebirth. Others roamed from one pilgrimage centre to another occasionally returning to Calcutta. There was little organization or discipline and those who lived together demonstrated an essentially orthodox pattern of religious activity. Narendranath attempted to engage them in a social programme focused on the education of women and peasants, the improvement of agriculture, and a campaign against child marriage. He failed and in 1890 abandoned his fellow monks. Narendranath sought aid from Hindu princes during the years 1890–3. In 1892 he travelled down the western coast of India and through the South where at the suggestion of the Raja of Khetri he took the name Swami Vivekananda. Having heard about the proposed World Parliament of Religions, Vivekananda raised funds for his travel expenses to the United States. He left Bombay on 31 May 1893 and arrived in Chicago on 11 September. Vivekananda did not return to India again until early 1897.

Swami Vivekananda's four years in the West greatly changed his position in contemporary Hinduism. News reached India of his success at the World Parliament and of his travels throughout the United States and England. He received a warm welcome from westerners, considerable publicity, and a small but growing circle of disciples. Vivekananda founded several Vedanta societies that disseminated his ideas. They also generated financial assistance both abroad and at home in India. The success of Swami Vivekananda stirred many Hindus with an example of spiritual superiority attested to by westerners themselves. From his new-found status as a Hindu celebrity, Vivekananda wrote extensively to the monks he had left behind, urging them to take up an active programme of social service with the promise that he would send them the necessary financial assistance.

When he arrived at Colombo in January 1897, Vivekananda was accompanied by a group of western disciples. He travelled north to

Calcutta in a triumphant procession. As soon as he had rejoined the monks, Vivekananda began to mould them according to his own ideas and priorities. He had been extremely impressed with the institutions he observed on his travels and wanted to establish an organization of Hindu monks along similar lines. He encountered considerable opposition, but managed, on 1 May 1897, to establish the Ramakrishna Mission. Using money collected in the West, Vivekananda purchased property for a new monastery, the Belur Math. He became president of this organization and Swami Brahmananda accepted the office as head of the new monastery. Vivekananda next created rules and regulations for the monastery. He also opened a second *math* at Mayavati in the Himalayas. Using his financial resources, Vivekananda introduced a famine relief programme, the first concrete expression of his concept of social service. Within a few months he had transformed the small group of devotees into the nucleus of a new organization devoted to a Hindu social gospel.[29]

Unfortunately Vivekananda's health worsened steadily. He suffered from diabetes and, in 1898, was advised to return to the West. Vivekananda reached New York in August 1899. He travelled throughout the United States, returned to England, and in 1900 visited the Congress of Religions held in Paris. In December 1900 Vivekananda returned to Belur Math, but his health was considerably worse from his incessant travels. He acted almost immediately to invest legal control over the growing organization and its property in a Board of Trustees. An election was held and on 12 February, Swami Brahmananda became president after Vivekananda resigned from that office. On 4 July 1902, Vivekananda died at the age of forty, leaving behind him a new type of Hindu religious organization, a blending of traditional monasticism and imported institutional concepts.

Vivekananda's vision of Hinduism was deeply divided between its glorious past and a degenerate present. In this he shared the perceptions of Rammohun Roy and other Hindu thinkers of the nineteenth century. Hindus were filled with superstition, with the trivia of elaborate rituals, rent by jealousy of anyone who might attempt to provide leadership or direction, and 'possessing the malicious nature befitting a

---

[29] Cyrus R. Pangborn, 'The Ramakrishna Math and Mission: a case study of a revitalization movement' in Bardwell L. Smith (ed.), *Hinduism, New Essays in the History of Religions* (Leiden, E. J. Brill, 1982), p. 113.

slave'.[30] Repeatedly he described a lack of manliness among Hindus and a feminine passivity. In disgust he blamed this on devotion to such figures as Radha, chief lover of Lord Krishna, with the result that 'the whole nation has become effeminate – a race of women!' The present state of Hindu decline stemmed from ignorance and their position as a subjugated people. Underlying Vivekananda's anxieties over Hindu degeneracy was the fear of possible extinction as conversion reduced the size of the Hindu community.

To counter this depressing description of contemporary life Vivekananda offered a complex set of ideas. First, he spoke of a past age of glory, of success, when Hindus acted as teachers to a world dependent on their spirituality. To Vivekananda the one universal religion was Vedanta, an expression of Hindu spiritual supremacy. He linked this concept to a dualistic division of the world between East and West. The West had positive achievements in the freedom and respect given women, in its emphasis on work, its organizational talents, and in its high level of material prosperity. It was, as well, 'gross, material, selfish and sensual'.[31] Vivekananda labelled the West as materialistic and contrasted it with a spiritual East by which he meant India and Hinduism. Technology, a work ethic, and new forms of organization were to be integrated into Hindu culture, for they were merely techniques. In turn Hindus would transfer their spirituality to the West. 'This is the great ideal before us, and everyone must be ready for it – the conquest of the world by India ... Up, India, conquer the world with our spirituality.'[32]

The restored Hinduism that Vivekananda wished for was not based on social criticism, but on selfless action by the dedicated followers of Ramakrishna, who would find their salvation through social service, and at the same time prove the superiority of their beliefs. Begun with the teachings of a traditional *sanyāsī*, this socio-religious movement drew into it young members of the English-educated elite thus creating an acculturative movement. It also proved to be successful among non-Hindus of the West under Vivekananda's leadership and in so doing was the first Hindu movement to explore a totally new source of

---

[30] Eknath Ranade (comp.), *Swami Vivekananda's Rousing Call to the Nation* (Calcutta, Centenary Publication, 1963). Quotes in this paragraph are from pages 26, 126, 94, and 101, respectively.
[31] *Ibid.*, p. 61.
[32] Prabha Dixit, 'The political and social dimensions of Vivekananda's ideology', *Indian Economic and Social History Review*, 12, no. 3 (July–Sept. 1975), 301.

support. When Vivekananda died, he left his ideas, plus the less structured teachings of Ramakrishna and a social service organization. The major pieces existed, but only in the twentieth century would these fuse together and create a successful socio-religious movement.

NINETEENTH-CENTURY BENGAL: A SUMMARY

A hundred years of religious developments in the Bengali region flowed in two main channels, one rural and Islamic, the other Hindu and urban. Among Bengali Muslims the Fara'izis and allied movements were transitional in nature owing nothing in their leadership or membership to the colonial milieu. Hindus, by contrast, created groups that drew upon the upper caste, urban, educated, for their leadership and much of their support. At times movements within each religious community produced communal conflict, a sharpening of religious definition, and of communal separation. Yet the forces behind major socio-religious movements depended heavily on the internal dynamics of each religious community and of Bengali society. Islamic leaders, speaking from their traditional role of 'ulamā, addressed a primarily peasant audience. They drew on the Islamic schools of philosophy and theology outside South Asia, particularly from the area of Sau'di Arabia, and from Muslim intellectual centres of north India. Bengali Muslims created one transitional movement and joined others from outside the region. The other Muslim societies in Bengal existed without direct opposition to the government.

The Hindu socio-religious movements, the Brahmos, the Ramakrishnas, and the followers of the neo-Vaishnavas drew symbols, concepts, and scriptural legitimization for the long history of protest within their religious heritage as well as limited elements of western civilization. Rammohun Roy adopted some concepts of ethics, theism, and rationalism from the West and Keshab Chandra Sen conscripted Christian symbols. Led by members of a rising educated-elite, the Hindu movements of return adopted imported organizational structure. In their reaction to Christianity, the Brahmo Samaj sought equivalence while the followers of Vivekananda and Keshab Chandra Sen held to Hindu superiority over all religions. The Ramakrishna Math and Mission also illustrates a fusion of social service with the ancient institution of the monastic order. These acculturative movements created new forms of Hinduism that met the social and psychological needs of an educated elite caught between two opposing poles of civilization, the indigenous Hindu and the intrusive Western.

Both sets of socio-religious movements, Hindu and Islamic, strengthened religious consciousness through competition between themselves and other groups within the same community. At the same time the boundaries between competing movements were defined and redefined by means of arguments placed in print, circulated and countered in pamphlet wars. Individuals were made aware of their own positions in terms of particular movements and other religions. To be a Hindu or a Muslim took on new meaning with the clarification and definition of religious terms, creeds, and rituals. In a multi-religious society such as Bengal or the South Asian subcontinent, the drive to establish or re-establish a purified form of religion led inevitably to the rejection of behaviour and beliefs attributed to other religions. Consequently, the distance between religions grew and communal lines hardened. Bengali religious movements, however, must be seen both in terms of the region and of other developments elsewhere in the subcontinent. To accomplish that, the next area for examination will be the central Gangetic plain, consisting of Bihar and the United Provinces.

CHAPTER THREE

THE GANGETIC CORE
UTTAR PRADESH AND BIHAR

THE SETTING

The vast northern plain of the Ganges–Jumna River system stretches from the banks of the Jumna River south-east to the edges of Bengal. To the North are the foothills and behind them the great barrier of Himalayan mountains. The southern borders of this plain are marked by another range of hills that merge into the Vindhya mountain chain, the line of demarcation between northern India and the Deccan plateau of the South. Within this geographic area evolved the Hindu-Buddhist civilization, beginning in the second millennium before Christ. After the conquest of northern India by Islamic armies, it also became the hub of Indo-Muslim civilization. This vast plain repeatedly provided the population and productivity needed to build and sustain major kingdoms and empires.

The population of the Gangetic basin reflects its history. Hindus live throughout the plains and foothills. Their society possessed a complex caste system encompassing all of the traditional *varnas* along with innumerable divisions of specific castes and sub-castes. Hindus predominated with 86 per cent of the population, while the largest minority were the Muslims with 13.7 per cent.[1] The Muslim population, however, showed distinctly different characteristics from the Islamic community of Bengal. In the North-Western Provinces they accounted for 38 per cent of the urban population. More concentrated in the cities and towns of the West, Muslims encompassed over 50 per cent of the urban dwellers in the area of Rohilkhand. Bihar held an even smaller percentage of Muslims; nevertheless, it too had a significant concentration of them in its towns and cities.[2] Many Muslims were drawn to urban life through their occupations in government service, trade, as artisans, and through Islamic learning or a preference for urban life

[1] Census, 1891, *North-Western Provinces and Oudh Report*, p. 171.
[2] Francis Robinson, 'Municipal government and Muslim separatism in the United Provinces, 1883 to 1916', *Modern Asian Studies*, 7, pt. 3 (1973), 394; Anil Seal, *The Emergence of Indian Nationalism: Competition and Collaboration in the Later Nineteenth Century* (Cambridge University Press, 1968), p. 58.

48

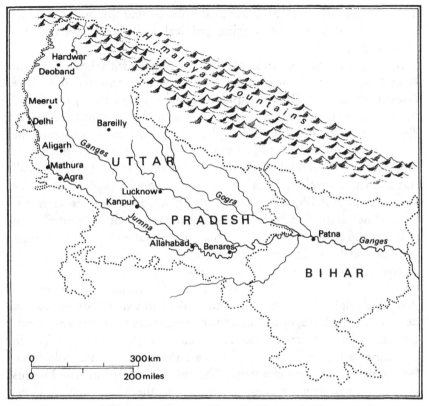

2 The Gangetic core: Uttar Pradesh and Bihar

demonstrated by many absentee landlords. Behind the two communities lay the centuries of Muslim political dominance when a new civilization arrived.

Bihar had already been absorbed by the English with the conquest of Bengal and over the next eighty-one years they annexed the entire Gangetic basin. The British acquired Benares in 1775, then paused, and in 1801, two extensive tracts were ceded from the kingdom of Awadh. Two years later, in 1803, the English extended their territory to the Jumna River and the foothills south of the plains. During the governor-generalship of Lord Dalhousie (1848–56) the English seized three small states on the southern edge of the plains and in 1856 annexed the kingdom of Awadh, thus completing their control of the Gangetic basin. The establishment of British rule brought with it a number of political and cultural changes, but their degree varied for different areas and for social divisions within those areas.

The arrival of British rule did not create as fundamental a restructuring of society as it had through the Permanent Settlement of Bengal. Roughly two types of land settlement existed, one based on dominant caste lineages within a given village who were classed as landowners and paid an annual tax. A second tax system existed in Awadh and Bihar where *taluqdārs* acted as a combination of tax-collectors, landowners, and petty chieftains. The culture of Muslims and Hindus of the plains was centred, however, in the cities and not the countryside.

The cities of this central plain illustrate the complex interaction of three civilizations. Benares was not only an early outpost of the British Empire, it was an ancient Hindu city as well, a place of temples, pilgrimages, and Hindu thought whose sanctity was recognized by all Hindus. A city of similar religious importance was Hardwar, located at the edge of the plains, where the holy Ganges emerged from the mountains. A place of pilgrimage and great religious festivals, Hardwar had little or no other function, either politically or economically. For South Asian Muslims, Delhi held greater importance than any other city on the Gangetic plains. It was the first capital of Islamic conquest and continued so under the Delhi Sultanate. In the Mughal Empire, Delhi shared that role with Agra to the South-East. Even after the Empire had disintegrated, Delhi remained a cultural and symbolic force in the subcontinent. The city also retained much of its vitality even in the late eighteenth century. In 1803 the British annexed Delhi and a new era of peace began. For Muslims, Delhi remained a source of Islamic thought and education, of poetry, prose and the arts. Many of the 'ulamā studied here and after departing disseminated its culture throughout the plains and beyond.

One example of Islamic education in Delhi was the Madrassah-i-Rahimiyah founded by Shaikh 'Abdu'r-Rahim (1644–1718). After the death of its founder the Madrassah continued under the leadership of his son, Shah Wali 'Ullah (see pp. 18–20). Those who received advanced education here carried with them the ideas of Wali 'Ullah, his condemnation of degenerate Islam, and his methods of returning it to past purity and past power. After studying in Sa'udi Arabia, Wali 'Ullah returned to Delhi convinced that numerous errors had crept into Islam both at the level of the 'ulamā and of popular practice. A blind acceptance of fiqh (the schools of law), ijmā (popular consensus), which justified many unacceptable rituals, customs and beliefs, and the use of questionable authorities, contributed to deviation from the true teachings of the Prophet. Wali 'Ullah accepted two forms of ultimate authority, the prophetic message as stated in the Qur'an and the hadīth or accounts of prophetic tradition.[3] Through the use of ijtihād (individual inquiry and reasoning), Islamic scholars could rediscover the proper forms of worship and behaviour, remove error, and restore Islam to its purity as exemplified during the life of Muhammad. For Wali 'Ullah the 'door to ijtihād' remained open and inquiry still valid, while to orthodox Sunnis such an approach was no longer acceptable since the four schools of law made this unnecessary. Shah Wali 'Ullah did insist, however, that ijtihād could only be conducted by Islamic scholars. Individuals with less education might fall into error and so should accept only the teachings and the judgments of the 'ulamā on points of law and practice.[4]

Concerned with strengthening Muslim unity, Shah Wali 'Ullah faced two divisive issues: Sufism, Islamic mysticism, and the Shi'ites. On the question of mysticism, he recognized the validity of Sufism and of its disciplinary techniques. He combined theological education and mystical training as two valid approaches to religious knowledge. Wali 'Ullah, nonetheless, rejected the excesses that Sufism was susceptible

---

[3] Aziz Ahmad, *Studies in Islamic Culture in the Indian Environment* (Oxford, Clarendon Press, 1964), pp. 203–4.

[4] Barbara Daly Metcalf, *Islamic Revival in British India: Deoband, 1860–1900* (Princeton University Press, 1982), pp. 37–9.

to in its more heterodox forms.[5] As to the Shi'ite beliefs in the authority of 'Ali and the *imāms*, he considered them unacceptable, but at the same time maintained that the Shi'ites were Muslims whom he wished to correct through persuasion rather than direct confrontation. Shah Wali 'Ullah died in 1763 and his son, 'Abdul 'Aziz (1746–1824), replaced him as head of the Madrassah-i-Rahimiyah. In 1803, after the British seized Delhi, 'Abdul 'Aziz issued a *fatwa*, that some understood as declaring India no longer *dār ul-Islām*, that is, under Islamic political control. It was instead *dār ul-harb*, an area under rule of non-Muslims. For 'Abdul 'Aziz the Mughal emperor no longer ruled in spite of the fiction maintained by the British. Thus the tie between Islam and political authority was severed. The question of 'proper' relations with the new British government was to divide and confuse Muslims throughout South Asia.

Delhi with its symbols of Islamic dominance was not simply a Muslim city. Hindus comprised the majority of its population. In 1847, Hindus accounted for 54.3 per cent of Delhi's people and in 1881 it had risen to 57.12 per cent. In the mean time the Muslims had fallen from 45.2 per cent to 41.82 per cent.[6] The divided nature of Delhi's population would have implications for communal conflict, but before examining this, it is necessary to survey the spread of printing as it paralleled the arrival of the British. By 1848, Indians owned and operated seventeen presses in the North-Western Provinces, two in Benares, and the remainder concentrated along the western edge of the province with seven in Delhi and five in Agra. These presses printed a stream of pamphlets, books, journals, and newspapers in Hindi and Sanskrit for Hindus, and in Arabic and Persian for Muslims. Both communities wrote extensively in Urdu. A variety of subjects were discussed: education, science, law, medicine, poetry, guides to social behaviour, yet the largest number of publications dealt with one or another aspect of religion. Many of these were reprints and translations of sacred literature.[7] The presence of Christian missionaries and socio-religious movements accounted, in part, for this focus on religious subjects.

[5] Istiaq Husain Qureshi, *The Muslim Community of the Indo–Pakistan Subcontinent, 610–1947* (The Hague, Mouton and Company, 1962), pp. 190–1.
[6] Sangat Singh, *Freedom Movement in Delhi, 1858–1919* (New Delhi, Association Publishers House, 1972), p. 15.
[7] Government of India, *Selections from the Records of the Government, North-Western Provinces* pt. 44 (Allahabad, Government Press, 1866).

The famine of 1837–8 stimulated the Church Missionary Society to reopen a mission in Agra. This mission also founded an orphanage and press. In 1841, K. G. Pfander joined the Church Missionary Society's Agra mission and began a campaign of proselytism aimed specifically at the Muslim community. In reaction to this campaign a stream of newspapers and tracts appeared in Agra, Delhi, and Meerut. Pfander continued to lead an aggressive conversion campaign until 1855, when he was posted to a mission station in Peshawar. The citizens of Delhi were drawn into similar controversy in the early 1850s. Ram Chandra, a Hindu teacher at the Delhi College, who would later convert to Christianity, clashed with the chief *qāzī* (a Muslim judge), of the city. Christians, Muslims, and Hindus struggled to defend their own beliefs in print and in public debates.[8] It was within this arena of cultural interaction and conflict, of Mughal decline and a newly emerging British government, that the first of the transitional movements arose to restore the fallen Muslim community to its rightful place as the ruling power of the subcontinent.

TRANSITIONAL MOVEMENTS AMONG THE MUSLIMS

Tariqah-i-Muhammadiyah

The founder of this socio-religious movement, Sayyid Ahmad Barelwi was born on 29 November 1786 in Rai Bareilly, a town near Lucknow (see p. 22). He received his early education at home. In 1806, he visited Delhi where he met Shah 'Abdul 'Aziz, was impressed enough to take *bai'at* (the initiation by a religious preceptor) from him, becoming in the process his religious disciple. He was, at the same time, initiated into three different Sufi orders. Sayyid Ahmad returned home and was back in Delhi in 1809. Next he travelled to Tonk in Rajasthan where he joined the Nawab's army. In 1817 he left and returned to Delhi. The Nawab of Tonk had made an alliance with the British and this act was unacceptable to Sayyid Ahmad. He dreamed of recreating an Islamic state, one that would follow a purified form of the religion and re-establish Islam to its proper position of political and cultural supremacy. Once again in Delhi, Sayyid Ahmad was accepted as a leader by the *'ulamā*. He gave *bai'at* to Muhammad Isma'il

---

[8] A. A. Powell, 'Muslim reactions to missionary activity in Agra' in C. H. Philips and Mary Doreen Wainwright (eds.), *Indian Society and the Beginnings of Modernisation c. 1830–1850* (London, School of Oriental and African Studies, 1976), pp. 142–52.

(1781–1831), the grandson of Shah Wali 'Ullah, and to 'Abdul Hayy (d. 1828), the son-in-law of 'Abdul 'Aziz. Because Sayyid Ahmad had visited Mecca in the years 1822–3, he had the authority of one who had concluded the *hajj* (the sacred pilgrimage). In addition, Sayyid Ahmad preached his own vision of a purified and restored Islam.

Sayyid Ahmad accepted the basic teachings of Shah Wali 'Ullah and, like him, called for the removal of erroneous innovations, all elements of polytheism, and idolatry. He rejected customs and rituals from the Indian, Roman, and Persian civilizations unless they were consistent with the Qur'an and Sunnah.[9] Sayyid Ahmad was adamant against the concept of an intermediary between God and man, telling his listeners that they could not seek aid from 'saints, apostles, imams, martyrs, angels, and fairies'. As with Wali 'Ullah, he accepted Sufism, acting himself as a Sufi teacher to his own disciples. Sayyid Ahmad was, however, more severe with the Shi'ah beliefs since he saw them as another source of error. His ideas were propagated through pamphlets and books. The first printed statement of his teachings was the *Sirāt ul-Mustaqīm* (The Straight Path) written in Persian by Muhammad Isma'il and published in 1819. The later publications were mainly in Urdu, since Persian could not reach a large audience of literate Muslims.

The ideology of Sayyid Ahmad Barelwi contained one basic difference from the teaching of Shah Wali 'Ullah and his disciples: Sayyid Ahmad intended to put his beliefs into action through a *jihād* (a sacred war against non-Muslims). He accepted 'Abdul 'Aziz's *fatwa* as declaring that British territory was *dār ul-harb* and, in accordance with Islamic law, *jihād* could only be conducted from an area of Islamic control. Consequently Sayyid Ahmad decided to begin his struggle on the north-west frontier of the Sikh kingdom. From April 1824, when he returned to Bareilly after his pilgrimage to Mecca, to January 1825, when he departed for the frontier, Sayyid Ahmad collected funds and recruits for the coming campaign. From his home town, he travelled west and then north, reaching Peshawar in November 1826 where he began fighting against the Sikhs from the tribal lands of the Yusufzai. In February 1827, Sayyid Ahmad was elected *imām*, enrolled *mujāhidīn* (religious warriors), gave *bai'at* to his adherents, and had his name

---

[9] Ahmad, *Studies in Islamic Culture*, pp. 210–11.

read in the *khutbah* (sermon).[10] The war waxed and waned as it became deeply involved with tribal politics of the frontier. In 1830 Sayyid Ahmad seized the city of Peshawar, but was forced to abandon it. In 1831, he was killed at the battle of Balakot along with many of his men and his disciple, Muhammad Isma'il.

In the wake of Sayyid Ahmad's death the movement faltered; its headquarters shifted first to Delhi and then to Patna in Bihar. New leadership arose from two brothers, Wilayat 'Ali and 'Inayat 'Ali, who were from a prominent Sadiqpuri family of Patna City, Bihar. Wilayat 'Ali first heard Sayyid Ahmad while a student at the Farangi Mahall in Lucknow. On his return from Mecca, Sayyid Ahmad stopped at Patna and gave *bai'at* to the entire family. The brothers joined him on the frontier, but were sent back after a short time to organize a system to gather finances and fighters. The brothers proved extremely able. Using itinerant preachers, they collected weapons, supplies, money, and recruits from the Muslims of eastern Bengal, the North-Western Provinces, Bihar, and Rajasthan. Wilayat 'Ali travelled to Bombay and as far south as Hyderabad in the Deccan, while 'Inayat 'Ali toured Bengal. By the mid-1840s both brothers returned to the frontier, where they faced a rapidly changing situation. After the death, in 1839, of the Sikh ruler, Ranjit Singh, his kingdom suffered from internal upheavals. Sikh control over the frontier weakened and their relations with the British became strained. In 1846, the Sikh kingdom fought the English and lost. The British then annexed the Jullundur Doab, and began to assist the Sikh state with its war on the frontier. In 1849 they absorbed the entire kingdom, bringing the English into a direct confrontation with the frontier *jihād*.

The fighting continued, but it proved increasingly difficult for the Muslim warriors. In 1853 Wilayat 'Ali was killed and his younger brother died in 1858. The uprising of 1857–8 brought some relief to the frontier, but after re-establishing control, the British were determined to end this frontier war. The Ambeyla campaign launched in the closing months of 1863 destroyed Muhammadi military power.[11] The British then dismantled the organizational and support system. In 1863 they arrested major figures in the movement and in the years 1864–5

---

[10] Harlan Otto Pearson, 'Islamic reform and revival in nineteenth century India: the Tariqah-i-Muhammadiyah', Doctoral Dissertation, History (Duke University, 1979), p. 51.

[11] Qeyamuddin Ahmad, *The Wahabi Movement in India* (Calcutta, Firma K.L. Muk-hopadhyay, 1966), pp. 200–9.

conducted a series of trials. A second round of arrests was followed by more trials in 1871–2. The British-Indian government managed to bring an end to the flow of money and men to the frontier, and this in turn made the resumption of warfare impossible. This movement did not end, however, but splintered into different sects and schools of thought that survived into the next century.

The death of Sayyid Ahmad divided his followers roughly into two groups. The more devoted and radical considered him to be the *imām–madhī* and expected that he would return to lead them once again. They gravitated to the Patna school created by the 'Ali brothers. Delhi housed the moderate thinkers who moved away from the concept of *jihād*, and did not accept Sayyid Ahmad as the *madhī* nor expect him to return. Meanwhile the Muslims of Delhi maintained the intellectual heritage of Shah Wali 'Ullah and 'Abdul 'Aziz.

Young Muslims continued to travel to Delhi for education, and one of them, Sayyid Nazir (d. 1902), became the leader of the Ahl-i-Hadith, a branch of the Tariqah-i-Muhammadiyah. Sayyid Nazir Husain first studied at Sadiqpur in Bihar and then in 1826 travelled to Delhi where he became a disciple of 'Abdul 'Aziz and his successor, Muhammad Ishaq (1778–1846). The intellectual respect given to Nazir Husain held together a network of *'ulamā* who saw themselves as inheritors of a line of thought stretching back to Shaikh Sarhindi. They accepted the teachings of the Shah Wali 'Ullah school, but were more uncompromising in their ideas. They rejected Sufism, and with it a variety of rituals and ceremonies associated with saintly shrines, including the pilgrimage to the grave of Muhammad. All forms of polytheism were condemned as well as the beliefs and practices of the Shi'ites. Nazir Husain had been a Shi'ite, but abandoned this when he studied with 'Abdul 'Aziz.[12] At the core of Ahl-i-Hadith doctrine lay an acceptance of 'God, His books, His prophets, and His angels as enjoined in the Qur'an'.[13] Their theological position denied the legitimacy of the four schools of law and advocated the use of *ijtihād* for members of a trained and educated elite. They were also separated from other Muslims by their use of a different form of prayer. The Ahl-i-Hadith advocated widow remarriage as Islamic and attacked the institution of the dowry as a non-Muslim innovation. Their position paralleled many

[12] Metcalf, *Islamic Revival in British India*, pp. 71–2.
[13] Aziz Ahmad, *Islamic Modernism in India and Pakistan, 1857–1964* (Oxford University Press, 1967), p. 115.

of the purification movements but did so primarily within the limits of the *'ulamā*.

Reform for the leaders of the Ahl-i-Hadith would be achieved through the literate elite and *ashrāf* Muslims. They looked for aid among Muslim princes, great landowners, and the *'ulamā*. They spread their vision of renewed Islam through publications, learned teachers, and formal debates. During the second half of the nineteenth century, the Ahl-i-Hadith comprised an effective voice in debates both within the Islamic community and without. They regarded the *'ulamā* as the class that would restore Islam to its proper status, an approach that dominated Muslim thinking in northern India during the second half of the nineteenth century. The prime question among Muslims remained just who would become the accepted leaders of this class.

The Tariqah-i-Muhammadiyah led by Sayyid Ahmad Barelwi aimed at restoring Islam to political dominance through the use of force, and drew upon all Muslims for support. Its vision of a restored and purified Islam was equalitarian rather than dependent on a single section of society and used military force as a method of achieving its ends along with the techniques of persuasion, debate, and publication employed by other Muslim movements of return. The failure of Sayyid Ahmad's military campaign and of the Indian Mutiny turned Muslims away from the use of military means to restore Islam to its proper place and from attempts to uplift the entire community. During the remainder of the nineteenth century, movements of return focused on the *'ulamā* and *ashrāf* Muslims of the upper classes.

The Dar ul-'Ulum Deoband

Throughout the centuries after the Muslim conquest of north India the *'ulamā*, as teachers, interpreters of religious law, and theologians, were closely linked to political power. In many ways they functioned similarly to the Brahman priests during the Hindu period. The decline of the Mughal Empire and its replacement by the British threatened them and, during the second half of the nineteenth century, led to movements of restoration based on a linking of *'ulamā* class interests with the fortunes of the Islamic community rather than the state, as had been the case in the era of Islamic political dominance. As a group the *'ulamā* saw little reason for adapting their own ideas to English culture, although they could not ignore British political-military power. The traditions of Islamic thought, especially as expressed by the Delhi school, provided the boundaries within which the majority of 'ulamā searched for a new world of purified religion and a resurgence of their own class. This approach to the challenges of the post-1857 years is exemplified by the Ahl-i-Hadith and the Deoband seminary movement.

Two major figures in the founding of the Deoband school were Muhammad Qasim Nanautawi (1833–77) and Rashid Ahmad Gangohi (1829–1905). Both had their homes in towns of the Doab, came from familes of the 'ulamā class, and were influenced by the intellectual life of Delhi. Because of a family feud, Muhammad Qasim was sent to stay with relatives in Deoband where he studied at the maktab (primary school) of Maulana Mahtar 'Ali and Shaikh Nihal Ahmad. By the 1840s he moved to Delhi for further education. Rashid Ahmad studied in his home town of Gangoh, then travelled to Karnal and Rampur, finally ending in Delhi where he met Muhammad Qasim. The two young students became disciples of Imdad 'Ullah (1815–99), a Sufi pīr, whose home was in the Doab and who shared a similar cultural background. They took bai'at from him and apparently became private students at Delhi College where they came into contact with the teachings of Sayyid Ahmad Barelwi and with the Delhi school of thought.[14] During their stay in Delhi the two young men returned to the Doab and in 1867 settled in Deoband where they opened a madrassah at the Chattah Masjid. Although the setting was similar to madrassahs throughout the subcontinent, a fundamental difference quickly became apparent. To begin with, they wanted their school to be a separate institution and not merely an appendage to the local mosque. The casual and personal teaching style used for centuries was replaced by a permanent teaching staff. Students enrolled in the school studied a defined curriculum with annual examinations. Much of the organizational form was adopted from British institutions and then modified to fit the needs of Deoband. The curriculum was not English. Instead they used the syllabus of the Farangi Mahall – a Muslim college associated with the court in Lucknow – as their guide in establishing the educational content of the school, while placing at the centre of their education the hadīth, the source of proper religious practice.

[14] Metcalf, *Islamic Revival in British India*, pp. 75–80. Unless otherwise indicated, the information on Deoband has been drawn from Professor Metcalf's detailed study of this school and movement.

Administratively they developed an Islamicized organization that borrowed heavily from the government colleges. It began with three officers: the *sarparast* (rector), 'a patron or guide of the institution; the *muhtamim*, or chancellor, the chief administrative officer; and the *sadr mudarris*, the chief teacher or principal, the person responsible for instruction'.[15] In 1892, Deoband added an officer whose duties stemmed directly from Islamic culture. This was the *muftī* who supervised the issuing of *fatwā*, a major task of traditional *'ulamā*. Questions of law, custom, and behaviour were submitted to the school and answered in the form of *fatwā*, issued by the assembled scholars. The final authority within this institution was vested in a Consultative Council that decided all questions of personnel, curriculum, finances, and organizational procedures. This administrative structure marked a sharp break from the older organization of Muslim schools, which were personal in nature and under the control of local leaders.

In the past, schools were supported by the institution of *waqf* (an endowment of land for charitable purposes). Deoband, by contrast, depended on public donations usually in the form of annual pledges. These came from a variety of individuals rather than a single source, further underscoring its wide base of support and the consequent independence of the institution from individual or local control. The breadth of its acceptance was demonstrated by the number of schools modelled after Deoband. By 1880, graduates had established over a dozen schools throughout the Upper Doab and Rohilkhand. The Deoband seminary was the centre of this expanding educational system. It provided advice, assistance, a central depot for records, and external examiners for the new schools. By 1900, this expanding educational system dispensed the Deobandi ideology in the North from Peshawar to Chittagong, and in the South-East at Madras.

Deobandis conceived of Islam as having two points of focus, *sharī'at* (the law, based on scriptures and religious knowledge), and the *tarīqah* (path, derived from religious experience). Thus they accepted Sufism with its forms of discipline and the role of the *'ulamā* in interpreting the four schools of Islamic law. The Qur'an, *hadīth*, *qiyās* (analogical reasoning), and *ijmā* (consensus) provided the foundation of religious knowledge, but understanding them required the *'ulamā* as guides. Uneducated Muslims could not make judgments on

[15] *Ibid.*, p. 95.

belief or practice. The Deobandis, while accepting Sufism, rejected numerous ceremonies and the authority of *pīrs* who claimed sanctity by their descent rather than by their learning. Knowledge granted authority and not inheritance. Pilgrimages to saints' tombs, and the annual death rites of a particular saint (the *'urs*), also lay outside acceptable Islamic practice. Along with types of behaviour seen as erroneous innovations, were classed any social or religious practice that appeared to come from Hindu culture.

The Deoband programme of study was originally set to cover ten years, but later reduced to six. Officially the school did not object to western learning or to the use of English, but neither was introduced. Instead, the syllabus focused on Islamic texts, covering 'Arabic and Persian grammar, prosody and literature, history of Islam, logic, Greco-Arab philosophy, *kalām*, dialects, disputation, medieval geometry and astronomy, Greco-Arab medicine, jurisprudence, the *hadīth* and *tafsīr* (Commentaries on the Qur'an)'.[16] In time Persian was de-emphasized; instead the seminary utilized Arabic as the language of the scriptures and Urdu as the language of north-Indian Muslims. The Deobandi curriculum was designed to prepare students for their role as members of the *'ulamā* and in doing so to strengthen that group as the link between Islamic religion and culture, and the Muslim population.

As the reputation of Deoband grew, students arrived from throughout the British-Indian Empire, but most came from Punjab, the North-Western Provinces, and Bengal. Once a student had enrolled he fell under the care and discipline of the institution. They lived nearby – until a hostel was constructed at the end of the century – were given supplies by the school, and treated if they fell ill. The students lived respectably, attended class regularly and, if they failed to work, were promptly dismissed. Their holidays were limited to every Friday and one month off each year. After six years at Deoband many of the students formed close ties with their fellows, ties that stayed with them for the remainder of their lives. Such bonds strengthened that section of the *'ulamā* sympathetic to Deobandi ideas, adding the dimension of an 'old boy' social network to this community.

The structure of Islamic society, especially of the *ashrāf*, greatly enhanced Deoband in its search for financial resources. They rejected the use of government grants-in-aid, since that assistance would be

[16] Ahmad, *Islamic Modernism*, p. 105.

suspect because it came from non-Muslims. Consequently, the school turned to imported methods of fundraising. Using the printing press and postal services, they developed a system of pledges and gifts complete with money orders, annual reports, and the publication of donors' names. The Deobandis also made special appeals on the celebration of various Muslim festivals. Donors included princes, government servants, religious leaders, merchants, and landowners. Many of these were associated with the school through their relatives or clansmen, through membership in a religious order or through a similarity of ideas. This success in finding widespread financial and ideological support ensured the continued growth of Deoband, but also generated strains within the movement.

The school faced two crises: one in 1876 and a second in 1895, both associated with its relationship to local Muslim leaders. The first controversy centred on erecting buildings separate from the mosque, an act that made a physical statement of Deoband's desire to remain an independent institution. In 1895 the conflict focused on staffing and control of the school's administration. Once again, the local leaders attempted to gain power. In both instances those who challenged the Deobandis lost and the school retained its wide base of support and its original leadership. Controversy did not, however, originate solely within the institution or its immediate environment.

Outside the school, Deobandis entered into debates with other Muslims to defend and explain their ideology. Their steady issuance of *fatwā*, 269,215 in the first century, earned the institution a reputation for authority in all aspects of Muslim life. Deobandis also participated in debates with both Christian and Hindu critics of Islam. Muhammad Quasim, a fine public speaker, defended Islam against Christian missionaries and Arya Samaj Hindus. In 1876 he entered a 'religious fair' against a Hindu convert to Christianity, the Reverend Tara Chand. He also challenged Swami Dayananda Saraswati, the founder of the Arya Samaj, to a public debate.

The impact of Deoband as a school and a transitional socio-religious movement grew first from its new style of Islamic education with an appointed staff, fixed curriculum, and regular examinations. This structure, as well as the methods used to raise funds, were adopted from the English model of education and the organization of voluntary associations. These techniques enabled the Deobandis to base their school on a broad support of the *ashrāf* Muslims, provide an effective Islamic educational system that promoted their ideas of return to proper Islamic practice, and create the foundation of a revived class of 'ulamā who could function without the patronage or power of a Muslim state. The Deobandis gained widespread respect and influence in the North and beyond through their students and the numerous fatwā on questions of proper religious practice. They also inspired the founding of schools modelled after the Deoband ul-'Ulum, debated with opponents of Islam and with those Muslims who rejected their vision of Islam. The Deobandis, as with other movements discussed in this section, were not products of the colonial milieu, but of the living tradition of Indo–Muslim thought and practice. The first Muslim acculturative movement also emerged from a Delhi environment, but with different goals and techniques.

THE CREATION OF THE COLONIAL MILIEU

The establishment of the English political sphere preceded the slow and uneven growth of a new colonial culture as it radiated out from urban areas. New knowledge was disseminated by government and missionary schools, but the North-Western Provinces and Bihar absorbed this education much more slowly than Bengal, Bombay, and Madras. An Orientalist attitude persisted in the schools of this area. Benares College, founded in 1791, and Delhi College, established in 1792, both focused on classical learning in Sanskrit, Arabic, and Persian. The British took over Delhi College in 1825 and three years later it began courses in English language and literature, and western science. Benares, however, continued its classical orientation. The study of English was not encouraged by a need to know it for professional purposes. Persian had been replaced in 1837 by Urdu as the language of administration, but Urdu remained dominant in government well into the second half of the nineteenth century. By 1865, some knowledge of English was required for upper level judicial posts, but not until 1889 was a Bachelor of Law degree needed before beginning a legal career.[17]

The acquisition of an English education followed different communal and social divisions here than in either Bengal or Punjab. The Muslims of the North-Western Provinces, Bihar, and Awadh, as

[17] David Lelyveld, *Aligarh's First Generation, Muslim Solidarity in British India* (Princeton University Press, 1978), pp. 95–6. The information on Sayyid Ahmad Khan and the Aligah movement will be from this work unless otherwise cited.

urbanized members of a middle- and upper-class minority, had a higher level of literacy and education than the Hindu majority. Consequently, Muslims absorbed English education and accounted for a greater percentage of students attending school than their proportion of the total population.[18] In spite of this acceptance of education in general, the number of English-speaking Muslims grew slowly through the nineteenth century.

The two parallel streams of education, Islamic and English, can be clearly seen in a single institution, the Delhi College. Students emerged from the Orientalist branch of this school prepared for careers as Muslim scholars and Urdu-speaking government servants. The Anglicist wing of the school produced students knowledgeable in western subjects, as well as the English language. This new education helped to create the 'Delhi Renaissance' that began in the 1830s and out of this came young radicals enthusiastic about western concepts, and critical of their own culture, who occasionally converted to Christianity. This was a period of cultural interaction and intellectual excitement that arrayed outspoken critics against the orthodox majority of their community whether it was Hindu or Muslim. The events of 1857–8 brought an abrupt end to the activities of young Anglicized radicals who were either killed or fled the city. It is against this background that we must examine the career of an Islamic leader, Sayyid Ahmad Khan, who sought an accommodation with the English as a political power and also as representatives of another civilization.

AN ACCULTURATIVE MOVEMENT AMONG THE MUSLIMS

Sayyid Ahmad Khan and the Aligarh experiment

Born into a prestigious family of Delhi, Sayyid Ahmad Khan (1817–98) spent his childhood in and out of the Mughal court. His family was connected to 'Abdul 'Aziz and he himself studied the work of Shah Wali 'Ullah. Sayyid Ahmad did not learn English, but according to the older pattern of education, studied Arabic and Persian, yet he was fascinated with western science, mathematics, and astronomy. He did not receive a religious education and instead demonstrated the person-

---

[18] Seal, *Emergence of Indian Nationalism*, pp. 305–6.

ality more akin to a courtier or government official than to an *'ulamā*. In 1838, Sayyid Ahmad entered British service and gradually advanced up the judicial ladder until his retirement in 1877. During these years he was posted in a number of cities and towns, mostly in the upper Gangetic plain with his longest stay in Delhi from 1846–54. During the Mutiny, Sayyid Ahmad remained loyal to the British, yet this event reshaped his life, and gave him a cause that he served until his death.

The uprising directly threatened Sayyid Ahmad and all those who served the British-Indian state. Had that power been swept away those who worked for it would also have been destroyed. Yet the restoration of peace brought with it neither tranquillity nor security for Sayyid Ahmad. The English were bitter, vengeful, and suspicious of the Muslim community whom they blamed for the revolt. Sayyid Ahmad belonged to a minority community, stripped of its past glories, ruled by a non-Muslim state, and faced with hostility. He reacted by writing three political statements, one was the *Asbāb-i-Baghvati-i-Hind* (Causes of the Indian Revolt), in which he laid much of the blame for the uprising on missionary activities and attempted to demonstrate that Islam as a religion was not responsible. Sayyid Ahmad produced two pamphlets in English under the title *Loyal Muhammadans of India* that contained accounts of Muslims who remained allied with the Raj. A third publication was his *History of the Revolt in Bijnor* telling of his own experiences during the revolt.

For Sayyid Ahmad Khan, the future of Islam rested with the fortunes of Muslims, particularly those in northern India. His writings soon began to draw others to him as he, in turn, founded a variety of public forums for his ideas. In order to end British suspicion and to create a bond with them, he organized a celebration in honour of the continuance of British rule and did so using public subscriptions. From ceremonies of loyalty he shifted to famine relief and by the mid-1860s had experimented with creating both a college and an orphanage. These projects failed, but through them Sayyid Ahmad learned the techniques necessary to mobilize individuals and resources. He became a leader of the Muslim community as well.

Sayyid Ahmad did not limit himself to the issue of loyalty. Instead he began to discuss the need to translate European works of science and the arts into the languages of north India. In 1863 he travelled to Calcutta and spoke before the Muslim Literary Society where he called for the study of European science and technology, arguing that nothing in Islam forbade such learning. His views stood in sharp contrast with Muslims who saw no value or utility in importing non-Muslim knowledge. Meanwhile the Scientific Society, which he had established earlier, moved its headquarters to Aligarh where he had been posted. Using Sayyid Ahmad's private press, the Society began publishing a weekly newspaper to disseminate his ideas. In 1866, Sayyid Ahmad created the British-Indian Association of the North-Western Provinces as another expression of his desire for closer relations with the British. Sayyid Ahmad, spurred by curiosity about English society, and a desire to locate material to refute Sir William Muir's *Life of Muhammad*, left for England with his son who went to acquire an advanced English education. He spent seventeen months, 1869–70, travelling and returned impressed, even shocked, by what he had seen.

For Sayyid Ahmad, this visit left him with a depressed vision of Muslim society in particular and India in general: 'The natives of India . . . when contrasted with the English in education, manners and up-rightness, are like them as a dirty animal is to an able and handsome man.'[19] To end this state of decadence Sayyid Ahmad felt that some of the characteristics of English society – its discipline, order, efficiency and high levels of education, along with science and technology – must be adopted by the Muslim community. His goal, in turn, raised funda-mental questions concerning the validity of the Prophet Muhammad and his message. Sayyid Ahmad approached these issues with two basic suppositions. First, he maintained that the Qur'an contained ultimate truth and existed prior to the knowledge of science. Secondly, science or natural law was itself true, thus there could be no contradiction between the Qur'an and natural law. If there was, then either the Qur'an was misunderstood or natural law in error.

Studying the Qur'an was both necessary and difficult, since it contained two types of verses, 'the "clear" and the "ambiguous", as "essential" and "symbolic", the former constituting the irreducible minimum of Islamic faith and creed, the latter being open to two or more interpretations, permitted deductions appropriate to other ages and circumstances different from those of Arabia in the early seventh century'.[20] Sayyid Ahmad argued that if a naturalistic and rational

[19] Lelyveld, *Aligarh's First Generation*, p. 106.
[20] Ahmad, *Islamic Modernism*, p. 45.

explanation could be found that did not directly clash with the Qur'an, it was to be used. Orthodox Muslims labelled Sayyid Ahmad and his followers as *nechārīs*, a term of derision and disgust.

Opposition to Sayyid Ahmad Khan grew from two levels, one of thought and the other of practice. Many disagreed with his interpretation of Islam. In addition orthodox Muslims were appalled when he insisted that 'it was all right to wear shoes for prayer in the mosque, to participate in Hindu and Christian celebrations [and], to eat at a European-style table'[21] Sayyid Ahmad defended his actions by the validity of *ijtihād*, and the need for new interpretations as a method of adjustment to changed circumstances. Few among the *'ulamā* accepted this, since they considered Sayyid Ahmad uneducated in religion, a man outside their class, and thus unfit to use the institution of *ijtihād*. Sayyid Ahmad addressed himself to members of the *ashrāf*, and stressed the importance of ancestry and of social status. The *ashrāf* were the rightful descendants of past rulers who should act to regain their proper and legitimate place even if cooperation with and adjustment to the British were required. Sayyid Ahmad used the term *quam* for Muslim society, first for the North and then to refer to Muslims throughout British India. As the nineteenth century progressed the Muslim *quam*, however, found itself facing a new threat. During the last quarter of the nineteenth century the spectre of an aggressive, expanding Hindu elite replaced the fears centred on the British-Indian government for Sayyid Ahmad and other Muslim leaders of the North.

The British conquests in the late eighteenth and early nineteenth centuries stimulated a growth of trade, while their legal system protected commercial activities. For urban Hindus of the upper castes this meant a new degree of prosperity and with that came an increase in aggressiveness and a pride in their culture. Wealthy Hindus built temples, sponsored the publication of Hindu religious literature, and founded organizations for a variety of purposes.[22] By 1867, Hindus demanded that Urdu be replaced by Hindi as the language of administration. Sayyid Ahmad acknowledged the threat of this movement when Babu Shiva Prasad of Benares requested that the Scientific Society replace Urdu with Hindi for its proceedings and reports. Shiva Prasad

---

[21] Lelyveld, *Aligarh's First Generation*, pp. 130–1.
[22] C. A. Bayly, *The Local Roots of Indian Politics, Allahabad, 1880–1920* (Oxford, Clarendon Press, 1975), pp. 363–5.

acquired his own press and organized a campaign promoting the use of Hindi.[23] The demands to replace Urdu with Hindi increased over the second half of the nineteenth century. In 1873 it was accepted for use in the lower courts of Bihar, and in 1881 received equal status to Urdu throughout that province. Language was not the only point of contention between Hindus and Muslims. During the last two decades of the century, Hindus became aggressive defenders of the cow and demanded that it be protected from slaughter either for food or at the Muslim ceremony of 'Id. The two issues of cow protection and Hindi stood at the forefront of competition between the Hindu and Muslim communities, one containing a rising elite, the other an elite struggling to regain its lost political and social status.

For Sayyid Ahmad the answer to the present dilemma of the Muslims lay in an education that disseminated elements of English knowledge within an Islamic context. In 1872 he organized a Select Committee charged with planning an education system. The Committee's reports discussed the educational needs of the various classes within Muslim society. Sayyid Ahmad, who acted as secretary, spoke of education for peasants, shopkeepers, artisans, and labourers, as well as Muslims who looked to government service or purely religious occupations. The Committee's work led to the concept of a school that was intended to serve all Muslims and cut across sectarian differences. A number of Hindus donated to this cause, and after 1873 Hindus were expected to participate in the student body. As planning advanced, this dream became in reality an education for sons of the respectable *ashrāf* Muslims.

In June 1875, the Muhammadan Anglo-Oriental College of Aligarh opened its doors. This institution enrolled students at the elementary levels, studying the standard government curriculum under an English headmaster, but doing so in a carefully constructed Islamic environment. In January 1878 college classes were initiated, but the young college faced serious problems. It needed students. Many of those who attended did so primarily because they were related to Muslims involved in the college movement, and consequently the student body grew slowly. After the first year Hindus attended, but their numbers peaked in 1889 and declined during the next decade. Meanwhile the contribution of Aligarh to the educated Muslim elite took on an

---

[23] For further information on Shiva Prasad, see Jurgen Lutt, *Hindu Nationalismus in Uttar Prades, 1867–1900* (Stuttgart, Ernst Klett Verlag, 1970), pp. 37–64.

increased significance: 'Between 1882 and 1902 Aligarh had sent up 220 Muslim graduates, or 18.5 per cent of the 1,184 in all of India ...[and] accounted for 53.6 per cent of the Muslim students from Allahabad University.'[24] The graduates from Aligarh became an impressive part of the limited number of Muslim degree holders in the subcontinent.

Sayyid Ahmad envisioned the college as preparing men to serve the *quam*. It would supply educated, honest, public-spirited leaders able to work with the English government, and to protect the Muslim community. In time this elite would lift the Muslims into a cooperative dominance, ruling India in partnership with the British. Theodore Beck, the English headmaster, accepted Sayyid Ahmad's educational vision, modifying it according to the ideas of the English public school. For Beck, Aligarh's graduates should be young men of character grounded in Islamic values; an Indian version of the educated gentry of England. This approach did not lead to intellectual and academic excellence as was demonstrated by Aligarh's uninspiring record in the annual university examinations. The activities of this college did not revolve around the classrooms or textbooks, but campus social-life. The presence of Beck and other Englishmen focused student energies on public speaking and debate. The core of student life became the Union where student factions fought to win elected offices with great energy and passion. Islam as a philosophical and theological system received little attention, although a consciousness of being a member of the Islamic community pervaded the entire institution.

Aligarh remained primarily an undergraduate college. Advanced degrees were offered to the MA level; however, these programmes attracted few students. In 1896 an LL B degree was instituted, but drew only a limited response. Problems of finance and factional strife slowed the development of Aligarh. During the late 1880s, a bitter and widely publicized dispute developed between Sayyid Ahmad and Sami 'Ullah, a distinguished jurist, over the method of choosing Sayyid Ahmad's successor. In 1889 the Muhammadan Anglo-Oriental Fund Committee passed a Trustee Bill, setting rules and procedures advocated by Sayyid Ahmad. As a result Sami 'Ullah withdrew from the college, taking many of the older and wealthier contributors with him. In this instance the British government offered the funds needed to maintain Aligarh. Another loss of support came with the departure of

[24] Lelyveld, *Aligarh's First Generation*, p. 185.

Shibli Nu'mani. He had joined the Aligarh faculty in 1883 to teach Persian and aid in Arabic instruction. As a scholar deeply committed to Islam and a teacher with close ties to his students, Nu'mani contributed a sense of Islamic devotion to the campus. He could not, however, be comfortable with the extensive role of foreign knowledge that existed in the Aligarh curriculum. He resigned from Aligarh, and with a group of 'ulamā founded the Majlis-i-Nadwah ul-'Ulum of Lucknow in 1893. Two years later he helped to open the Nadwah Dar ul-'Ulum, a seminary intended to unite all Muslims through a single institution that transcended sectarian differences.

For the rest of Sayyid Ahmad Khan's life, Aligarh was his most important cause. He dedicated much of his time and energy to administering the college. Sayyid Ahmad functioned as a one-man managing committee, overseeing all budgets, college publications, correspondence, teaching, and student discipline. After 1887, with the addition of several young men from Cambridge to the college faculty, Sayyid Ahmad gradually abandoned some of his responsibilities, although he remained extremely active until his death. Beyond the college he continued his public campaign to revive the fortunes of the Islamic community. In 1886, he founded the Muhammadan Anglo-Oriental Educational Conference to popularize and encourage the fusion of English and Islamic education.[25] That same year he spoke out against the Indian National Congress and Muslim participation in this openly political organization. To Sayyid Ahmad, the Congress offered nothing for the embattled Muslim community except the possibility of rekindled British hostility. Two years later, in 1889, along with Theodore Beck, he organized the United Indian Patriotic Association as a counter to the Congress. Once more he sought to emphasize loyalty to the British.

The difficulties faced by Sayyid Ahmad and the graduates of Aligarh were expressed in 1890 by Mustafa Khan in *An Apology for the New Light*. He discussed the shortcomings of Indo-Muslim culture, the pride of his fellow students, as well as their relative isolation, and the value of English education. He described how their style of dress, the fez and a Turkish coat, had given his fellow students a 'national identity'.[26] Aligarh's new generation of leaders, he wrote, would unite the dispersed Muslims into a single *quam*, a community no longer divided

[25] Ahmad, *Islamic Modernism*, pp. 37–8.
[26] *Ibid.*, pp. 248–50.

by sectarian strife, class tensions or linguistic pluralism. This dream of internal tranquillity remained unfulfilled. Aligarh and Sayyid Ahmad faced opposition from numerous Muslim movements and they in turn competed with each other.

The efforts of Sayyid Ahmad Khan to defend and then strengthen the Muslim community marked a sharp break with previous attempts to purify Islam and return it to its past glory. Sayyid Ahmad envisioned the creation of an administrative elite which would govern in cooperation with the British rather than focus its attention on the 'ulamā. He incorporated western knowledge including science, looked to a new type of education as the prime tool of his campaign, and justified this through his own system of scriptural interpretation. Sayyid Ahmad was concerned with the fate of the Muslims as a religiously defined community. This concentration on Muslims as a group of people rather than on proper religious practice led him to reject the Indian National Congress, oppose aggressive Hinduism, and to lay the foundation for a consciousness that evolved into religious nationalism. He was opposed by Muslim movements that did not accept his inclusion of western learning into Islam. Perhaps the most uncompromising of all were the 'ulamā led by Maulana Ahmad Riza Khan.

The Barelwi 'Ulama in defence of Islamic orthodoxy

At a polar opposite to the acculturative movement of Sayyid Ahmad Khan and the transitional movements that advocated degrees of change in Islam stood the Barelwi 'Ulamā, who defended contemporary religion from criticism within and beyond the community. This group was led by Ahmad Riza Khan (1856–1921), an effective exponent and apologist for Islamic customary practice. His family migrated from Afghanistan, became attached to the Mughal court, and finally settled on a landed estate near Bareilly. Ahmad Riza descended from a line of distinguished scholars and soon established his own reputation for learning in the area of *fiqh*, for an impressive memory, and for his linguistic abilities. He joined and then became a *shaikh* in the Qadiri order of Sufis. In this role he gained a reputation for skills in divination and in the construction of numerical charts for similar purposes. He also began a long career in opposing all those who were critical of Islamic customs, beliefs and practices. These he labelled 'Wahhabis', both a theological and political condemnation. Ahmad Riza drew around him an expanding circle of disciples.

Ahmad Riza Khan placed at the centre of his teachings the figure of the Prophet who possessed total knowledge of spiritual truth and for whom Ahmad Riza had the greatest respect. He could brook no criticism of Muhammad, celebrated the Prophet's birthday, and saw him as unique among all men. He also gave his respect and public deference to all *sayyids* since they were descendants of the Prophet. In his conception of Islam, saints, retained a bodily existence after death. They could thus both hear prayers and grant requests from the grave. This position led him to accept the celebration of *'urs*, revere saints, tombs, and the rituals associated with these powerful figures. The Prophet, saints, *pirs*, and *shaikhs* could all act on behalf of Muslims who sought their assistance. In addition Ahmad Riza accepted as valid, customs and parochial cults as long as they were not in contradiction to established sections of *hadīth*. His teachings then supported the pro-British religious leaders who were under attack by many leaders of transitional and acculturative Islamic movements.

An erudite scholar, Ahmad Riza answered questions on proper behaviour, issued an impressive number of *fatwā*, and entered into controversies with the Ahl-i-Hadith and the Deobandis. For him these were the greatest danger to Islam. He wrote condemning their ideas and made fun of their programmes. He labelled them *kāfirs* and Wahhabis. Ahmad Riza also attacked one element of contemporary Islam and that was the Shi'ites. He even forbade his followers to wear black and green during Mohurram. He 'wanted to preserve Islam unchanged; not as it was idealized in texts or the historical past, but Islam as it had evolved to the present'.[27]

As an orthodox, defensive movement, the Barelwi 'Ulamā rejected those who would reinterpret Islam or who wanted to challenge the existing religious status quo. They did not limit their activities to debates or the issuance of rulings on particular questions, but also founded schools to instruct future members of the 'ulamā. One madrassah was established in Bareilly, another in Lahore (1887), and a third in Philibhit (1920). As with other movements that placed religion at the centre of an individual's existence, they rejected political action including the Khilafat movement in which Indian Muslims attempted to defend Turkey and the symbolic head of Islam, the Khalīfah, as well

---

[27] Metcalf, *Islamic Revival in British India*, pp. 296–314.

as Gandhi's campaigns. Politics was a distraction from the demands of a truly religious life.

Ahmad Riza Khan was a *mujaddid* to his followers, a religious figure of great authority who deserved reverence and respect. He won disciples mainly from the rural areas and among the uneducated, with a small sprinkling of government servants. The Barelwis accepted a wide variety of customary practices, defended the established religious elite, and demonstrated no interest in adopting elements of western knowledge. They did, however, contribute to the hardening of lines between Sunnis and Shi'ahs. Outside the Islamic community they entered into controversy with aggressive Hindu groups such as the Arya Samaj and with Christian missionaries. Nevertheless, their main opponents remained Islamic movements of return that condemned many of the customs defended by the Barelwis. Their position was then similar to movements of orthodox defence in other religions. Although acculturative socio-religious movements called for change, not all did so in an outwardly aggressive manner, as was exemplified by the Radhasoami Satsang of the Hindus with its inward orientation.

ACCULTURATIVE MOVEMENTS AMONG THE HINDUS

The Radhasoami Satsang

The beginnings of the Radhasoami Satsang are to be found in the life of Swami Shiv Dayal, later known as Soamiji Majaraj (1818–78). Shiv Dayal was born in Agra into a banking family of the Khatri caste. Originally they came from Punjab and were Nanakpanthis, a sect that revered Guru Nanak.[28] The family's *guru*, Tulsi Sahib of Hathras, 'recognized' the spiritual uniqueness of Shiv Dayal, and consequently the young man was left to follow his own preferences, which included periods of lengthy meditation. He secluded himself in a small room isolated from others for days at a time. Apparently, Shiv Dayal had no formal education and only a short career as a tutor to one of the Indian princes.[29] Shiv Dayal was married at a young age to Naraini Devi,

[28] Mark Juergensmeyer, 'Radhasoami reality: the logic of a new modern faith' (unpublished manuscript), ch. 1, p. 2.
[29] S. D. Maheshwari, *Radhasoami Faith, History and Tenets* (Agra, Radhasoami Satsang, 1954), p. 13.

later called Radhaji. As he matured Swami Dayal began to draw to him a circle of disciples. He taught a path of devotion, Sūrat Shabad Yoga, by which a person could follow the sound, *shabd*, that emanated from the Supreme Being back through various levels of consciousness to its point of origin, and in so doing find eternal peace through union with the ultimate. Shiv Dayal drew on the *sant* tradition and on such figures as Kabir and Guru Nanak (see pp. 12–13). He utilized the Sikh scriptures, the Guru Granth Sahib, and the writings of Tulsi Sahib.[30]

One of Shiv Dayal's disciples, Salig Ram (later known as Huzur Maharaj), urged him to found a public society and so, in January 1861, the Radhasoami Satsang was launched. Its daily meetings consisted of readings from either the Satsang sacred books or the writings of various north-Indian saints. Also used were prayers, hymn-singing, and a talk by Shiv Dayal or, if he could not be present, by one of his followers. In such instances a portrait of the Swami was worshipped. The use of pictures was an early development in this movement. Shiv Dayal presented his disciples with a photograph of himself and his wife so that they might have it as an aid to their meditation. The role of the *guru* in the Swami's teaching was of the utmost importance, since he alone could direct disciples in their quest for the Supreme Being. Members of the Satsang depended totally on their teacher, spent as much time as possible with him, and centred their devotion on his personage.

He remained the focal point of an unstructured group during his life. Shiv Dayal was responsible for two versions of a single book, the *Sār Bachan* (Essential Utterances), one in prose and the other in poetry.[31] In 1876 the Satsang built him a new residence at Soami Bagh, a permanent camp of Radhasoami mendicants, approximately three miles outside Agra. This became the headquarters of the movement and also a place of pilgrimage. Here Shiv Dayal died and a small *samādhi* or memorial was built in his memory. The loss of its founder left the Radhasoamis without a single leader. One of the disciples, Sanmukh Das, supervised the mendicants encamped at Soami Bagh, property rights were held by the Swami's younger brother, and women within the movement were told to obey Radhaji as their leader. Just before his death Shiv Dayal recommended that his disciples should look to Salig

---

[30] Juergensmeyer, 'Radhasoami reality', ch. 1, p. 3.
[31] J. N. Farquhar, *Modern Religious Movements in India* (New York, Macmillan Company, 1919), p. 166.

Ram for advice in spiritual matters, but no one was named as successor to Shiv Dayal.[32]

Nevertheless, there existed two strong candidates, Salig Ram and Jaimal Singh. Salig Ram was born in Agra on 14 March 1829. His family were Kayasthas from Mathura who had moved to Agra where Salig Ram was educated first in a local *maktab* and learned Persian. He next attended Agra College and, in March 1847, joined government service in the office of the Postmaster General. His career was highly success-ful. In 1871 the government bestowed the title of Rai Bahadur on him and ten years later he was appointed the first Indian Postmaster General in the North-Western Provinces. It was during these years of govern-ment service, in November 1858, that Salig Ram first met Shiv Dayal. He became a devoted disciple of the Swami and later an active member of the Satsang.

Baba Jaimal Singh (d. 1903) was a Punjabi, born into a Jat Sikh family who met Shiv Dayal in 1856.[33] While serving in the army, he gained a reputation for spiritual leadership and began to attract his own dis-ciples. In 1884, Jaimal Singh started to initiate members of his own Satsang as disciples of Shiv Dayal. When he retired from the army in 1889, Jaimal Singh turned his full attention to tending his growing band of followers.[34] Similarly Rai Salig Ram, after his retirement from government service in 1887, returned to Agra to become the recognized *guru* of one section of the Satsang and a successor to Shiv Dayal. He served as such from his retirement in 1889 until his own death in 1898. During these years another line of succession emerged within the main Agra section of the Radhasoamis.

Salig Ram brought to the Satsang a sense of organization and doctri-nal development lacking under Shiv Dayal. Ideology was standardized through a series of publications. Salig Ram wrote the *Prem Bāni*, four volumes of verse in Hindi, the *Prem Patra*, six volumes of prose also in Hindi, the *Rādhāsoāmī Mat Prakāsh*, a prose statement in English, and several smaller treatises in Hindi and Urdu. This body of literature gave members of the movement a more detailed exposition of its ideology

[32] Juergensmeyer, 'Radhasoami reality', ch. 2, p. 3.
[33] Philip H. Ashby, *Modern Trends in Hinduism* (New York, Columbia University Press, 1974), p. 76.
[34] Om Parkash, 'Origin and growth of the Radha Soami movement in the Punjab under Baba Singh Ji Majaraj, Beas (1884–1903)', *Punjab History Conference: 12th Proceedings* (1978), 227–8.

and spiritual practices.[35] Since the Satsang did not proselytize, their publications also assisted in winning new members. Recruits were welcomed from any sectarian or religious background and membership included Hindus, Sikhs, Muslims, and Jains of all classes.[36] The one requirement for membership was an acceptance of the *guru* and his authority.

Salig Ram managed to hold the loose coalition of leaders together, but this unity was weakened further with the death of Radhaji in 1894. When Salig Ram died in 1898, the question of a succession again placed strain on the Satsangis. One faction in Agra favoured Ajudia Prasad, the Swami's son, while a larger section preferred Brahm Shankar Misra, who was recognized as the replacement for Salig Ram. Born Brahm Shankar Misra in Benares on 3 March 1861, the new leader was from a Bengali Brahman family. He received an advanced English education. In 1884 Brahm Shankar earned a Master of Arts degree at Calcutta University. Later he joined Bareilly College as a teacher and still later served in the Accountant General's Office in Allahabad.[37] In 1885, Brahm Shankar read a copy of *Sār Bachan* and then joined the Satsang. He soon became a prominent member and even developed his own Satsang meetings in Allahabad. When Salig Ram died, Brahm Shankar replaced him and became known as Maharaj Sahib. He held this position until his death on 12 October 1907.

In an attempt to create formal unity among the various branches of the movement and the contending leaders, Brahm Shankar introduced the Central Administrative Council in 1902. This body was intended to regulate the conduct of business for the Satsang and its branches, to preserve and administer all properties given to Swami Dayal or acquired by the Satsang, and to execute any other tasks 'in accordance with the directions and mandates of the Sant Sat Guru'.[38] The Council was intended to strengthen Brahm Shankar's authority and also was something of a compromise with other leaders. Members of the Council were elected, ten out of a slate of twenty-eight, by the entire membership. The youngest brother of Shiv Dayal became its first president, with Misra and Salig Ram's son serving on the Council. These three had the right to initiate new members into the Satsang. This

---

[35] Maheshwari, *Radhasoami Faith*, p. 46.

[36] Juergensmeyer, 'Radhasoami reality', ch. 1, p. 4.

[37] See both Maheshwari, *Radhasoami Faith*, p. 49, and Farquhar, *Modern Religious Movements*, p. 165.

[38] Maheshwari, *Radhasoami Faith*, pp. 97–8.

right was extended to Jaimal Singh, and to the leaders of Satsangs in Bengal and Benares.[39] In accordance with the Council's goals, the relatives and heirs of Shiv Dayal signed over all property to the Council on the basis that it belonged to the Sant Sat Guru who was then leading the community and not to him or to his descendants. Two years later the Radhasoami Trust was established and it held all property under the management of a somewhat smaller body. Thus control and administration became centralized, at least in theory. Jaimal Singh, however, refused to turn his records over to the Council and acted independently because he believed himself the sole spiritual heir of Shiv Dayal.

Brahm Shankar also introduced a new sense of discipline to the functioning of the Satsang. He insisted that discourses be delivered at a set time regardless of the seasonal changes. Men and women were seated separately at the Satsangs and he even instituted a system of separate child care. In addition Misra attempted to restructure the role of the *sādhus* (begging mendicants). The Radhasoamis taught a form of *grihastha dharma* (a religious path for householders), and discouraged anyone from leaving his family for religious ends. Brahm Shankar maintained that those who were already *sādhus* should settle down, abandon begging, and their ochre robes, and then the Satsang would provide them with a monthly stipend. In addition to his organizational changes he added one, not quite finished book, to the literature of the Satsang. This was a 300-page volume entitled *Discourses on Radhasoami Faith*. By this time the doctrine of the Satsang had grown in detail and structure.

In the eyes of the Radhasoami Satsang the whole of creation consisted of the three descending spheres. The highest was one of total spirituality, the second a mixture of spiritual-material, and the last a reverse combination of the material-spiritual. The Supreme Being dwelt in the first level and man at the lowest subdivision of the last. Man must find his way up through levels and sublevels to the ultimate spirit that rules over all and it is the *guru* on earth who has the knowledge and techniques needed for the journey. This ideology centred on two principles from which were constructed a moral code of action. First, 'all acts including spiritual practice which tend to free the spirit from matter and raise it towards its sources are good works', and second, 'all acts which tend to degrade the spirit by weighing it down-

[39] Juergensmeyer, 'Radhasoami reality', ch. 2, p. 9.

wards deeper and deeper into matter are bad works'.[40] In practice, this meant a vegetarian diet free from liquor and drugs, a moral life, and a strong emphasis on the devotional practice of religion.

The Radhasoamis entered the twentieth century as a divided religious movement held together loosely by the personality of Brahm Shankar Misra. It possessed doctrines of worship and an organizational structure that borrowed concepts from English society and fused them to the ancient institution of the *guru*. It exhibited a strong sense of social justice and a successful entrepreneurial drive by businesses acting on behalf of the community and not the individual. The Radhasoamis tended to ignore whatever did not directly affect their own vision of life and the universe, and to search for social and religious changes within their various Satsangs.

In defence of Hindu orthodoxy: the Bharat Dharma Mahamandala

Unlike the Radhasoami Satsang with its focus on a particular religious vision, the Bharat Mahamandala strove to defend Hindu orthodoxy against all opponents whether they lay outside of, or within, Hinduism. The first fifteen years of the Mahamandala were closely tied to the life of its founder, Pandit Din Dayalu Sharma.[41] Born in May 1863 in the town of Jhajjar, the young Gaur (a subcaste of the Brahmans) learned Persian and Urdu in local schools. Din Dayalu also studied Sanskrit. He next attended the government school in Jhajjar. Din Dayalu worked for the census of 1881, and in the following year founded his first Hindu association, the Panchāyat Taraqqi Hunūd (The Council for the Advancement of the Hindus). In 1883 its name was changed to the Society Rafah-i-'Am in an attempt to include Muslims and thus to serve all religions. The society published a monthly paper, *Hariyānā*. In 1885, Din Dayalu accepted a position as editor of the *Mathurā Akhbār*, an Urdu monthly dedicated to expressing Hindu religious principles. The following year he left Mathura and travelled to Lahore where he shared the editorship of the Urdu weekly, *Koh-i-Nūr*, with Munshi Har Sukh Rai. Through his travels and work on two newspapers, Pandit Din Dayalu met prominent Hindus of both Punjab and

---

[40] Farquhar, *Modern Religious Movements*, p. 162.
[41] Pandit Harihar Swarup Sharma, an untitled, unfinished and unpublished Hindi biography of Pandit Din Dayalu Sharma, pp. 5–9. Information in this section will be from this source unless otherwise cited.

the North-Western Provinces. Using his contacts, Din Dayalu turned again to establishing an expressly Hindu organization.

In 1886 the young pandit called a meeting in Hardwar and founded the Gau Varnashrama Hitaishini Ganga Dharma Sabha (The Religious Association for the Benefit of the Cow, Social Order, and the Holy Ganges). The immediate issue that stimulated this organization rested with boxes set up along the banks of the Ganges by the Arya Samaj. After they had bathed in the river the pilgrims dropped donations into these receptacles. In this way, the money collected at an orthodox pilgrimage site aided Hindu critics of orthodoxy. This new society, after electing officers and establishing its own organization, urged the priests of Hardwar to end this practice that allowed their enemies to profit from orthodox rituals. Discussion then turned to questions of respect for the holy Ganga (i.e. the Ganges River), cows, Brahman priests, and places of pilgrimage. All agreed that Hindus were divided and so there must be an attempt to create a greater degree of unity, and that they must work for the preservation of *sanātana dharma*. At the close of this first meeting, the new society had constructed an organizational structure with officials, a headquarters in Hardwar, and a set of published rules. The Sabha had articulated the view of Brahman priests as to the type of social and cultural tasks facing them and their allies, but little else was accomplished.

In the aftermath of the Hardwar meeting, Din Dayalu travelled extensively organizing Sanatana Dharma Sabhas, *goshālās* (homes for cattle), and Sanskrit schools. He toured Punjab, the Gangetic plain, and went as far east as Calcutta. During this period he and others spoke of creating an organization with broad goals, one that would represent all Hindus. At a meeting held in April 1887 in the Princely State of Kapurthala, a small group of Din Dayalu's associates joined with him to plan a new organization, the Bharat Dharma Mahamandala, with the purpose of bringing together all leaders of the orthodox Hindu community. A welcoming committee was organized with Pandit Din Dayalu as its chairman. It met in Hardwar on 4 May 1887, sent out letters and circulars announcing the new society, and the date of its first meeting, 29–31 May 1887. They invited individuals to attend and suggested that anyone with a question concerning the Vedas, Shastras, Puranas, or other Hindu scripture should submit it in writing so that it could be answered by the assembled priests.

The first gathering of the Mahamandala was set for the Hindu holy day, Gaṅgā Dashmī, when Hardwar was filled with pilgrims.It began with ritual bathing, followed by other ceremonies, numerous speeches, and the passing of resolutions. These focused on the need to protect *varnāshramadharma*, the traditional pattern of religious duties as expressed in the caste system, on the urgency for religious preaching, for Sanatana Dharma Sabhas, and for the defence of Hinduism from critics both within the community and outside of it. Din Dayalu spoke on the need for Sanskrit schools and for Hindi to be the language of education and administration. The Mahamandala agreed to send out *updeshaks* (paid missionaries) to propagate its goals and act to tie this organization with local Sanatana Sabhas. This first meeting ended with great enthusiasm and renewed hope that orthodoxy could protect itself in an era of apathy and degeneracy. The Mahamandala was sustained by members of the ruling Hindu aristocracy, landowners, priests, heads of Hindu societies as well as the Theosophists who were represented by Colonel Olcott (see pp. 167–79).

The Mahamandala held its second meeting 24–7 March 1889, at the Shri Govinda Deva temple in Brindaban. This time the announcement was written in Hindi according to a decision taken at the first meeting to use Hindi for all Mahamandala proceedings. The notice claimed that prior to their first gathering there were fewer than 100 Hindu religious organizations in India, but that in the last two years their number had risen to over 200. Once again the Mahamandala met at the same time as a major religious fair in order to guarantee as large a gathering as possible. It reported that over 500 delegates attended with more than 5,000 visitors. This assembly resembled the first meeting with a combination of rituals, speeches and resolutions. Similar results came from the 1890 gathering in Delhi. The Mahamandala met there on 14–16 November 1890, in a much grander and more elaborate setting than the two earlier gatherings. The conference site was on the banks of the Jumna River. Two pavilions, one small and one large, stood at the meeting place. The smaller contained 125 Brahmans reciting the *gāyatrī mantra*, the larger had a platform for priests with a throne holding the sacred scriptures. There was a speakers' podium as well upon which sat the high-ranking officers of the Mahamandala. It was a grand setting that illustrated the dreams and hopes of orthodox Hindus.

Although the Delhi gathering followed previous patterns, two resolutions showed new directions: one which objected to government interference with Hindu customs. This issue grew from the proposed

Age of Consent Bill then being widely discussed. A second resolution condemned the use of dowries for marriages, and thus placed the Mahamandala in the role of a critic of, at least, one contemporary practice. Din Dayalu had already spoken against 'bad customs' such as the singing of obscene songs, as an example of Hindu degeneracy. Another departure from previous practice appeared on the fifth day when the conference was open only to delegates. Problems of organization and administration had created serious internal tension. After a lengthy discussion the delegates decided that ten representatives should be chosen as trustees for the Mahamandala, and that each delegate should return to his home association to ask its members where they thought the organizational headquarters should be established. In response to an invitation from Pandit M. M. Malaviya, they agreed to hold their next meeting in Benares.

The conference at Benares began on 29 February 1892, and lasted fifteen days. On the fifth day a Mantran Sabha or Advisory Council was chosen, and for the next four days discussion focused on the functioning of this council. These deliberations failed to solve the various organizational and administrative problems facing the Mahamandala. On 2–4 November 1893 it returned to Delhi, but unlike all previous meetings this was an organizational work-session limited to official delegates. After lengthy discussions they managed to choose a Karyakarina Sabha or Working Committee. Pandit Din Dayalu pushed for the founding of a Hindu college, but received only partial support for this idea. Later an office of the Mahamandala was established in Delhi with Din Dayalu overseeing it.

The Mahamandala continued its conferences: at Amritsar in 1896, Kapurthala in 1897, and Mathura in 1899. Din Dayalu remained secretary, but turned much of his attention toward the creation of a college in Delhi. The question of where such a college might be located became an issue among the supporters of the Mahamandala. Finally with the assistance of the Vaishya Conference of Delhi, Din Dayalu opened the Hindu College, Delhi, on 15 May 1899. The College survived, but was plagued by a continuing struggle to find funds for its maintenance.

In August 1900 the Mahamandala returned once more to Delhi. It claimed an attendance of delegates from over 800 Dharm Sabhas. Again there was a series of grand events. The Maharaja of Dharbanga arrived on his special train to take the office of conference president. A procession carrying the Vedas, a performance of the *sandhya* ritual, speeches, and resolutions demonstrated the growing importance of the Mahamandala. Yet beneath the surface tensions between rivals for leadership emerged following the Delhi conference. In 1896 Swami Gyanananda founded the Nigamagama Mandali in Mathura. This organization became part of the Mahamandala in March 1901. Swami Gyanananda then began to issue regulations and make decisions concerning the Mahamandala. He was supported by several Hindu leaders and also the Theosophical Society. In 1902 Pandit Din Dayalu Sharma resigned his position as secretary and gradually withdrew from the Mahamandala.

Under Swami Gyanananda's leadership, the headquarters moved to Mathura and in 1903 to Benares where it remained. In addition Swami Gyanananda became secretary and a new constitution was adopted.[42] In the next three decades the Mahamandala evolved into a subcontinental organization. By 1930 it had provincial bodies as far east as Calcutta, to the South in Madras, to the West at Karachi, and to the North in Srinagar; 950 branch societies were registered with the Mahamandala and accepted their rules. Another 150 sabhās of various kinds were associated with the main organization. The Mahamandala maintained its goals through periodic conferences and the celebration of religious sacrifices. They lobbied with the government over issues that supported orthodoxy and on questions that threatened their interests. The Mahamandala sent delegations to the Viceroy and fought various legislation on marriage, divorce, cow protection, and opposed dams on the Ganges River, in short anything that appeared to threaten the practise of 'proper' Hinduism. They could and did mobilize public opinion through their extensive organizational structure.

The Mahamandala was organized into various departments that focused on preaching by paid missionaries of Hindu orthodoxy, the establishment of Sanatana Dharma schools, the publication of supporting literature, journals such as Suryodya and the Mahamandala Magazine, religious texts, and approved rules of conduct. A major division of the Mahamandala conducted rituals, established religious centres, managed them, and carried out an extensive programme of repair to numerous existing temples, pilgrimage sites, and monasteries. They also fought the 'unjust' building of mosques. Funds for this and other

[42] All information on the Mahamandala in the twentieth century is drawn from the Sri Bharat Mahamandala Directory, 1930, published in Hindi by the Mahamandala office in Benares.

Mahamandala projects rested heavily on large donations from Hinda princes. Their activities also included efforts to uplift women through education, founding almshouses for indigent women, widows' homes, and the publication of journals, books, and tracts for women.

The Bharat Dharma Mahamandala had grown from its roots in the societies founded by Din Dayalu Sharma into a widespread organization that claimed, with some justification, to represent Hindu orthodoxy. Funded by Hindu rulers, wealthy landowners, and merchants, this was perhaps the most successful orthodox organization in the subcontinent. Its impressive programme touched all major interests of the Hindu religious establishment, provided a body to pressure the government on issues that affected Hinduism as they envisioned it, linked diverse regional groups, and attempted to standardize religious practices throughout the Hindu community. Most successful north of the Vindhya Mountains, the Mahamandala was able to establish numerous bases in the Deccan and even to penetrate the Dravidian South. As an orthodox society it also created and maintained an extensive organizational structure, a feat few orthodox groups, in any religion, were able to emulate.

THE GANGETIC CORE IN THE NINETEENTH CENTURY: A SUMMARY

Socio-religious movements of the Gangetic plains drew on the long-standing customs and ideals of each religious community. They did so in a region of South Asia where the power of two traditional religious elites, the Brahmans and the 'ulamā, restricted direct challenges to established customs more than in either Bengal or the Punjab. What interaction existed between the two religious communities was largely defensive and acted to clarify the lines that divided Hindus and Muslims. There is little evidence of influence from one community helping to shape a particular movement within the other.

By the end of the nineteenth century, Muslims of the Gangetic plains had produced socio-religious movements designed to restore their community to its rightful position in society. All, save the Barelwis, advocated various alterations in contemporary religion, and legitimized their programmes through different versions of religious authority. Four ideological approaches and concomitant patterns of action were clearly discernible. The Tariqah-i-Muhammadiyah attempted to re-establish Islamic supremacy through war and thus to elevate the entire Muslim community. Egalitarian in their approach, the Muhammadis appealed to all levels of Islamic society. After the defeat of the Muhammadi *jihād* and British suppression of the Mutiny, Muslim movements were primarily concerned with the loss of status and power of the elites. The Deobandis, Ahl-i-Hadith, and founders of the Nadwah Dar al-'Ulum focused on the role of the *'ulamā* as 'natural' leaders of the Muslims. They all dealt with the loss of Islamic political power by creating an Islamic community that would retain its cohesion through an appeal to the individual's conscience, rather than state authority. The *'ulamā* would instruct their fellow Muslims and thus lead the way to a religious revival as well as to the maintenance of their own class status. By contrast, Sayyid Ahmad Khan envisioned the re-emergence of a bureaucratic and administrative elite who would guide their fellow Muslims into cooperation with the British-Indian government, and do so on the basis of a mixture of Islamic and western education. Finally the Barelwis defended orthodoxy in an alliance with the hereditary *pīrs* of the countryside. Muslims, in their encounter with foreign conquest and civilization, fragmented into opposing schools of thought and action that represented different constituencies within their society and expressed contrasting perceptions of their historic dilemma. These movements also extended beyond the Islamic community, in reaction to challenges from an increasingly aggressive Hindu elite that saw itself as the spokesman for the majority community.

During the second half of the nineteenth century, Hindus of the Gangetic plain created two types of socio-religious movement within this region, both acculturative, but one also defensively orthodox. They were also influenced by the Brahmo Samaj, as Bengalis moved north-west in search of employment. The Hindus of the Gangetic basin first turned to their traditional institutions. The Radhasoamis refurbished the *guru*, adding to this ancient institution such innovations as photography and new forms of organization. They offered a flexible approach to social and cultural change, for whatever problem or question might arise, the living *guru* provided an answer. Religious authority was alive and available for those who accepted it, and such authority covered all aspects of life. The Radhasoamis appealed to a rising vernacular, literate group and to a lesser degree to English literates. Through their publications and meetings, they promised a form of spiritual enlightenment and a new psycho-social order. For the remaining issues of change and of cultural adjustment, they either adopted what they needed for their religious community or ignored them as irrelevant to the search for spiritual progress. By contrast, the Bharat Dharma Mahamandala, as with the Barelwis, attempted to defend established religion with an organization based on the pre-British elite of aristocrats, priests, landlords, princes, and merchants. They maintained that if each individual would adhere to *varnāshra-madharma*, then Hinduism would once more flourish as it had prior to the arrival of Islam. Members of both religious communities turned first to their own traditions of thought and action, and only in the second half of the nineteenth century was there the beginning of conscious interaction with British culture. Struggles with the opposing communities played a less important role here than the communal conflicts of Punjab and the North-West.

CHAPTER FOUR

PUNJAB AND THE NORTH-WEST

THE SETTING

The Punjab encompasses the land west of the Sutlej to the Indus River, and from the Himalayan foothills south to the confluence of the Panjnad and Indus Rivers. North of the Punjab are the foothills and the Himalayan mountains that include the Kashmir valley. To the West lies the edge of the Iranian plateau with its sharp hills, tribal groups, and key passes. To the South of eastern Punjab is Rajasthan with its dry, hilly topography that merges to the East with the great Indian desert. Beyond Rajasthan, at the lower end of the Indus River, is Sind, a semi-desert land at the edge of South Asia.

The Hindu-Buddhist cultures of the North-West extend back in time to the third millennium BC and were the first to be incorporated into the Islamic world, Sind in AD 712, and the Punjab by the end of the twelfth century. Majorities of Muslims lived in Sind, western Punjab, and Kashmir. Hindus remained the majority in eastern Punjab, Rajasthan, and the Punjab hills. The religious structure of this region was given a new dimension when Guru Nanak founded Sikhism (see p. 13). In 1799, under the leadership of Ranjit Singh, they established a Sikh kingdom that ruled Punjab and Kashmir.

In 1803 British victories brought them to Delhi and the eastern border of the Sikh kingdom, as the lands between the Sutlej and Jumna Rivers came under British control. After 1818 the princes of Rajasthan accepted British supremacy, and in 1843 Sind was annexed to the Bombay Presidency. The two Anglo-Sikh wars led to the acquisition of the Jullundur Doab in 1846, and of the entire Sikh kingdom in 1849. The British Empire expanded to its geographic limits with a fluctuating border in the trans-Indus territory. This vast surge of the British political sphere, the last such expansion in South Asia, was followed by a much slower uneven growth of the cultural milieu.

Delhi during its pre-Mutiny 'renaissance' became the source of cultural interaction for the Punjab until it was replaced by Lahore. In between these two cities, Ludhiana gained prominence after 1834

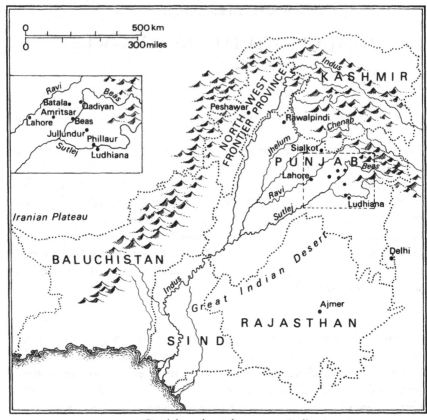

3 Punjab and north-western India

when the American Presbyterian Mission established its new head-quarters there. The next year the Mission acquired a printing press and proceeded to publish tracts, translations of the scriptures, grammars, and dictionaries in Punjabi, Urdu, Persian, Hindi and Kashmiri. As with the Baptists of Serampore, the Ludhiana missionaries did much to standardize the languages of this region. They also introduced new forms of religious organization and aggressive proselytism. For the missionaries, Ludhiana was a forward base from which they quickly expanded after the Punjab was annexed on 29 March 1849. The growth of Christian missions was interrupted briefly by the Mutiny, but during the 1860s they created a chain of missions throughout the North-West. Theirs was an aggressive and uncompromising Christian-ity, which was expressed in print and through open preaching in the streets. During the second half of the nineteenth century, Christian converts rose from 3,912 in 1881 to 37,980 by 1901 – small numbers for Punjab, but percentage increases that frightened indigenous religious leaders. The Christian missionaries were seen as part of a government machine that first defeated the Punjabi, next sought to govern him, and then to convert him. This comprised a 'hard' impact in contrast with the experience of Bengalis during the period when Christianity and government could still be seen as somewhat separate. It is against this framework that we must view the first of the socio-religious move-ments of Punjab.

The Nirankaris

Baba Dayal Das (1783–1855) founded the Nirankaris, a movement of purification and return. Dayal Das was born into a Malhotra Khatri family in Peshawar and raised as a pious, religiously oriented boy, but beyond this we know little of his early life. After his parents died, Dayal Das moved to Rawalpindi where he opened an apothecary shop. Ap-parently disenchanted with contemporary religion, Dayal Das con-cluded that Sikhism was decadent, filled with falsehood, superstition and error. Sometime during the decade of the 1840s, he called for the return of Sikhism to its origins and emphasized the worship of God as nirānkār (formless). Such an approach meant a rejection of idols, rituals associated with idolatry, and the Brahman priests who conducted these rituals.[1] A repudiation of Brahman priests meant also a rejection of those Sikhs allied with them. Dayal Das quickly ran into opposition from the established religious authorities; consequently, the movement progressed in secret until the British gained control of the Punjab.

The Nirankaris focused more on deficiencies in religious practice than on a critique of theology. The appropriate path to God was through worship based on meditation rather than complex ritual. Dayal Das urged his disciples to meet each morning for daily worship in their *dharmshālās*. He stressed the importance and authority of Guru Nanak and of the Adi Granth (the source of all authority and knowledge). His disciples were 'to worship the formless God, to obey the *shabad* of the guru [in the Adi Granth], to clean the shoes and feet of the congregation [as an act of humility], to serve one's parents, to avoid bad habits, and to earn one's livelihood through work'.[2] In accordance with Sikh tradition, Dayal Das taught a religious code for the house-holder, that is, an individual who retained his familial and social ties and had not withdrawn into the role of a mendicant.

In addition Dayal Das taught that women should not be treated as unclean at childbirth; disciples should not use astrology or horoscopes in setting the time for ceremonies; the dowry should not be displayed at marriages; neither lighted lamps nor blessed sweets, *prasād*, should be placed in rivers; and no one should feed Brahmans as payment for conducting rituals. Eating meat, drinking liquor, lying, cheating, using false weights – all were forbidden. Each should follow a strict moral code and use only the proper life-cycle rituals as taught by Dayal Das. The new ceremonies included those of birth, naming of a child, a shortened marriage ceremony that had at its core a circumambulation of the Adi Granth, and a death-rite requiring that the body be immersed in a river or cremated. All ceremonies eliminated the services of a Brahman priest.

Slowly the Nirankaris attracted new members. Because of persecution, Dayal Das purchased land on the edge of Rawalpindi where he constructed a *dharmshālā*, which became a centre of worship and was known as the Nirankari Darbar. Baba Dayal Das died on 30 January 1855 before he could bring organization and cohesion to this

---

[1] There is some disagreement on just when Baba Dayal Das began to preach and draw to him disciples, see John C. B. Webster, *The Nirankari Sikhs* (Delhi, Macmillan Company, 1979), p. 10; information from this section will be from Webster or it will be cited specifically.
[2] *Ibid.*, p. 14.

movement. The Nirankaris of Rawalpindi placed his body in the Lei River at a spot where he used to meditate. Later it was known as Dayalsar and considered sacred by the Nirankaris. Before his death Dayal Das named his son, Baba Darbara Singh (1814–70), to succeed him.

Darbara Singh, born under the name of Mul Rai, was an energetic and persuasive leader who was determined to cut all ties with Hinduism. A year after he had replaced his father, Darbara Singh began to issue *hukamnāmās* (statements describing both doctrine and approved rituals). He toured the Rawalpindi area and while travelling preached, converted, and married his followers according to their own rites. In 1861 he visited Amritsar and asked permission to perform the Nirankari marriage ceremony at the Golden Temple. This request was rejected; however, he conducted such a service in Amritsar on 17 April 1861.[3] In fifteen years Darbara Singh opened forty new subcentres as the number of disciples continued to grow: under him the Nirankaris had their most rapid period of expansion. He died on 13 February 1870, and his younger brother, Rattan Chand, succeeded him.

Rattan Chand established new centres and appointed *bīredārs* (leaders) for each congregation or *sangat*. The *bīredārs* oversaw these groups and were charged with reciting the *hukamnāmās* every fifteen days. Thus they provided a tie between the head of the Nirankari movement and its members. Rattan Chand developed Dayalsar into a religious hub as new *bīras* (congregations) were added to the surrounding towns and villages. In 1903 he wrote a will leaving all property of the association to his successor, and before his death on 3 January 1909 he named his son, Baba Gurdit Singh, to fill that office. Gurdit Singh headed the movement until his death on 26 April 1947.

The historical impact of the Nirankaris remains a matter of some debate, since even the most basic information is open to question. The census of 1891 stated that there were over 60,000 Sikhs in this movement. John Webster considers these figures exaggerated, and those of the 1921 census as too low with the more realistic estimate of around 5,000 members.[4] Drawing on Sikh tradition, the Nirankaris focused on Guru Nanak, on Sikhism before the establishment of the Khalsa by Guru Gobind Singh at Anandpur, and the militarization of the faith. In this they pursued a path open to both orthodox, *keshadhārīs*, Sikhs and

---

[3] Man Singh Nirankari, 'The Nirankaris', *Punjab Past and Present* (April 1973), 5–6.
[4] See Nirankari, 'The Nirankaris', pp. 6–7, 10; and Webster, *The Nirankari Sikhs*, p. 16.

to the non-baptized ranks of the *sahajdhārīs*, but drew members mainly from the urban non-Jat section of the Sikh community. The Nirankaris stressed proper religious practice, issued *hukamnāmās* to define its concepts of what was correct and built a series of worship centres staffed by their own priests. They did not clash with or oppose the British, but grew in part through the establishment of British rule in the Punjab since that freed them from the restriction of the Sikh government. The Nirankaris thus became a permanent subsection of the Sikh religion and in doing so helped to clarify the lines dividing Sikhs from Hindus. Their dependence on Guru Nanak and early Sikhism for their model of 'pure' religion separated them from another transitional movement, the Namdharis.

The Namdharis

Baba Ram Singh (1816–85) founded this transitional movement. He was born into a poor carpenter's family in the village of Bhaini Arayian in Ludhiana district. Little is known about Ram Singh's early life. Apparently he received no formal education and was married at the age of seven. Later his wife was addressed as 'Mata' or mother by members of the Namdhari movement.[5] In 1836, when Ram Singh was twenty, he joined the army of Ranjit Singh and served until 1845. While a soldier he demonstrated a deep commitment to religion and began to attract his own following. In 1841, he met Balak Singh of Hazru in Campbellpur district and became his disciple. Balak Singh urged his listeners to live a simple life and to reject all ritual except for repeating God's name. Those who accepted Balak Singh's leadership saw him as a reincarnation of Guru Gobind Singh. Before his death, Balak Singh chose Ram Singh as his successor.

In 1855 Ram Singh returned to Bhaini, where he reopened the family's shop and lived there until his exile in 1872. Gradually disciples flocked to Bhaini where Ram Singh ran a free kitchen and preached his ideas of a purified Sikhism. In 1857, he formally inaugurated the Namdhari movement with a set of rituals modelled after Guru Gobind Singh's founding of the Khalsa. Ram Singh used a recitation of *gurbānī* (hymns from the Granth Sāhib), *ardas* (the Sikh prayer), a flag, and baptism for entry into the new community. Each of the baptized Sikhs

[5] Fauja Singh Bajwa, *The Kuka Movement: An Important Phase in Punjab's Role in India's Struggle for Freedom* (Delhi, Motilal Banarsidass, 1965), pp. 5–6; this is the basic source used for the Namdharis and any other sources will be cited.

was required to wear the five symbols with the exception of the *kirpān* (sword) no longer allowed by the British government. Instead of the sword, Ram Singh required them to keep a *lāthī* (a bamboo stave). In addition the Namdharis wore white clothes with a white turban and carried a rosary to further set them apart from all others.

Ram Singh demanded that his adherents abandon the worship of gods, goddesses, idols, graves, tombs, trees, and snakes. Popular saints were rejected along with the rituals conducted by Brahman priests and the authority of the hereditary custodians of the Sikh *gurdwārās* (centres of worship). He also condemned the claims to special status by the Sodhis and Bedis, descendants of the Sikh *gurus*. The Namdharis were told to abstain from 'drinking, stealing, adultery, falsehood, slandering, back-biting and cheating'.[6] The consumption of beef was strictly forbidden, since protection of cattle remained one of the Namdaris' most ardently held values. Proper behaviour was enforced by *panchāyats* (village courts), which dispensed the appropriate punishment for a particular transgression. Ram Singh condemned beggary and thus the role of mendicants. His was a householder's religious path that stressed hard work, cleanliness and a moral life.

The Namdharis granted women a degree of equality. They too were initiated through baptism, allowed to remarry when widowed; dowries were rejected, and child marriage forbidden. For men, there was an emphasis on strength and martial qualities drawn from the teachings of Guru Gobind Singh and, no doubt, from Ram Singh's years as a soldier. As he articulated his ideas, the movement grew and the village of Bhaini became a point of pilgrimage later known as Bhaini Sahib. In time Namdhari worship acquired a new dimension. Hymns were accompanied with shouts of joy (*kūks*), as the worshipper slipped into a state of ecstasy. This form of worship resulted in the Namdharis being referred to as *kūkās* (shouters). Many outside the Namdhari community saw them as peculiar and extreme, but they considered themselves as bearers of the only true Sikhism.[7]

Ram Singh attracted many of his disciples from the peasant and untouchable castes and transformed them into a disciplined community. *Sangats* were organized in any village that had a group of Namdharis. Each *sangat* had its own place of worship, a *granthī*

[6] *Ibid.*, pp. 24–5.
[7] Khushwant Singh, *A History of the Sikhs* (Princeton University Press, 1966), vol. 2, pp. 128–9.

(scripture-reciter), and a free kitchen. The *granthī* taught Gurmukhi and the Sikh scriptures to both children and adults. *Sangats* were grouped together and administered by *sūbās* (governors), *nāib sūbās* (assistant-governors), and *jathedārs* (group leaders), whose primary function was to collect funds and remit them to the headquarters at Bhaini. The Namdharis also maintained a system of preachers to spread their message and their own postal runners to ensure communications within the community. Among the Namdharis, prophetic letters appeared that described a reincarnation of Guru Gobind Singh in the person of Ram Singh, and predicted the re-establishment of the Sikh kingdom.[8]

The Punjab government became sufficiently uneasy with the Namdharis that on 28 June 1863 they interned Ram Singh in his village where he was held until the end of 1866. By 1863, the Namdharis were estimated to have between 40,000 to 60,000 members and approximately 100,000 by 1871.[9] The impressive growth of this movement as well as its militant ideology led the Punjab government to keep them under close surveillance and to prohibit Namdhari missionaries from preaching to Sikh troops of the British-Indian army. The period from 1867 to 1870 remained quiet as the Namdharis continued to make converts. Yet some type of conflict with the government seemed almost inevitable. When Ram Singh visited Amritsar in 1867, he arrived with nearly 3,500 followers, converted 2,000, and conducted himself as a prince. He travelled with an escort of soldiers, held court daily, and exchanged gifts with local rulers. The clash, when it finally exploded, was not over Ram Singh's acquisition of secular status, but the issue of cow protection.

Under Ranjit Singh the slaughter of cattle had been outlawed, but the British lifted this ban. Cattle once more became a source of meat for the British and for Punjabi Muslims. The latter also publicly sacrificed cattle on the Islamic festival of 'Id. Both Hindus and Sikhs objected to this and found offensive the presence of slaughter-houses and meat shops. The Namdharis were pledged to protect cattle and to end their slaughter. In 1871 two incidents occurred as Namdharis put their beliefs into practice. On the night of 15 June, a small band attacked a

---

[8] *Ibid.*, p. 130.
[9] Estimates of size vary; Bajwa claims between 300,000 to 400,000 by the end of the 1860s, but the lower, 100,000 figure is given in G. S. Chhabra, *Advanced History of the Punjab* (Ludhiana, 1962), p. 370.

Muslim slaughter-house in Amritsar. One month later a second attack took place in Raikot, Ludhiana District. The British arrested those involved and hung eight of them; however, this did not quiet matters. Another band marched on the small Muslim state of Malerkotla in January 1872. They intended to seize weapons and possibly begin an uprising against the government. To this threat the British reacted with speed and viciousness. The Deputy Commissioner of Ludhiana, Mr L. Cowan, rushed to Malerkotla, arrested the Namdharis, and on 17–18 July executed sixty-five of them.

In the aftermath a mixed military and police force raided Bhaini and arrested Ram Singh; he was exiled to Burma where he died in 1885. The government stationed a police post in the village of Bhaini where they remained until 1922. With the removal of Ram Singh, his younger brother, Baba Budh Singh, became head of the Namdharis. During the remainder of the nineteenth century studies of Namdhari attempts to find allies against the British in Nepal, Kashmir and Russia illustrated their enduring hostility toward the British government. Pilgrims continued to reach Bhaini, but the movement was effectively curtailed. The census of 1891 counted 10,541 Namdharis and in 1901 the number had risen to only 13,788.[10]

The teachings of Ram Singh and his *guru*, Balak Singh, promised a return to purified Sikhism, not of Guru Nanak, but of Guru Gobind Singh. Both leadership and membership came from the Jat peasant class of Punjab, the same segment of society that had supported Guru Gobind Singh and his version of Sikhism. They shared with the Nirankaris the belief that Sikhism was decadent and degenerate and they too sought to return it to past purity. The Namdhari vision of a restructured Sikhism, however, called for a total reshaping of the Sikh community into a militant, religious–political dominion that threatened established religious authority and brought them into direct conflict with the British–Indian government. With their ecstatic devotionalism, a millennial vision of the future, a tightly organized religious community that contained elements of a parallel government they, like the Tariqah-i-Muhammadis, struck against British political dominance and in return were suppressed. Neither Namdharis nor Nirankaris, both transitional movements, were concerned with

---

[10] Chhabra, *Advanced History*, p. 379.

adjusting to the cultural influences of the colonial milieu, a world that had only begun to penetrate the Punjab.

THE CREATION OF THE COLONIAL MILIEU

Once again we must look to Delhi and Ludhiana for sources of imported knowledge, technology, and the beginnings of cultural interaction in the North-West. After the annexation of 1849 and the uprising of 1857, Lahore became the premier city of the North-West; the centre of provincial administration as well as a place of social, educational, and religious ferment. Students travelled to Lahore from throughout the province. There they received an education, participated in the culture of Lahore and then disseminated it throughout the North-West when they departed for jobs in other cities and towns.

The conquest of the Punjab generated a sudden need for educated Indians to staff government offices and the institutions erected by Christian missionaries. Brahmans and Kayasthas were recruited from Bengal and from the North-Western Provinces. Their arrival created an elite situated below the English rulers, but above Punjabis who lacked an English education or an understanding of the new colonial world. Bengalis provided three models for emulation: one as orthodox Hindus, a second as converts to Christianity, and a third as members of the Brahmo Samaj. Of the three types, the Brahmos were the most outspoken, aggressive, and articulate. In 1863 a few Bengalis and Punjabis founded the Lahore Brahmo Samaj. Much of the dynamics of this society derived from the leadership of Babu Novin Chandra Roy, a Bengali employed as paymaster of the North-Western Railway offices in Lahore. He wrote extensively as an advocate of socially radical Brahmoism, fought for increased use of Hindi, and succeeded in recruiting new members among Bengalis and Punjabis. The Lahore Brahmo Samaj was aided by visits from leading Bengali Brahmos. Keshab Chandra Sen spoke in Lahore in 1867 and 1873, Debendranath Tagore in 1867, 1872 and 1874, and Protap Chandra Majumdar in 1871.[11]

Islamic influences also reached Punjab and the North-West from the Gangetic plain and particularly from Delhi. The career of 'Abdul-

[11] Kenneth W. Jones, *Arya Dharm, Hindu Consciousness in 19th-Century Punjab* (Berkeley, University of California Press, 1976), p. 16; and Sivanatha Sastri, *History of the Brahmo Samaj* (Calcutta, R. Chatterjee, 1911), vol. 2, p. 395.

Minan Wazirabadi illustrates the diffusion of Islamic ideas. He was born in Jhelum, travelled first to Bhopal and then to Delhi for his education. In Delhi he studied under Nazir Husain and when he returned to the Punjab, he brought the ideology of Ahl-i-Hadith with him, becoming one of this movement's most effective exponents.[12] Another prominent supporter of Ahl-i-Hadith in Punjab was Maulawi Muhammad Husain of Batala (Gurdaspur district), who began publishing the newspaper, *Ishāʿat-i-Sunnah*.[13] At an extreme of movements of return, the Lahore Ahl-i-Qur'an, founded by 'Abd 'Ullah Chakralawi, rejected orthodox Islam as well as all movements such as the Ahl-i-Hadith that accepted forms of authority other than the Qur'an. Chakralawi and his few followers clashed with all other Muslim groups, remaining as they did on one end of a continuum of advocates for religious and social change.

New types of Islamic organization began to appear in the years after the Mutiny. In 1866 the Anjuman-i-Himayat-i-Islam (the Society for the Defence of Islam) was founded in Lahore by Muhammad Shafi and Shah Din, both followers of Sayyid Ahmad Khan. This society opened schools that included western education and required the study of English. They emphasized female education, loyalty to the British-Indian government, and opposed the Indian National Congress. This organization was not limited to Lahore. The parent association established branches throughout the subcontinent.[14] Three years later the Anjuman-i-Islamiyah (the Islamic Society) was organized in Lahore to teach Muslim youth the principles of Islam and elements of western knowledge. Thus influences from Muslim movements outside of the North West flowed into that area and beyond through societies and organizations created in the North-West. The largest of the Hindu acculturative socio-religious movements, the Arya Samaj, also demonstrated the inward and outward flow of ideas and organizations.

The Arya Samaj

The career of one man, Swami Dayananda Saraswati (1824–83), changed the face of the Punjab and the territories surrounding it. He

---

[12] Barbara Daly Metcalf, *Islamic Revival in British India: Deoband, 1860–1900* (Princeton University Press, 1982), p. 292.

[13] Spencer Lavan, *The Ahmadiyah Movement, a History and Perspective* (Delhi, Manohar Book Service, 1974), p. 10.

[14] J. N. Farquhar, *Modern Religious Movements in India* (New York, Macmillan, 1919), pp. 347–8; Lavan, *Ahmadiyah Movement*, p. 10.

was born in Tankara (Gujarat), a town in the small Princely State of Morvi. His father, a Samavedi Brahman of the Audichya caste, had considerable status and wealth. Young Dayananda, born Mul Shankar, was educated in his home by local tutors. He studied religious texts and Sanskrit in preparation for his life as an orthodox Shaivite. He questioned and then rejected his expected role. After delaying the marriage his parents wanted, the young Mulji fled from his home to begin the life of a wandering mendicant. He was initiated into the order of Saraswati Dandis, taking the name Dayananda and then dedicated his life to searching for release from rebirth.[15]

His life's direction changed in November 1860, when he met and became the disciple of Swami Virajananda. After nearly three years with Virajananda, Dayananda emerged with a new set of goals, namely to purify Hinduism and save it from its contemporary degenerate state. He also had devised a method of accomplishing this. For Dayananda all truth was to be found in the Vedas by anyone who used the proper analytic and grammatical tools needed to understand Vedic Sanskrit. Dayananda separated all Hindu scriptures into two categories: *ārsha* and *un-ārsha*. The former included the Vedas and any text based on a proper understanding of the Vedas. The latter were the products of the post-Mahabharata period of history when true Vedic knowledge was lost and ignorance prevailed. The Vedas then comprised the yardstick against which all other scriptural texts were judged, as were questions of religious custom and ritual.

Dayananda began to preach a 'purified' Hinduism, one that rejected the popular Puranas, polytheism, idolatry, the role of Brahman priests, pilgrimages, nearly all rituals, and the ban on widow marriage – in short, almost all of contemporary Hinduism. He still dressed and lived as a *sādhu*, spoke in Sanskrit, and debated with orthodox priests. Dayananda visited Calcutta in 1872 where he met Debendranath Tagore as well as other Brahmos. When he left Bengal, Dayananda had abandoned the dress of a mendicant and spoke in Hindi to reach an audience of middle-class, often educated Hindus. Among them his message found a much greater acceptance. One of his new disciples, Raja Jai Kishen Das, suggested he record his ideas, with the result that, in 1875, Dayananda published his first edition of the *Satyārth Prakāsh* (The Light of Truth), in which he elaborated his concepts of true

---

[15] See J. T. F. Jordens, *Dayananda Saraswati, His Life and Ideas* (Delhi, Oxford University Press, 1978), pp. 1–23.

Hinduism. Dayananda condemned all that he considered false, i.e. orthodox Hinduism, Christianity, Islam, Buddhism, Jainism and, Sikhism. For him there was only one true faith, Vedic Hinduism.

In 1874 Dayananda travelled to Gujarat and Bombay. On 10 April 1875 he established the Bombay Arya Samaj (Noble Society). It survived and became the first successful organizational expression of his ideas. Turning north Swami Dayananda reached Delhi in January 1877. Once there sympathetic Hindu leaders, primarily Brahmos, invited him to visit Lahore. After arriving in Delhi on 19 April 1877, Dayananda attacked idolatry, child marriage, elaborate rituals, the Brahman priests, and, at the same time, insisted on the infallibility of the Vedas. Orthodox Hindus were outraged and critics, such as the Brahmos, disturbed by his insistence on Vedic truth.[16]

Swami Dayananda remained in the Punjab until 11 July 1878, when he left for the North-Western Provinces. During these months he criss-crossed the Punjab. In Lahore he quickly attracted a group of dedicated disciples, many of whom were students and graduates of the Lahore colleges. On 24 June 1877, after three months of public lectures and private discussions, the Lahore Arya Samaj held its first meeting. The lengthy statement of belief was rewritten by Punjabi Aryas and reduced to ten simple principles that became the universal creed of the Samaj. Soon Arya Samajes were organized in different cities of the province. In the meantime Dayananda left for the North-Western Provinces. He toured primarily the western Gangetic plain until the spring of 1881 when he departed for Rajasthan. Here he spent the last two years of his life in a vain attempt to persuade the Rajput princes to accept his vision of a purified world. In this he failed; yet on his death in Ajmer on 30 October 1883, he left behind him Arya Samajes scattered throughout the Punjab and the North-Western Provinces plus a few in Rajasthan and Maharashtra.

The Arya Samaj lacked any central organization and each Samaj was independent. Dayananda's death, however, did not lead to disintegration, but to a burst of energy, as numerous Samajes sought to honour their departed teacher. They were nearly unanimous in the desire to found a school that would impart his Aryan form of Hinduism, and thus be safe from Christian influence. The Lahore Samaj drafted plans for this institution and on 6 December 1883 set up a

---

[16] Jones, *Arya Dharm*, pp. 34–7; information has been taken from this source unless otherwise cited.

subcommittee to raise funds. Initially they were quite successful, but by 1884 enthusiasm waned. In 3 November 1885 the Antarang Sabha (Executive Committee), of the Lahore Samaj, received a letter in which Lala Hans Raj promised to serve as principal of the school without pay. Hans Raj, a Bhalla Khatri, had joined the Arya Samaj while a student at the Lahore Government College. His act of selflessness rekindled the desire for a school. Events then moved quickly. The newly organized Dayananda Anglo-Vedic Trust and Management Society held its first meeting on 27 February 1886 and the school was opened on 1 June of that year. Within one month 550 students had enrolled and on 18 May 1889 the Punjab University granted affiliation to the new Dayananda Anglo-Vedic College. The high school and college taught a curriculum similar to the government schools, but did so without government support or the participation of Englishmen on the faculty. It was highly successful, as students trained in this institution demonstrated the quality of their education in the annual examinations.

The Dayananda Anglo-Vedic Trust and Management Society was the first centralizing organization within the Samaj, with representatives from many branch *samājes*. Still it was limited to issues concerning the school. Consequently, a formal representative body convened in October 1886, the Arya Pratinidhi Sabha, Punjab. Delegates to this Sabha came from throughout the province and in time from branches in Sind and on the trans-Indus frontier. It dealt with a wide variety of questions and provided a degree of centralization missing since Dayananda's death. As the Samaj expanded, other provincial *sabhās* were established: the North-Western Provinces (1886), Rajasthan (1888), Bengal and Bihar (1889), Madhya Pradesh and Vidarbha (1889), and Bombay (1902). Organizational developments, however, could not prevent the rise of internal tensions.

Serious strains first appeared among the Aryas as the Dayananda Anglo-Vedic school progressed from a set of ideals to their concrete expression. A militant party, led by Pandit Guru Datta, began to separate itself from more moderate Aryas. Pandit Guru Datta Vidyarthi was born of a wealthy Arora family in Multan. He earned both a BA and MA degree at the Government College. Guru Datta joined the Arya Samaj and was deeply committed to Dayananda and his message. For Guru Datta this was a religious experience. He considered Dayananda a *rishi* (a divinely inspired prophet), and the *Satyārth Prakāsh* a text that must be taken literally and could not be questioned. He and those, such as Pandit Lekh Ram and Lala Munshi Ram, who shared his vision, wanted the proposed school to focus on Aryan ideology, on the study of Sanskrit and the Vedic scriptures. For them it must be modelled after the ancient Hindu universities, and would thus produce the new 'pure' Hindu youth. The school, once established, expressed the ideas of more moderate Aryas who wished to provide an English education safe from non-Hindu influence and relevant to careers within the colonial milieu.

Tensions between adherents of opposing Aryan concepts erupted in the late 1880s, as the question of who would become principal of the Dayananda Anglo–Vedic College was debated in the Managing Committee. The militants wanted Pandit Guru Datta and a change in the curriculum; the moderates preferred Lala Hans Raj and the existent form of education. The moderates won, but out of this struggle came two clearly defined parties. The militants, later known as the 'Gurukul' wing, stressed the religious nature of the Samaj and the moderates, the 'College' party, saw Dayananda as a great reformer, but not as a divinely inspired *rishi*. The issue of vegetarianism came to symbolize these internal differences. Militant Aryas insisted on a strict vegetarian diet, while the moderates maintained that this question was one of personal choice and irrelevant to membership in the Samaj. By 1893, the Arya Samaj was formally divided. The militants gained control over most of the local Arya Samajes and the Arya Pratinidhi Sabha, Punjab. The moderates kept their hold on the Managing Committee and the school. They established rival local organizations and in 1903 founded the Arya Pradeshik Pratinidhi Sabha as their own provincial representative body. Power and leadership for them remained focused on the Managing Committee and education their primary cause.

The division of 1893 left the moderates and supporters of the College in severe difficulties. They had lost the organizational structure that supported their educational work. Slowly they rebuilt it and were able to provide the necessary money, not only to maintain the Dayananda Anglo-Vedic College, but to expand it. The student body grew to 961 by 1914. More importantly, the Lahore school became the model for other Aryas as local *samājes* established elementary and secondary schools throughout the Punjab. By 1910, the Managing Committee framed rules and regulations governing schools affiliated to it, and thus became the formal head of a growing educational system.

Moderates added to their educational activities other forms of service to the Hindu community. As early as 1877 Rai Mathura Das opened the first Arya Samaj orphanage in Ferozepore. It grew slowly until the famines of the late 1890s. In response to Christian relief measures that both saved starving children and converted them, Lala Lajpat Rai, a leading moderate in the Arya Samaj, announced that the Samaj would shelter any orphan sent to them. In February 1897, he began a campaign to collect funds for orphan relief. This opened a struggle between the Aryas and Christian missionaries over legal control of Hindu orphans. In the meantime, Aryas travelled to the Central Provinces and brought back children who were sent to Ferozepore and to other newly established orphanages throughout the Punjab. Orphan and famine relief illustrate the tendency of moderate Aryas to view Hindus as members of a community rather than a religious sect and then act for the benefit of that community. Militant Aryas, however, developed a somewhat different set of priorities.

With the division of 1893–4 the militants replaced their main purpose, education, with an emphasis on *Ved prachār* (proselytism and preaching). After the death of Pandit Guru Datta on 18 March 1890, leadership fell into the hands of Lala Munshi Ram and Pandit Lekh Ram. Under their guidance the Arya Pratinidhi Sabha created a plan for professional missionaries. The entire province was divided into circles (*mandalīs*), and in November 1895, six full-time missionaries were hired to preach and work with local Arya Samaj branches. Volunteers aided them, tracts were published, and newspapers printed in both English and the vernaculars. The Arya Samaj borrowed the institutional forms and techniques of the Christian missionaries needed to counter the challenges presented by the three conversion religions, Christianity, Sikhism and Islam, as they made inroads into the Hindu community.

Traditionally, Hinduism lacked a conversion ritual. After the introduction of a decennial census in 1871, religious leaders began to focus their attention on the issue of numerical strength. For Hindus the census reports pictured their community as one in decline, its numbers falling in proportion to those of other religions.[17] Christian success in converting the lower and untouchable castes furthered Hindu fears and led the militant Aryas to develop their own ritual of conversion, *shuddhi*. Initially *shuddhi* was employed to purify and readmit Hindus

---

[17] Kenneth W. Jones, 'Religious identity and the Indian census' in N. G. Barrier (ed.), *The Census in British India: New Perspectives* (Delhi, Manohar, 1981), pp. 73–101.

who had converted to Islam or Christianity. During the 1880s and early 1890s, Aryas conducted individual reconversions; however, considerable opposition existed to this practice and it was often difficult for a reconvert to find admission to Hindu society. In the wake of the 1891 census that reported an increase in Christian converts of 410 per cent for the previous decade, Aryas and their Sikh allies in the Singh Sabhas began to expand the use of *shuddhi*. Individual conversions gave way to group conversions. The first of these was performed on 31 March 1896, when the Shuddhi Sabha purified five people, and on 5 April another six. During the 1890s larger and larger groups were purified and the meaning of *shuddhi* reinterpreted. Originally *shuddhi* applied only to those converted, but soon it was performed for anyone whose ancestors had once been Hindus. Aryas also used *shuddhi* to purify untouchables and transform then into members of the clean castes. During the first decade of the new century, Aryas purified a number of Rahtias, a caste of Sikh untouchables, as well as Hindu Odes and Meghs.

Shuddhi and Arya proselytism challenged the other religious communities, creating tension and discord between them. The most dramatic of all such clashes resulted from the career of Pandit Lekh Ram (1858–97). He was born in Peshawar near the north-western frontier; educated in Persian and Urdu by Muslim teachers. He joined the Peshawar Arya Samaj in 1880 and travelled to Ajmer, where he was at Dayananda's bedside when he died. The next year, Lekh Ram resigned from the police to devote himself completely to the Samaj. He wrote extensively in condemnation of Islam in general and the Muslim leader, Mirza Ghulam Ahmad, in particular. In 1892 he published *Risāla-i-Jihād ya ya'nī Dīn-i-Muhammadī kī Bunyād (Jihād*, the Basis of the Muhammadan Religion). In it, Lekh Ram portrayed Islam as a religion of murder, theft, slavery, and perverse sexual acts. Repeated writings by the Pandit angered Muslims who responded in kind. Islamic leaders appealed to the courts, but failed to silence Lekh Ram. On 6 March 1897, the Pandit was assassinated and the resulting furor tore apart the Punjab, as Muslims and Hindus moved to the edge of communal violence. On the surface conditions quieted in the next few months, but tensions remained embedded in north-western society.

In addition to *Ved prachār* and *shuddhi*, militant Aryas turned their attention to education. By the early 1890s Lala Munshi Ram (later known as Swami Shraddhanand), Lala Dev Raj, and their fellow Aryas in Jullundur, had established a girls' school, the Arya Kanya Pathshala, to provide an education safe from missionary influence. They also founded the Kanya Ashram or women's hostel. Both the school and the hostel were considered controversial to most of the Hindu community, whether orthodox or moderate Aryan. The success of the Kanya Path-shala stimulated discussions among its supporters for expansion towards higher education, with the result that on 14 June 1896, they founded the Kanya Mahavidyalaya. Initially this was an extension of the older school, but it grew steadily, becoming a fully developed high school and finally a women's college. By 1906, the Mahavidyalaya enrolled 203 students in all grades and the Ashram housed 105 students, a mixture of unmarried, married, and widowed women. Gradually the school became the core of an educational movement, as its alumnae opened their own girls' schools. The Kanya Mahavidyalaya published literature for women's education and founded the Hindi monthly, *Panchal Panditā*, in 1898, 'to preach and propagate about female education'.[18] For the militant Aryas, education was intended to produce a new ideal Hindu woman.

Along with their attempts to educate women the militants also advocated widow remarriage. They launched societies to support such marriages and to put these ideals into practice. Over the next decade widow remarriage became increasingly acceptable among Punjabi Hindus. There was, however, a line drawn between virgin widows, those who had not lived with their husbands, and non-virgin widows, especially women who had borne children. Only the remarriage of virgin widows was beginning to be accepted in the late nineteenth century. The cause of widow remarriage drew adherents from a wide spectrum of the Hindu community, yet leadership was often provided by militant Aryas who wished to create the 'new' Hindu as envisioned by Dayananda.

Pandit Guru Datta's dream of a school system modelled after the ancient Hindu universities survived his death, since Lala Munshi Ram and other militant Aryas shared this vision. In the late 1890s Munshi Ram dedicated himself to the creation of a new educational institution, one where students would follow a life of celibacy, discipline, and Vedic learning. In 1898 the Arya Pratinidhi Sabha of the Punjab voted to establish such an institution. On 22 March 1902 the Gurukula Kangri opened in Hardwar, with Lala Munshi Ram as its manager and

[18] Jones, *Arya Dharm*, p. 217.

moral guide. Students at the Gurukula entered the first grade and remained there through college. They lived on the campus under strict faculty discipline, and learned selected western subjects through the lens of Aryan ideals, Hindu scriptures, and the vernacular languages.

With the establishment of the Gurukula, militant Aryas had completed their own system of religiously oriented education for both women and men. The Samaj had become a major acculturative movement with its purified Vedic Hinduism that rejected almost all contemporary Hinduism. Drawing its leadership and members from educated Hindus, primarily of the upper castes, the Arya Samaj adopted an imported organizational structure and parliamentary procedures. The two wings of the Samaj created a wide variety of institutions, offered new forms of worship, introduced proselytism, including paid missionaries, a conversion ritual, and reduced their teachings to a fundamental creed. Commitment to Aryan ideals focused the energies and wealth of their devotees into a variety of fields. It also provided the necessary psychological strength to publicly oppose existing rituals and customs. The ideals of the Samaj were not only preached, but put into action. The Samaj with its aggressive defence of Vedic Hinduism reinforced the lines drawn between Hindus and other religions. They also created escalating religious conflict. The Samaj entered the twentieth century divided over interpretations of Dayananda, his message, and the methods of putting those ideas into concrete form. In the process, Aryan Hinduism had become a creedal religion, repeatedly defined and explained through a system of proselytism and conversion. The Aryas were not, however, the only Punjabi socio-religious movement to follow this pattern of creed and conversion.

The Dev Samaj

As with many of the first Aryas in Lahore, the career of Pandit Shiv Narayan Agnihotri as a religious leader grew from his involvement with the Lahore Brahmo Samaj. Pandit Agnihotri was born into a family of Kanauji Brahmans on 20 December 1850.[19] At the age of sixteen Agnihotri enrolled in the Thomson College of Engineering at

---

[19] P. V. Kanal, *Bhagwan Dev Atma* (Lahore, Dev Samaj Book Depot, 1942), p. 51. J. N. Farquhar states that Agnihotri was born in 1850, but gives no source for this information. The remaining dates in Kanal's work are uncontested and so it has been used as the standard biography for this section. Other sources will be cited.

Roorkee. As a student he was introduced to Vedanta through the teachings of Shiv Dayal Singh who, in 1871, formally initiated Agnihotri and his wife as his own disciples. Two years later Agnihotri left Roorkee for Lahore where he accepted a position as drawing master in the Government School.

After settling in Lahore, Pandit Agnihotri was attracted to the Brahmo Samaj through the influence of his *guru* and of Munshi Kanhyalal Alakhdhari. He joined the Samaj in 1873 and quickly became a major figure in that organization. The Pandit was a dramatic speaker, prolific writer, and a successful journalist. While a member of the Brahmo Samaj, he spoke and wrote in favour of marriage reform and vegetarianism. He expounded the rationalistic and eclectic Brahmo doctrine. Gradually he committed more of his time to the Samaj and, in 1875, Agnihotri became an honorary missionary of the Samaj.[20] Five years later, he travelled to Calcutta where he was ordained as one of the first missionaries of the newly established Sadharan Brahmo Samaj.

Pandit Agnihotri met Swami Dayananda in 1877 and, although many of their ideas were compatible, they clashed with each other on a personal basis. Afterwards Agnihotri repeatedly attacked Dayananda and the Arya Samaj. Writing in Hindi, Urdu, and English, Agnihotri borrowed criticism from European scholars to reject Dayananda's interpretation of the Vedas. Aryas replied with a stream of tracts condemning Agnihotri, first as a Brahmo, and later as leader of his own religious movement. Pandit Agnihotri became increasingly involved in the work of the Brahmo Samaj. He took a modified Brahmo form of *sanyās* on 20 December 1882 and changed his name to Satyananda Agnihotri. As a full-time practitioner of religion, Agnihotri left his post as drawing master, but still retained his married life. Friction developed within the Brahmo Samaj and doubts in the Pandit's own mind so that in 1886 he resigned from the Punjab Brahmo Samaj.

On 16 February 1887 Agnihotri founded the Dev Samaj (Divine Society). At first this organization was considered an extension of the Brahmo Samaj, but it soon began to deviate from their doctrines. Agnihotri rejected Brahmo rationalism and taught instead that only the *guru*, in the person of Agnihotri, could provide a path of eternal bliss. At the upper end of an evolutionary ladder, he possessed the 'Complete Higher Life', a stage of being beyond the dangers of degeneracy and

---

[20] Farquhar, *Modern Religious Movements*, p. 173.

disintegration. A soul moved up this ladder of life or down it. Degeneracy could be achieved by anyone, but progress upward required the guidance of an enlightened soul, and in this world the only guide was Pandit Agnihotri. In 1892 he initiated the dual worship of himself and God. Three years later, the worship of God was dispensed with, leaving the *guru* as the sole point of attention for members of the Samaj.

The Dev Samaj held regular services consisting of hymns, a sermon, and readings from the *Deva Shāstra*. *Mūrti pūjā* (idol worship) was combined with these other types of worship. Agnihotri or his portrait replaced the traditional idol. In its patterns of worship and its ideology, the Dev Samaj fused traditional concepts with demands for radical social change. It taught a code of honesty in public and private. The Dev Samajis were forbidden to lie, steal, cheat, accept bribes or gamble. They should take neither liquor nor drugs and were expected to be strict vegetarians. Adultery, polygamy, and 'unnatural crimes' were outlawed and each member was expected to follow a useful life – that is, to work and live as a householder. All levels of membership looked to Agnihotri, known later as Dev Bhagwan Atma, for guidance in their lives and in their search for fulfilment.

The Dev Samaj demanded that its members abandon all caste restraints; they were expected to practise intercaste dining and intercaste marriage. Pandit Agnihotri also wished to restructure the role of women. He attempted to eliminate child marriage by setting the age of marriage at twenty for boys and sixteen for girls. Agnihotri discouraged excessive dowries, the seclusion of women, and their traditional mourning rites. He taught that widow marriage was acceptable and married a widow himself after the death of his first wife. The Dev Samaj encouraged the education of women and opened a coeducational school in Moga (Ferozepore district) on 29 October 1899.[21]

The emphasis on a stern moral standard plus considerable social radicalism appealed to educated Punjabi Hindus, 'graduates, magistrates, doctors, pleaders, money-lenders, landlords and Government servants', who comprised the membership of the Dev Samaj.[22] The Dev Samajis were almost totally educated men and even contained a large percentage of literate women. This, and their position in society, gave the movement far greater influence than sheer numbers would allow. This acculturative socio-religious movement was always an elite organ-

---

[21] Kanal, *Bhagwan Dev Atma*, pp. 345–6; and Census, 1911, *Punjab Report*, p. 139.
[22] Census, 1911, *Punjab Report*, p. 139.

ization drawing its membership from the highly educated upper caste Hindus of Punjab. Centred on a *guru*, the Dev Samaj produced a mixture of religious tradition and radical social change, especially in the role of women. The Samaj peaked in 1921 when it had 3,597 members. After the death of Pandit Agnihotri the Dev Samaj declined, but it did not disappear. It continued to practise the Vigyan Mulak Dharma (Science Grounded Religion).[23] The radicalism of the Dev Samaj, Brahmo Samaj, and Arya Samaj, the attacks by individual critics, such as Kanhyalal Alakhdhari, and the criticisms of the Christian missionaries stirred orthodox Hindus to defend their religion from all who opposed it.

SANATANISTS IN DEFENCE OF HINDU TRADITION

Pandit Shraddha Ram Phillauri

The first nineteenth-century leader of Hindu orthodoxy in Punjab was Pandit Shraddha Ram who was born in 1837 at Phillaur (Jullundur district). His family belonged to the Marud Joshi Brahmans and served the Bhandari Khatri community of Phillaur. His father, a worshipper of *shakti*, earned his living as a priest. The young Shraddha Ram was educated to follow the same profession, but in a manner unique to the North-West. He studied both Sanskrit and his native tongue of Punjabi, but because of the long Islamic dominance in this area, he also learned Persian and Urdu from a local *maulawī* (Islamic scholar).[24] By the time he was nineteen, Shraddha Ram had begun to perform his priestly role. One evening after reciting a part of the Mahabharata in public, Shraddha Ram was arrested and expelled from Phillaur by the police who thought he was preaching revolution. This was either just before or at the beginning of the Mutiny. Shraddha Ram travelled to Patiala, then Hardwar and back to Ludhiana, where he found employment with the Reverend J. Newton of the American Presbyterian Mission. The young Pandit translated tracts and books into the languages of the North-West. His work included parts of the New

---

[23] Census, 1931, *Punjab Report*, p. 301.
[24] Tulsi Deva, *Shraddha Prakash, Pratham Bhag, Shri Pandit Shraddha Ram Ji Ka Jivan* (Lahore, Punjab Economical Press, 1896), pp. 3–12. This is the only biography of Shraddha Ram.

Testament and the Qur'an, the latter translated from Persian. Later he broke with Newton and returned home. Yet this tie with the English rulers was maintained, as he continued to write books for the use of government officials.

After his return to Phillaur, Shraddha Ram began to preach Vaishnava Hinduism. He called for forsaking liquor, flesh, theft, gambling, falsehood, and vanity. He condemned 'bad customs', such as public bathing, and urged his listeners to maintain all the signs of an orthodox Hindu. Each should follow the rituals of purification, learn the *gāyatrī mantra*, wear a red mark on the forehead, a necklace of Tulsi beads, and greet each other with '*jayatrī harī*' ('Victory to God'). Shraddha Ram went from town to town where he preached and organized hymn-singing. His travels took him to Kapurthala in 1863–4 along with other Hindu leaders. It was rumoured that the Maharaja of Kapurthala was about to succumb to the preaching of a Christian missionary, Father Golaknath, and convert. Shraddha Ram, so it is claimed, persuaded the Maharaja to remain a Hindu, thus defeating the missionaries. In 1867–8, he joined with Munshi Yamuna Prasad in establishing a Hindu school in Ludhiana that taught both Sanskrit and Persian. They also organized a Hindu Sabha to sustain *sanātana dharma* (the eternal religion).

Pandit Shraddha Ram continued to defend orthodox Hinduism and bitterly condemned Christianity as 'trivial and gross'. He maintained 'there are only two things you can get from being in the Christian religion that are not possible in Hindu *dharma*, one is liquor and the other is eating left over food and meat'.[25] Shraddha Ram visited Amritsar in 1872–3 and preached at the Guru ka Bagh. He excoriated the Namdharis and also claimed that Ram Singh was one of his disciples. He spoke against the Anand Marriages (reformist Sikh marriage ceremonies), the killing of Muslim butchers, and for the necessity of Brahman priests and their rituals. A number of Sikhs who heard him felt that Shraddha Ram had denied the sanctity of the Sikh *gurus*. A near riot erupted and for the remainder of his stay Shraddha Ram required police protection to ensure his safety.

Shraddha Ram published a number of books and tracts that explained his beliefs and criticized his opponents. Perhaps the most significant of all his works appeared in 1876. This was *Dharma Rakshā*

---

[25] *Ibid.*, pp. 31–2.

(In Defence of Religion). Here he defended orthodox Hinduism by references to various scriptures given in the text in Sanskrit and then explained in Urdu. He rejected the idea that human reasoning had any validity, only the scriptures counted, and yet when it came to customs he considered unacceptable – such as Ras Dhārī with its erotic adventures of the young Krishna – Shraddha Ram discounted them through the authority of his own personal logic. As with many a Sanatanist, he asked for change, but its scope remained extremely limited.

In 1872, as a member of the Amritsar Dharma Sabha, Shraddha Ram joined with other Hindu leaders including the critic of contemporary Hinduism, Kanhyalal Alakhdhari, in an attempt to purify Hindu social and customary practice. The two men cooperated until 1873 when Alakhdhari founded the Niti Prakash Sabha in Ludhiana. Shraddha Ram with his followers attended the initial meeting, delivered a devastating condemnation of Kanhyalal, and then left with his followers. The two leaders became enemies and also typified the division among Punjabi Hindus into critics and defenders of their religion. The year 1877 brought a new and more dangerous opponent to Shraddha Ram with the arrival of Swami Dayananda Saraswati. Dayananda's success stirred Shraddha Ram to action. He followed Dayananda around the province to counter his call for a restructuring of Hinduism. In all their travels the two men never met, although supposedly challenges to formal debates were issued by both sides. After Dayananda left for Rajasthan, Shraddha Ram continued to argue against the Arya Samaj. He also turned his attention to establishing organizations to protect orthodoxy.

On 13–15 March 1880, a celebration was held at Phillaur to mark the founding of the Hari Gyan Mandir. Along with this temple Shraddha Ram opened a school where the four Vedas would be taught. That same year Shraddha Ram organized the Hardwar Sabha with a rest-house for mendicants visiting the holy city and Brahman pilgrims. His third accomplishment of 1880 was the establishment of the Gyan Mandir in Lahore; it too had a school attached. Shraddha Ram fixed the pattern of services for this temple and arranged that the temple property would not be inherited by his relatives. He was able to do no more since he died in the first quarter of 1881.

Shraddha Ram had laid the foundation for later Sanatanist movements, but he himself created only a few small organizations uncoordinated and without central authority. He did, however, leave behind him a collection of writings that expounded Sanatanist ideas and defended them from a variety of critics. Typical of adherents to Punjabi culture, Shraddha Ram clashed with other religions including Christians and Sikhs. He found support from pre-British elites among them Brahmans, landowners, princes, and merchants. Orthodox Hindus of Punjab would have no movement until the young Brahman, Din Dayalu Sharma, began his own organizational efforts in 1887 (see pp. 77–82). Shraddha Ram's defensive campaign was the first attempt to protect orthodoxy in Punjab and was a natural outgrowth of socio-religious movements that threatened the entrenched religious establishment of the Hindu community. Paralleling these critical movements within Hindu society were similar ones among the Sikhs of Punjab.

ACCULTURATIVE MOVEMENTS AMONG THE SIKHS

The Singh Sabhas

A series of events led to the founding of the first Singh Sabha at Amritsar. The Sikh community had been shaken by Namdhari unrest, the speeches of Shraddha Ram, and by Christian conversions. In the beginning of 1873, several Sikh students at Amritsar Mission School announced that they intended to become Christians. This incident stirred a small group of prominent Sikhs to form the Singh Sabha of Amritsar, which held its first meeting on 1 October 1873. Among those who helped to establish the Sabha were Sir Khem Singh Bedi, Thakur Singh Sandhawalia, Kanwar Bikram Singh of Kapurthala, and Giani Gian Singh. Sandhawalia became its president and Giani Gian Singh its secretary. The Sabha intended to restore Sikhism to its past purity, to publish historical religious books, magazines and journals, to propagate knowledge using Punjabi, to return Sikh apostates to their original faith, and to involve highly placed Englishmen in the educational programme of the Sikhs.[26]

The Singh Sabha was directed by an Executive Committee consisting of the president and secretary plus a few members. As the Sabha expanded, new officers were appointed, a vice-president, assistant secretary, a *giānī* (scholar of the Sikh scriptures), an *updeshak* (preacher), a

[26] Harbans Singh, 'Origins of the Singh Sabha', *Panjab Past and Present* (April 1973), 28–9.

treasurer and a librarian. They were elected each year and could be re-elected. Members had to be Sikhs with a strong belief in the teachings of the *gurus*. They paid a monthly subscription and were asked to pledge themselves to serve the community and to be loyal to Sikhism. All the original members were baptized Sikhs, although no requirement for this was written into the constitution of the Sabha.[27] They met every two weeks, held anniversary celebrations, and special meetings on festival days or in response to specific challenges by other religious groups. The Sabha soon began to issue *hurmatās* (records) of its decisions, each of which was the result of a majority vote. The Sabha also kept records of its income and expenditures, and produced annual reports.

The Singh Sabha represented the leaders of the Sikh community. It was joined by members of the landed gentry, the aristocracy, and by various types of temple servants: *pūjārīs* who conducted rituals, *granthīs* who recited the Sikh scriptures, *mahants* who administered the *gurdwārās, giānīs* and descendants of the *gurus*.[28] The Sabha prepared a calendar that listed the correct dates of the births and deaths of the ten *gurus*. They embarked on the preparation of a definitive text of the Dassam Granth; however, this task proved so demanding that a separate organization, the Gurmat Granth Pracharak Sabha, was founded to finish it. The Singh Sabha published numerous tracts and books and in 1894 organized the Khalsa Tract Society to popularize Punjabi, the Gurmukhi script, and to issue monthly tracts on the Sikh religion.[29] Soon the Singh Sabha of Amritsar was emulated by a new organization that also proved to be a competitor for leadership within the Sikh community.

The Lahore Singh Sabha held its first meeting on 2 November 1879. This new society was led by Professor Gurmukh Singh (1849–98) and Bhai Ditt Singh (1853–1901). Gurmukh Singh drew others into the Lahore Sabha through his personality, his extensive writings, and his efforts in the field of journalism.[30] This new Singh Sabha announced goals similar to those of the Amritsar society. They also wanted to

[27] Gurdarshan Singh, 'Origin and development of the Singh Sabha movement, constitutional aspects', *Panjab Past and Present* (April 1973), 46.
[28] See Teja Singh, 'The Singh Sabha movement', *Panjab Past and Present* (April 1973), 31–2; and N. G. Barrier, *The Sikhs and Their Literature* (Delhi, Manohar Book Service, 1970), p. xxiv.
[29] Teja Singh, 'Singh Sabha movement', p. 32.
[30] Barrier, *Sikhs and Their Literature*, p. xxvi; and Chhabra, *Advanced History*, pp. 382–3.

return Sikhism to its past purity by expunging all elements of non-Sikh origin. The Lahore Sabha intended to publish literature on Sikhism and authentic texts of the various Sikh scriptures. They wished to impart 'modern' knowledge through the vehicle of Punjabi, and published journals and newspapers to achieve these ends. The first president of this Sabha was Diwan Buta Singh, and Bhai Gurmukh Singh served as its secretary. The Lahore Singh Sabha formed an Educational Committee to encourage Sikh learning and also invited sympathetic Englishmen to join in the Committee's project. Another of the early acts of this Sabha was to affiliate with the Singh Sabha of Amritsar.

Differences between the Lahore and Amritsar societies quickly surfaced. The Lahore Sabha was more democratic and accepted members from all castes including untouchables. Their programme of purifying Sikhism directly opposed the vested interests of the Amritsar Sabha. The career of Bhai Ditt Singh illustrates the type of friction that erupted between the two organizations. Ditt Singh, himself of low-caste status, wished to remove the 'evils of caste' and 'guru-dom' from the Sikh community. Because he was an effective writer, he became the main propagandist for the Lahore Sabha. His publications chided high-caste Sikhs for denigrating converts, especially from the lower castes; Ditt Singh also attacked the hereditary priests and claimants to special status as descendants of the *gurus*. His tract, *Sudān Nātak* (A Dream Drama), ridiculed the religious establishment and resulted in a court case, the first of many that grew from his writings.[31] The Lahore Sabha soon confronted considerable opposition within the Sikh community, and were banned from meeting in many local *gurdwārās*. Consequently, the Singh Sabhas found it necessary to erect their own *gurdwārās* served by priests who accepted the Singh Sabha ideology.

The Lahore Sabha expanded with local branches in many of the Punjab towns. The Amritsar Sabha developed its own societies, but its growth was far slower than the Lahore society. In 1880 a General Sabha was established in Amritsar to provide a central organization for all Singh Sabhas. On 11 April 1883 this was renamed the Khalsa Diwan, Amritsar. It included thirty-six to thirty-seven different Singh Sabhas as well as the Lahore association. The officers reflected an attempt to bring all groups together to heal the differences between them. Raja Birkam Singh of Faridkot accepted the title of patron, Baba

---

[31] Barrier, *Sikhs and Their Literature*, p. xxvi.

Khem Singh Bedi, president, Man Singh, officer-in-charge of the Golden Temple, Bhai Ganesh Singh and Bhai Gurmukh Singh as joint secretaries. This effort at unity lasted but a short time. In 1886 the Lahore Singh Sabha created its own Khalsa Diwan (Sikh Council). Only the Sabhas of Faridkot, Amritsar, and Rawalpindi allied with the original Diwan; the rest turned to the Lahore leadership and to its radical ideology of social and religious change.[32]

The Lahore Khalsa Diwan received assistance from the Maharaja of Nabha as its patron, while Sir Attar Singh served as its president and Bhai Gurmukh Singh as its secretary. At first they had good relations with the Arya Samaj. Several young Sikhs joined the Aryas, seeing in it many of the same ideals that motivated members of the Singh Sabha. The two organizations appeared to be moving along parallel paths. Dayananda criticized Sikhism, but the Aryas had not emphasized this until the Lahore anniversary celebrations of 25 November 1888. On this occasion Pandit Guru Datta attacked Sikhism and labelled Guru Nanak 'a great fraud'. Other Aryas, including Pandit Lekh Ram and Lala Murli Dhar, joined this denigration of Sikhism. As a result, three young, educated Sikhs, Bhai Jawahir Singh, Bhai Ditt Singh Giani, and Bhai Maya Singh, departed the Samaj for the Lahore Singh Sabha. They became staunch defenders of Sikhism against all external criticism, especially from the Aryas. Arya–Sikh relations ranged from vicious tract-wars to cooperation in the area of *shuddhi*, but as the two movements matured they tended to draw further and further apart.

The Singh Sabhas continued to expand, new branches were founded that, at times, created their own distinct ideas and programmes. The Bhasur Singh Sabha became a hub of Sikh militancy under the leadership of Bhai Teja Singh. Members of this Sabha were required to wear the five symbols of orthodoxy, to accept strict religious discipline, and if they did not do so, were expelled. Its members were treated as equals regardless of their class or caste origins. The Bhasur Singh Sabha was aggressive in its missionary zeal and extreme in its ideology. In time it developed into the Panch Khalsa Diwan and competed with other Khalsa Diwans. Not all deviation or enthusiasm by local Singh Sabhas proved as controversial. Under the leadership of Bhai Takht Singh (1860–1937), the Ferozepore Singh Sabha opened a girls' high school and hostel when the education of women was still unacceptable to

---

[32] Gurdarshan Singh, 'Origin and development', pp. 48–9.

many Sikhs. Other Sabhas connected with the Lahore Diwan built orphanages, opened schools for all classes and castes, and produced a stream of literature, tracts, journals and newspapers.[33]

Although strong differences in membership, ideology, and programmes divided the Amritsar and Lahore Diwans, they did cooperate in establishing a Sikh college. Representatives of both Khalsa Diwans met in Lahore to draw up plans for the proposed college. A *hukam-nāmā* (ruling) was issued from the Golden Temple that requested each Sikh to give a tenth of his income for the college project. Sympathetic Englishmen organized a committee in London to raise funds and donations were requested from the Sikh ruling families. This institution became a degree-granting college in 1899 and the foremost success of Sikh efforts in higher education.

During the 1890s, Sikhs in both wings of the Singh Sabha movement became increasingly concerned with the question of Sikh identity; were they or were they not part of the Hindu community? Competition with Hindu movements had done much to fuel this discussion. Western scholars, involved in translations of different Sikh scriptures, added further stimulus to controversy surrounding the role and meaning of Sikhism. In 1898, the Sikh philanthropist, Sardar Dayal Singh Majithia, died leaving his wealth to the Dayal Singh Trust. His widow contested his will with the result that an English court had to decide whether the deceased was a Sikh or a Hindu. Throughout 1898, 1899, and 1900, the lawsuit and the question of Sikh identity were argued in public meetings, in the press, and through numerous publications. The more radical Sikhs claimed that Sikhism was separate from Hinduism, while others maintained it was a subdivision of Hinduism. The Arya Samaj added more fuel to this debate.

Sikh leaders of the Rahtia community, untouchable weavers from the Jullundur Doab, demanded that the Singh Sabhas remove their social and religious liabilities. Sikhism rejected caste, they maintained, and so this error of ignorance and Hindu influence should be extinguished. Since the Singh Sabha leaders did not respond to their pleas, they turned to Lala Munshi Ram of the Arya Samaj. He welcomed them and, on 3 June 1900, the Samaj conducted a public ceremony of *shuddhi* in the city of Lahore for 200 Rahtias. The Aryas gave each of them a sacred thread signifying his pure status, shaved their beards and hair, and

---

[33] For a discussion of Sikh papers, books and tracts, see Barrier, *Sikhs and Their Literature*.

introduced them to the proper rituals of worship. In short, the Rahtias were transformed into clean-caste Hindus. The Sikhs, who witnessed this spectacle, became enraged, seeing it as sacrilege and a threat to their community. In the following months Aryas continued to purify members of the Rahtia caste and Sikh leaders pulled further away from the Hindu community. In 1905 Sikh reformers struck back as they succeeded in 'cleansing' the Golden Temple of Brahman priests, idols, and Hindu rituals. This action strengthened the argument that Sikhs were separate from the Hindu religion, an idea which gained wider and wider acceptance among educated Sikhs during the twentieth century.[34]

Meanwhile leadership within the Sikh community shifted. The Lahore Singh Sabha lost many of its prominent members. Sir Attar Singh died in 1896, Bhai Gurmukh Singh in 1898, and Bhai Ditt Singh in 1901. Attention moved to a new organization, the Chief Khalsa Diwan founded in Amritsar, where it first met on 30 October 1902. A constitution and an elaborate structure of organization were adopted and, in 1904, the society was registered with the government. Sikh leaders again attempted to unite the diverse organizations within their community under one umbrella. Yet only twenty-nine of the 150 Singh Sabhas then in existence agreed to join the Chief Khalsa Diwan. Membership was limited to baptized Sikhs and the organization depended on individual subscriptions for financial support. The Chief Khalsa Diwan failed to transcend internal divisions among the Sikhs, divisions that surfaced in the decade after World War I.

Initially Sikhs had responded to the loss of political domination much as had the Muslims of north India, but they differed in the models of Sikhism used for their socio-religious movements. The Singh Sabhas sought an adjustment to British control, but the two wings differed in their membership within the Sikh class and caste structures. These differences were manifest in the competing ideologies each group articulated. The Lahore Singh Sabha spoke for a rising educated elite and the Amritsar Sabha, while calling for changes in religion, rejected any fundamental restructuring of authority within the community. It paralleled many of the orthodox defensive movements of the Hindus and of Islam which drew upon the strengths of pre-British elites and members of the religious establishment. The Amritsar Singh Sabha wanted only limited adjustment of British culture. Both wings realized the need to

[34] Kenneth W. Jones, 'Ham Hindu Nahin: Arya-Sikh relations', 1877–1905, *Journal of Asian Studies*, no. 3 (May 1973), 468–75.

gain a command of western knowledge if Sikhs were to compete successfully with Hindu and Muslim Punjabis, but here again they differed on the extent of this education and who should receive it. In the development of their ideas the two branches of the Singh Sabhas helped to redefine the 'true' Sikhism and to draw lines between it and the other religious communities in Punjab. In the twentieth century the Singh Sabhas were overwhelmed by other organizations. In the first decade they were supplanted by the Khalsa Diwans and then in the 1920s by the struggle for control over the Sikh place of worship. Paralleling the Arya Samaj and Singh Sabhas, a socio-religious movement among Punjabi Muslims also added to this general process of self-definition that characterized so much of the nineteenth century.

AN ACCULTURATIVE MOVEMENT AMONG PUNJABI MUSLIMS

The Ahmadiyahs

The Ahmadiyahs began with the career of one man, the messianic Mirza Ghulam Ahmad (1835–1908). Mirza Ghulam was born in the village of Qadiyan on 13 February 1835.[35] His family once held extensive estates that were seized by the Sikhs when they gained control of the Punjab. A few villages remained, but the young Ahmad grew up in an atmosphere of frustration over the decline in his family's status and wealth. He was educated by private tutors, the first of whom was Fazl Ilahi, a resident of Qadiyan and a scholar of the Hanafi School of Law. In 1845 he studied with Fazl Ahmad, a member of the Ahl-i-Hadith, who tutored him in Arabic grammar. At seventeen he began to work with the Shi'ah tutor, Gul 'Ali Shah of Batala, and became acquainted with Muhammad Husain, a fellow student of Gul 'Ali Shah.

After finishing his education Mirza Ghulam's father sent him to Sialkot. There he read law and oversaw a number of legal cases instituted to regain the family's lost estates. While in Sialkot Mirza Ghulam met several Christian missionaries. In 1868 he returned to Qadiyan and in 1876 his father died. Little is known of his life during

[35] This date is given by Lavan in his recent study of the Ahmadiyahs. Farquhar states that he was born 'about 1838'. See Lavan, *Ahmadiyah Movement*, p. 22, and Farquhar, *Modern Religious Movements*, p. 137. Lavan's is presently the most authoritative study of the Ahmadiyahs and so will be used as the basic source of this section unless otherwise cited.

the years 1868 to 1876, but after his father's death Ghulam Ahmad ceased to concern himself with the family estates and turned his attention to religion. He debated, mostly through newspapers, with Pandit Kharak Singh, a Christian convert, and with Pandit Shiv Narayan Agnihotri, then a leader in the Brahmo Samaj. In May 1879 Mirza Ghulam announced his forthcoming book, the *Barāhīn-i-Ahmadīyah* (Proofs of Ahmadiyah) in the pages of Muhammad Husain's journal, *Ishā'at-i-Sunnah*. The *Barāhīn* appeared in six issues of *Ishā'at* and was published in four volumes from 1880–4.

Ahmad described his basic ideas, his claims to special authority, and his programme for rejuvenating Islam in *Barāhīn*. He stressed the fundamental principles of Islam and the duties of all Muslims. His claims to religious authority rested on the visions and messages he received from God. Mirza also refuted the doctrines of other religious leaders both within and outside Islam. The Arya Samaj and its founder provided him with a dramatic enemy and one close to home. Mirza Ghulam clashed with Sharampat Rai (1855–1932), a resident of Qadiyan and secretary of the local Arya Samaj. In a registered letter he offered to send a copy of the *Barāhīn* to Swami Dayananda and to debate him over the truth of Islam and its superiority over Hinduism. Dayananda failed to respond. In August, Mirza reported a vision in which he saw that Dayananda would die in the near future, a prophecy that was fulfilled in October. Nevertheless confrontations between Mirza Ghulam Ahmad and the Arya Samaj lasted until his death in 1908.

Controversies within the Islamic community developed at roughly the same time. In March 1882 Mirza Ghulam Ahmad announced that he had received a divine command that he should be a *mujaddid* (a renewer of the faith).[36] He did not make additional claims or take further steps to initiate his own disciples until 12 January 1889. On that date his son, Bashir ud-Din Mahmud Ahmad, was born thus fulfilling one of his prophecies. He chose then to announce conditions on which he would grant *bai'at* to his disciples. In 1890–1 he published three works and publicly claimed that he was the *masih mau'ūd* (promised messiah) and the *madhī*. Mirza Ghulam was thus the future saviour of both Islam and Christianity. Different *'ulamā*, including Muhammad Husain of Batala, 'Abd al-Haqq Ghaznavi of Amritsar, Nazir Husain

---

[36] Lavan, *Ahmadiyah Movement*, p. 36.

of Delhi, and Ahmad 'Allah of Amritsar immediately condemned him. Muhammad Husain arranged for *fatwā* against Mirza Ghulam that were signed by a number of *'ulamā* representing different groups within the Islamic community. Public debates quickly followed. On 20 July 1891, Mirza Ghulam disputed with Muhammad Husain in Ludhiana. In September, he travelled to Delhi where he debated with Nazir Husain, the distinguished leader of the Ahl-i-Hadith movement. This confrontation took place in the Jama'a Masjid and culminated in a near riot, a fairly common occurrence and one that grew from the extremely bitter personal, as well as theological, differences expressed in speech and writing.

Partly out of response to the critical statement issued by various *'ulamā*, a meeting of Ahmad's adherents was held in Qadiyan on 27 December 1891. This was the first general gathering of the movement. Eighty individuals attended and such a meeting was held each year afterwards. In 1892 500 members travelled to Qadiyan from Punjab and the North-West. People came from as far east as Aligarh and from as far west as Mecca. At the 1892 meeting, the Ahmadiyahs declared their goals: 'To propagate Islam; to think out ways and means of promoting the welfare of new converts to Islam in Europe and America; to further the cause of righteousness, purity, piety and moral excellence throughout the world, to eradicate evil habits and customs; to appreciate with gratitude the good work of the British Government.'[37] The Ahmadis attempted to expand their membership through proselytism and continually engaged in contests with a wide variety of opponents. In 1897 they began publishing the newspaper, *al-Hakam*, to explain the Mirza's doctrines and attack those who disagreed with him.

Controversy with other Muslims reached its height in the years 1898–9 over Mirza Ghulam's claim to messiah status, his interpretations of the word *jihād*, and over numerous other theological issues. Finally the British Government intervened, impelled to act by his habit of prophesying the demise of his opponents. On 24 February 1899, after a court-hearing, Muhammad Husain signed a statement in which he promised to stop using abusive language against Mirza Ghulam who in turn agreed to cease predicting the death of his critics. This did not end controversy, but did diminish somewhat the intensity and open

---

[37] Quoted *ibid.* p. 93.

animosity that characterized the 1890s. In the process Mirza Ghulam came to consider his own followers as separate from the body of Sunni Muslims. On 4 November 1900, he called for the Ahmadiyahs to list themselves separately on the census of 1901. At this time *al-Hakam* listed 1,098 members who now comprised their own officially recognized religious society.

Paralleling his tussles with different Islamic groups, the Mirza engaged in a struggle with various Christians, particularly the Punjabi converts, Imad al-Din, Thakur Das, and 'Abd 'Allah Asim. One public dispute with 'Abd 'Allah lasted for fifteen days. It was held in May–June 1893 at the village of Jandiyala. At the root of this controversy lay the Mirza's claim to be the *masih mau'ūd*. He argued that Christ did not die on the cross, but survived, and travelled to Kashmir where he lived until the age of 120 administering to the lost tribes of Israel who had settled there. Christ was thus, a man, a prophet, but not the son of God, and Mirza Ghulam was also a prophet fulfilling a similar historic role. Christian leaders rejected Ahmad's claims through a series of polemical tracts and by condemning him in their public lectures.

From the late 1880s Pandit Lekh Ram spoke and wrote extensively against Islam and with special vehemence against Mirza Ghulam Ahmad. In 1887 Lekh Ram published his answer to the claims of Mirza Ghulam in *Takzib-i-Barāhīn-i-Ahmadīyah* (Accusing as False the Proofs of Ahmadiyah). Nur ud-Din Ahmad answered in 1890 with *Tasdīq-i-Barāhīn-i-Ahmadīyah* (Verifying the Proofs of Ahmadiyah), and Mirza Ghulam in 1891 with *Ta'īd-i-Barāhīn-i-Ahmadīyah* (Confirming the Proofs of Ahmadiyah). A year later Lekh Ram condemned all Islam in his treatise on *Jihād*. Ahmad responded with numerous attacks against different elements of the Arya Samaj ideology. He found a particularly vulnerable point with Dayananda's concept of *niyog*, the idea that barren women or virgin widows might have children without being married. This was one of Dayananda's teachings that found little or no acceptance among members of the Arya Samaj, but was often used to embarrass the movement. Ahmad published *Radd-i-Niyog* (The Rejection of Niyog) in 1895. He also predicted that Pandit Lekh Ram would not live long, a prophecy that was fulfilled in 1897.

During these years of conflict, the Ahmadis continued to make converts and a community formed around Mirza Ghulam at Qadiyan.

The ideology of the Ahmadiyahs shared many elements of other nineteenth-century Muslim movements of return. Mirza Ghulam condemned the worship of tombs and numerous other customs as *shirk* (polytheism). He interpreted the Qur'an to justify the gradual elimination of slavery. He explained *pardah* (the seclusion of women), and the Muslim institution of divorce as solutions to worse evils, and redefined *jihād* to exclude the concept of holy war as often accepted by theologians. He taught his followers to perform the five daily prayers, obey God and his Prophet, and to conduct themselves righteously and ethically. As long as he was alive the Ahmadiyah community was united partly through the Sufi institution of *bai'at*, as each member was initiated at the hands of Mirza Ghulam and by his person.

The ideology of the Ahmadiyahs appealed at first to middle-class, literate Muslims; however, because of its location in Qadiyan, the Ahmadiyahs began to attract more members from the less educated, poorer rural classes. The origins of its members produced with the Ahmadis a bipolar pattern. Among the literates were doctors, attorneys, landowners and businessmen. They tended to come from the district towns rather than from the few major cities, and were somewhat separated from a growing rural and less affluent membership. As with other Islamic movements of return, the Ahmadis attempted to remove all error and to return to what they considered the 'true' fundamentals of their religion. The role of Mirza Ghulam, however, led to clashes within Islam, particularly with the *'ulāma* who did not consider Mirza a qualified religious leader. The aggressive, militant stance of the movement brought it into direct conflict with Hindus, Sikhs and Christians among others. The acculturative Ahmadis adjusted their doctrines to the reality of British power and the fact of western civilization as was most clearly illustrated by their reinterpretation of *jihād*. Conversion and proselytism became the main goals of the Ahmadis as they proved uniquely able to win converts from outside of the subcontinent. Success was accompanied in the twentieth century by internal division and drove their community into two distinct organizations, and conflict at all levels continued to be a byproduct of the Ahmadis as it has been of Punjabi movements in general.

PUNJAB AND THE NORTH-WEST IN THE
NINETEENTH CENTURY: A SUMMARY

The diversity of religious communities in the Punjab led to a greater number of socio-religious movements than in any other region of South Asia. In addition, divisions within and among religious communities appeared repeatedly. The two Sikh transitional movements grew from the crises within this community, by the turmoil among the Sikhs after the death of Ranjit Singh, and by the British conquest of the Sikh kingdom. They reflected the long-standing differences that existed among the Sikhs. The major Sikh acculturative movement, the Singh Sabha, was bifurcated between a pre-British elite centred in Amritsar and a new rising group at Lahore.

The Sikhs were not the only Punjabi community at war with itself. Punjabi Hindus too were rent by opposing visions of what should be done to save degenerate Hinduism from further decline. The founding of the Lahore Arya Samaj in 1877 brought to the North-West an aggressive movement of return, one that was uncompromising in its insistence that it alone possessed truth and its willingness to condemn all other systems of belief. This stance echoed existing conflicts between proponents of radical change and defenders of orthodoxy. It brought the Samaj into conflict with the Brahmo Samaj, among reformers, with orthodox Hindus, and with the smaller Dev Samaj. Aryas also accepted the mantle of defenders of Hinduism against the challenges of Christian missionaries, Muslim religious leaders, and eventually both wings of the Singh Sabha movement.

Punjabi Muslims were influenced by movements of return from the Gangetic basin and reactions to those movements by orthodox Muslims added to religious controversy through the leadership of Mirza Ghulam and his claims to a prophetic role. The Ahmadis demonstrated a similar set of dynamics as they fought against the 'ulamā, the Ahl-i-Hadith, Sayyid Ahmad Khan's organization, and Muslim orthodoxy. They, like the Aryas, also attempted to defend their parent religion, Islam, and their unique 'truth' against the condemnation of other religious groups including the Christian missionaries.

All Punjabi religious communities created acculturative movements that began in one of its cities and then expanded to the others, to smaller towns, and occasionally to the villages. Each had the Punjabi tendency to see their ideas as the absolute, unbending truth. Such movements were aggressive with the exception of the Dev Samaj. They adopted western organizational techniques with which they created a wide variety of institutions. Each possessed missionaries, tract societies, parochial schools, centres of worship, systems of fund-raising, bureaucracies, and central associations. Lines dividing one religion from another and one socio-religious movement from all others were defined, and aggressively defended. By the end of the nineteenth century, religious identity was in the process of expressing itself in combinations of symbols based on language, script and religion. This newly strengthened communal consciousness was exported from the Punjab by such movements as the Arya Samaj and the Ahmadiyahs. The Punjab was not only influenced by religious associations outside of it, particularly from movements within Bengal and the Gangetic core, but also itself became an exporter of movements. The North-West was a region on the periphery of the Hindu-Buddhist civilization and one historically unsettled by invaders. Here the religious elites strong in the Gangetic basin and in the South could not maintain control over their respective communities and were repeatedly challenged by individuals and groups that demanded radical change in the status quo. It was a region in turmoil that during the twentieth century added a political dimension to its forms of religious consciousness. In the four decades before Independence the attitudes, strategies and organizations predominant in the Punjab spread to other areas of the subcontinent, carrying with them forms of aggressive religious competition. Further to the South the dynamics of socio-religious movements changed in part, although not totally.

CHAPTER FIVE

THE CENTRAL BELT AND MAHARASHTRA

THE SETTING

Below the Gangetic basin and to the east of the Indus plain a series of steep hills and valleys run eastwards separating the northern subcontinent from its peninsular South. This central region of hills and jungles has impeded north-south movement, acting as a cultural and political barrier. On the western coast lies the Kathiawar peninsula and the immediate mainland attached to it. Together they comprise the region of Gujarat, which is partially isolated from the rest of the subcontinent. A narrow strip of land runs north and south connecting mainland Gujarat to the coast below it and through this coastal band passes the trade routes from the Gangetic plain. To the East are the Central Provinces containing a rich agricultural tract, Chhattisgarh, surrounded by hills, separated from the Deccan and the northern plains. The river valley and delta of the Mahanadi constitute the eastern region of this transitional belt, the area of Orissa. Bordered by hills to the North-West and South-West, Orissa is the site of a regional society created from a mixture of indigenous cultures, influenced from Bengal to the North, and the Telugu region to the South. Below this chain of hills is Maharashtra, an area composed of three geographic features: the Konkin coast, the western Ghats, an escarpment beginning at the Tapti River, and the Deccan, a dry inland plateau broken by numerous hills that extend south across the Godavari River, the linguistic border between the Deccan and the Dravidian South.

The culture and social system of Gujarat, the Central Provinces, and Orissa showed affinities with northern India. These areas had castes and subcastes representing all levels of the *varna* system. In Gujarat the two most powerful caste clusters were the merchants and members of the ruling elites, both Hindus and Muslims. A further feature of Gujarati society was the tight, hierarchical control maintained by elders within each caste. Gujarat was the home of a Hindu majority and small minorities of Jains, Muslims, and Parsis. Muslims from the North conquered Gujarat in AD 1297, yet the Islamic community accounted

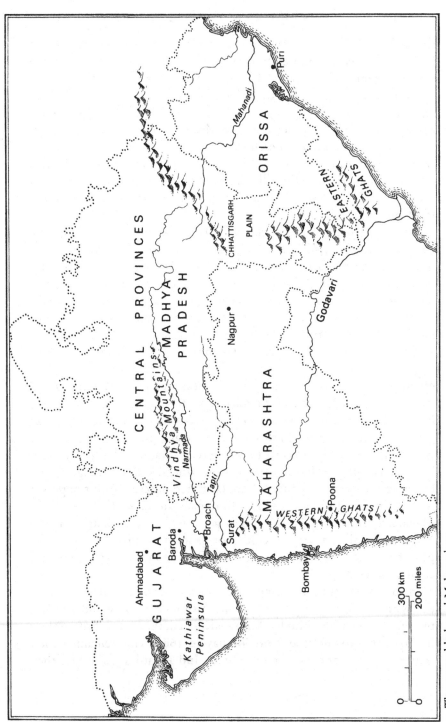

4 The central belt and Maharashtra

for only 10.3 per cent of the population in 1881. Muslim penetration in the central hills was limited to only 5 per cent and in Orissa to a mere 2.29 per cent.[1] The Central Provinces and Orissa both had Hindu majorities, but also significant tribal populations who were only partially assimilated into the high culture of South Asia. British conquest began in 1803 with the defeat of the Maratha ruler, Raghuji Bhonsla, Raja of Nagpur. At that time Orissa fell under English control. Gujarat was taken in 1819 as a result of the defeat of the Maratha state. British power then moved into the hill tracts of the Central Provinces. Yet in all three areas the British controlled considerable tracts of land through local rulers.

South of Gujarat and the central hills lay Maharashtra, a linguistic and cultural region with its own distinct social structure. Beginning in the thirteenth century, a series of *bhakti* saints standardized the Marathi language, aiding in the development of an extensive religious literature. As an Indo-European language, Marathi was tied to northern culture; however, in its caste system, Maharashtra showed a similarity to the society of the South. Essentially the Maratha social structure was divided into three classifications, Brahmans, non-Brahmans and untouchables. The non-Brahmans, whether functionally rulers or not, were considered Sudras or peasant castes. Merchants and traders active in Maharashtra tended to be from other regions or were Maratha Brahmans. Maharashtra was effectively dominated by a small group of three Brahman castes, the Chitpavans and Sarawats from the coast, and the Desharthas from the Deccan. Maratha Brahmans often held overlapping roles as priests, landowners, estate managers, and government servants. Thus they concentrated different forms of power within this group of castes. The Brahmans stood at the apex of the Maharashtrian social system, its largest single-caste cluster was the Maratha–Kunbis, a peasant cultivator group who provided the manpower for the creation of the Maratha Empire in the seventeenth and eighteenth centuries.

In 1612 the East India Company established its first trading centre on the west coast at the port of Surat. Although they would retain a presence there as the Mughal Empire declined, the British shifted their headquarters to the island of Bombay in 1687. This remained their centre of trade and power in western India until 1818, when they

[1] Census, 1881, *Central Provinces Report*, p. 10.

defeated the Marathas and annexed much of the lands under Maratha control. Gujarat, the Deccan as far east as the Nizam of Hyderabad's kingdom, the coast lands south to Goa, and the corridor north to Rajasthan, all came into the sphere of British political and military dominance. Within this central band of the subcontinent three transitional movements appeared in the nineteenth century.

TRANSITIONAL MOVEMENTS AMONG HINDUS

The Swami Narayana Sampradaya of Gujarat

One of the future leaders of Gujarat was born in 1781 in the village of Chhapaia near Ayodhia in the North-Western Provinces. He came from a Brahman family and was named Ghanashyam Pande. Little else is known about his early life except that he left home in 1793 in search of a *guru*.[2] After five years of wandering he changed his name to Nilakantha Brahmachari.[3] According to legend he travelled the great pilgrimage route from Nepal and the Himalayas, south to Rameshwar visiting many religious sites along the way. Returning to Nasik, he met a group of holy men who were followers of Ramananda Swami (1739–1802). The Swami was born in the North-Western Provinces, but located his headquarters in Lojpur, Gujarat. The young Nilakantha joined this band and travelled to Gujarat where he became an ardent disciple of Ramananda Swami. By 1800 Nilakantha had settled in Gujarat and changed his name to Sahajananda Swami, a name he retained until his death in 1830. The new disciple impressed his *guru* with skills in yoga, with an extensive religious knowledge, and with his dedication. Also he was able to place many of the devotees into states of trance, a talent that impressed the members of this sect. In 1802 Sahajananda succeeded as *āchārya* (spiritual preceptor) upon the death of Ramananda. Once in charge, Sahajananda built an expanding movement based on devotion to Krishna as he followed the path laid down by Ramananda Swami. This was a popular and well-established form of Hinduism in Gujarat.

Sahajananda Swami preached a puritanical ideology both of belief

[2] Raymond B. Williams, *A New Face of Hinduism: The Swaminarayan Religion* (Cambridge University Press, 1984), pp. 8–10.

[3] M. J. Mehta, 'From Sahajanand to Gandhi: role perception and methods', and Vijay Singh Chavda, 'Social and religious reform movements in Gujarat in the nineteenth and twentieth centuries', both in S. P. Sen, *Social and Religious Reform Movements* (Calcutta, Institute of Historical Studies, 1979), pp. 230–1, 202–3.

and practice. He taught his disciples to abandon the singing of vulgar songs at weddings and on such festivals as Holi, and to refrain from luxurious or licentious behaviour. He advocated vegetarianism and condemned the use of liquor and drugs. Sahajananda instructed his adherents to bathe daily, not to eat before performing their worship, and not to use water or milk without first straining it.[4] He attacked the actions of the Vama-Margas who worshipped female power (*shakti*), and practised animal sacrifices, meat-eating, drinking, and sexual rituals.[5] On the role of women his message was somewhat ambiguous. He insisted that men and women be seated separately at all religious gatherings. He taught that a woman should obey her husband, accept his behaviour no matter how insulting it might be, and to worship him as a deity. Yet Sahajananda also attacked the restrictions on widow remarriage, the institution of *sati*, and the practice of female infanticide. It is possible that he was influenced by British officials and Christian missionaries on the questions of *sati* and infanticide, since both institutions were openly condemned by Englishmen in Gujarat.[6] Women were also given a place in his movement as *sankhyāyoginīs* (female religious mendicants). Sahajananda formed a special order of women aesthetes whose prime responsibility was preaching to and proselytizing women.

The ideology of the Swami Narayana movement was explained in the *Shikshāpatrī* (Conduct of Disciples) published by Sahajananda in 1826. In later years a number of books and pamphlets appeared explaining and elaborating on the beliefs and practices advocated by Sahajananda. The movement expanded rapidly under Sahajananda's leadership. He toured Gujarat extensively and created a network of disciples. He also made contact with many of the feudal rulers of both mainland and peninsular Gujarat.[7] Sahajananda was a charismatic leader who performed miracles and inspired many individuals to accept his spiritual guidance. He was assisted by bands of holy men who travelled widely and disseminated his message.

The Swami Narayana movement developed a hierarchical structure. At its apex was Sahajananda, the *āchārya*. Religious mendicants were recruited from all castes, but the future *āchāryas* had to be Brahmans.

---

[4] Chavda, 'Social and religious reform', pp. 230–1.
[5] Williams, *New Face of Hinduism*, pp. 24–5.
[6] M. J. Mehta, 'The Swami Narayana sect (a case study of Hindu religious sects in modern times)', *Quarterly Review of Historical Studies*, 17, no. 4 (Calcutta, April 1978), 229.
[7] Mehta, 'From Sahajanand to Gandhi', p. 227.

The mendicants were divided into three hierarchical orders, the *brahmachārīs*, *sādhus*, and *pālās*. The first two orders' primary responsibility was to proselytize. The *brahmachārīs* had no caste mark and only ate food acquired through begging. *Sādhus*, by contrast, maintained caste restrictions and were limited to non-Brahmans of the second and third *varnas*. These two orders travelled together in missionary bands. The third category were the *pālās* who acted as temple servants and attendants. They were drawn from the Sudras (peasant castes). No untouchable was allowed to become a *pālā* or to enter the Swami Narayana temples except for the two specifically built for their use.[8]

Sahajananda Swami first attracted disciples from among the traditional genealogists and bards of Gujarat who served in many of the Princely Courts of that region. Members of the warrior, merchant, artisan castes and members of tribal groups joined as the movement expanded. Growth meant two things, greater wealth and projects made possible by these resources. Income was generated by *bhets* (gifts) given by devotees and by cash contributions. Followers of Sahajananda were expected to make two annual donations of one-half rupee on the festival days of Ram Navami and Divali. By 1847, this amounted to an annual income of Rs 175,000, which made the construction of temples and guest houses possible.[9] Sahajananda built three temples during his tenure as leader. With the construction of the temple at Gadhada (1829) he also built a *dharmshālā*, and moved his headquarters here from Lojpur. Smaller temples were also erected in numerous towns and villages. In addition a number of *sabhā mandaps* (assembly halls) were constructed where both mendicants and members of the laity could stay. The buildings and mendicant orders comprised a network that held this growing religious movement together.

Since Sahajananda Swami was celibate the question of succession was unanswered. Sahajananda took two steps towards solving this potential problem. First, he declared that the office of *āchārya* could be held by a householder and secondly, in 1816, he invited his two brothers to settle in Gujarat with their families. After they arrived, he adopted two of his nephews, Ayodhya Prasad and Raghavir Prasad, whom he appointed as his successors to the office of *āchārya*. When Sahajananda died in 1830, the two nephews divided the movement. One took the position as *āchārya* of the Uttaraji or northern section, headquartered at

8 *Ibid.*, p. 227. 9 *Ibid.*, p. 228.

Ahmadabad. This subdivision included part of Gujarat, Ujjain, Benares and Calcutta; the other subdivision, the Dakshina Bhag, or southern section, included southern Gujarat, Broach, Surat, and Bombay. Sahajananda Swami was deified during his lifetime and an idol representing him was worshipped beside Vishnu and Lakshmi.[10] In 1872, the Swami Narayanas claimed 380,000 members.[11] By the twentieth century, this movement had achieved the status of a recognized subdivision of Gujarati Hinduism.

The transitional socio-religious movement of Swami Narayana drew upon the religious traditions of limited dissent from the Gangetic basin and the Gujarati region. Swami Narayana Sampradaya's dissent, however, was limited to a few aspects of Hindu custom, particularly with regard to the marriage customs, infanticide, and the Vam-Margist sectarian form of Hinduism. Mostly, the Swami Narayana Sampradaya acted to reinforce Hindu values and practices, and to encourage Hindu devotionalism.[12] This movement had a broad appeal for pure-caste Hindus, tribals and some untouchables. Its followers were divided into religious practitioners and laity, given a network of religious institutions managed by an organization of hereditary Brahmanical leaders and built largely on pre-British forms. The Sampradaya became a permanent feature of Gujarati Hinduism and during the years following Independence spread abroad through Indian immigration. To the east of Gujarat a transitional movement among untouchables arose in the early nineteenth century, briefly attacked society in general, and then retreated to become a part of that society.

The Satnamis of Chhattisgarh

Two decades after Sahajananda Swami settled in Gujarat, a socio-religious movement came into being on the Chhattisgarh plain of the Central Provinces. Its founder, Ghasi Das, was a native of Bilaspur district, probably a Chamar, an untouchable leather worker. Nothing is known about his early life. On reaching adulthood he became a servant in the village of Girod (Raipur district). Sometime during the 1820s, Ghasi Das and his brother set out on a pilgrimage to the Vaishnava temple of Puri in Orissa. They did not complete this journey

---

[10] *Ibid.*, p. 232.

[11] Mehta, 'The Swami Narayana sect', p. 225.

[12] For a discussion of the twentieth-century development of the Swami Narayana movement, with particular emphasis on the spread abroad after India's Independence, see Williams, *New Face of Hinduism*.

and, after reaching Sarangarh, they returned joyously shouting '*sat nām*', proclaiming the concept of a single 'true' god. Ghasi Das abandoned his normal life and became a religious ascetic. He retired to the forest for meditation and periodically reappeared making himself available to individuals who sought spiritual inspiration and moral aid. Gradually his reputation grew and he gathered a group of disciples. Although anyone could come to Ghasi Das, almost all of his followers were from the Chamar caste.[13]

The religious career of Ghasi Das moved to a new stage when he withdrew to the forest for six months and then returned to preach a new religious doctrine. Ghasi Das urged his followers to abandon idol worship and all that it entailed. He maintained that all men were equal, thus striking against the system of caste. Ghasi Das also asked for a restructuring of dietary practices. Meat along with liquor and anything that resembled flesh or blood were forbidden, a ban that included tomatoes, lentils, and chillies. Beyond the issue of diet and basic belief, Ghasi Das taught his disciples to abstain from using cattle for ploughing after midday or from taking food out to the fields. The use of cattle for farm work in the afternoons was frowned upon by the local Brahmans. Through the dietary changes he advocated, Ghasi Das brought his untouchable disciples into conformity with upper-caste customs. Until his death in 1850, the Satnamis focused primarily on improving the status of the Chamars through adjustments within the untouchable community.

Balak Das, Ghasi Das's eldest son, became the next leader of the Satnamis. Balak Das was aggressive and radical in his attitudes to caste discrimination. He adopted the sacred thread worn only by the first three *varnas*. The twice-born Hindus were deeply affronted by what they considered his extreme presumptuousness. In the 1860s, a group of Rajputs retaliated by assassinating Balak Das. This murder sparked a dimension of social protest and rebellion against the upper castes among the Satnamis. Many refused to pay their land-taxes as the conflict escalated to include riots and further murders. Meanwhile, Balak Das was replaced by his son Sahib Das as leader of the Satnamis, although real power rested with Agar Das, a brother of the founder. On the death of Sahib Das the line of succession shifted to the two sons of Agar Das, Ajab Das and Agarman Das, who became high priests of the

---

[13] Central Provinces, *District Gazetteer, Raipur, 1909*, p. 81. This is the main source for the Satnamis and if any other sources are used they will be cited.

movement. They divided all property and the right to collect a rupee from each of the Satnami households. Leadership then passed down these two lines of descent.

In addition to this formal bifurcation of authority, the Satnamis suffered an earlier split over a ban on tobacco and smoking. Popular among many Chamars and other inhabitants of the Central Provinces was the *chungī* (leaf pipe). Ghasi Das banned all smoking along with the use of liquor and drugs. One section of the Satnamis maintained that Ghasi had lifted the ban before his death and broke away from the parent group. The new subsect was known as *chungīas*. Another subdivision of the Satnamis were the Jahorias, named so from the term *johar* (essence), and composed of those Satnamis who took vows of mendicancy. They ate only pulses and rice, never slept in a bed and wore only uncoloured clothes.

In time the Satnamis were linked to the Hindu *bhakti* saint, Ramananda. It was claimed that Rohi Das, a Chamar disciple of the great northern saint, was the true inspiration for the Satnamis. Those who accepted this story adopted the name, Rohidasi, rather than Satnami. This account has no historical foundation and a more likely source of influence on Ghasi Das was Jagjivan Das (d. 1761), a Rajput who founded the Satnamis of the Gangetic plains. It is reasonably certain, however, that the Satnamis of Chhattisgarh were an extension of the Ramanandi movements of the North. The Chhattisgarh area had been influenced by the teachings of Kabir, and by the first decade of the twentieth century the Kabirpanthis of this area claimed 685,672 members in their own movement. In the same period the Satnamis had grown to 477,360. Of this number only 2,000 or so were not members of the Chamar caste, and within that community 52 per cent of the Chamars were Satnamis. Chhattisgarh remained the centre of this movement with 42 per cent of the Satnami concentrated within it.[14]

The Satnamis became a permanent subdivision of the Hindus of the Central Provinces. Lawrence Babb, who conducted field research among the Satnamis in 1966–7, describes them as essentially a single-caste movement with its own hierarchical system of priests, its sacred centres, and a calendar of ritual events.[15] As a transitional socio-

---

[14] Census, 1911, *Central Provinces Report*, p. 77.
[15] Lawrence A. Babb, 'The Satnamis – political involvement of a religious movement' in Michael Mahar (ed.), *The Untouchables of Contemporary India* (University of Arizona Press, 1972), pp. 144–5; and see also by the same author, *The Divine Hierarchy, Popular Hinduism in Central India* (New York, Columbia University Press, 1975).

religious movement the Chhattisgarh Satnamis followed the well-established path of Ramanandi Hinduism, then for a brief period of extreme radicalism attempted to strike out against the caste system and society in general, but finally returned to an existence within that very system. This movement persisted as an untouchable form of Hinduism with its own priests, its hereditary leadership and its followers almost solely from one untouchable caste, with its area of impact limited to the Chhattisgarh plain. They, like the Swami Narayanas, were an extension of the religious and cultural developments within the Gangetic basin, a dimension that sets these two movements apart from Satya Mahima Dharma, a third transitional movement.

The Satya Mahima Dharma of Orissa

The early history of Satya Mahima Dharma revolves around three key men. The first was Mukand Das later known as Mahima Gosain. We have little information on his early life, his family or the sources for his ideas. He evidently spent the years 1840–50 living in Puri as an Achari Vaishnava. At the end of this decade he left for the hills where he wandered and meditated for approximately twelve years. In 1862 he reappeared as a *siddhi* (enlightened teacher), and journeyed throughout Orissa with a new message of revived Hinduism. His travels took him to the *āshram* of the second key leader, Govinda Baba. The two men quickly became friends and toured together throughout Orissa. Govinda Baba was a talented organizer and provided much of the skill necessary to establish a new religious movement. They recruited Bhima Bhoi, a young, blind, illiterate cowherd from the Khond village of Kankanapada, who became the third crucial leader of Mahima Dharma. He was a prolific poet who composed hymns for the movement and who inspired numerous disciples with his songs and his personality.[16]

During the 1860s and 1870s, this movement gained considerable strength. Because of its condemnation of orthodox Vaishnavism and its Brahminical supporters, there was also an increasing opposition. In 1873, the Commissioner of the Orissa Division received a petition charging Mahima Gosain with luring women from respectable families away from their homes and into orders of nuns within Mahima Dharma. Little came of this, but the next year witnessed a violent clash at the village of Malativiharpur between supporters and opponents of

---

[16] N. K. Sahu, 'Bhima Boi' in Daityari Panda (ed.), *Mahima Dharma O Darshana* (Koraput, Orissa, Dayananda Anglo–Vedic College, 1972), p. 17.

the new movement. In the aftermath of this riot, the government attempted to arrest Mahima Gosain. He escaped, but fell ill and died in 1876 at Kamaksha Nagar in Dhenkanal state.[17] His body was taken to Joranda and buried there. After this Joranda became the sacred and administrative centre of Mahima Dharma.

Mahima Gosain taught his disciples to worship one deity, Alekh Param Brahma, an eternal being who was without end and without form or description. This deity assembled the universe, dissolved it, and reassembled it again. All other deities were rejected since they did not exist, and the worship of idols was proclaimed useless. Brahman priests and their rituals were also invalid. Not surprisingly Mahima Gosain appealed heavily to the lower castes, to untouchables, and to members of the tribal communities.[18] His followers were required to perform a simple combination of prayer and ritual twice daily. In the morning they conducted *sārānām*, which consisted of praying seven times while facing east and sitting in certain yogic positions. In the evening they performed *darshānān*, and on this occasion prayed seven times while facing west.[19] Mahima Gosain divided his adherents into laity and monastic–mendicant orders. The laity (*ashrīkas*) wore yellow clothing, married according to simple ceremonies, refrained from killing animals, but could eat the meat of goats and deer if someone else supplied them. They also observed some of the normal caste restrictions. Mahima Dharmis did not cremate their dead, but buried them in a sitting position. Mourning was restricted to ten days and on the eleventh a rite of purification signalled a return to normal social life.[20]

The disciples of Mahima Gosain, who had taken vows of renunciation, were divided into three classes each representing a stage of religious advancement. The first group, originally called *niskāmīs*, and later known as *tyāgī bhairāgīs*, consisted of initiates who lived under the discipline of senior monks whom they served. The *tyāgī bhairāgīs* acted as cooks, cared for the temples and *āshrams*, and in general waited on the other classes of mendicants. The *aparā sanyāsīs* came second in this religious hierarchy. They were under the supervisiuon of the *parā sanyāsīs*, the senior group, and participated both in travel and preach-

---

[17] Sahu in 'Bhima Bhoi' gave this date as 1876, p. 18, and the Census, 1911, *Orissa Report*, p. 212, gives the date of his death as 1875.
[18] K. M. Patra, 'Religious movement in modern Orissa, "Satya Mahima Dharma"', *Journal of Indian History*, 55, pts. 1–2 (April–August 1977), 275, 280.
[19] *Ibid.*, 277.
[20] Census, 1911, *Bengal, Bihar and Orissa Report*, p. 212.

ing. When touring, the *apara* and *para sanyasis* begged for food from a single house. The *para sanyasis* represented the highest level of monastic achievement. They were the core of the movement and managed its various institutions. All three levels were open only to men. Women could join the movement as devotees, but they were forbidden to enter the monastic orders.[21]

With the expansion of the movement, Joranda took on an increasing importance as a centralizing force. It became a place of pilgrimage and the site of an annual festival on which the Mahima Dharmis came to honour their founder. Various ceremonies were conducted at two temples, the Sunya Mandir and the Dhuni Mandir. Perhaps of even greater significance was the annual feast, the Satsang Ghost, in which all participated. All *sanyasis* and *bhairagis* were expected to confess their failings to one of the *para sanyasis* before they could join the feast. After such confessions they received punishments, if necessary. Lay members also made their confession, although the punishments given them were minimal.[22] This common meal demonstrated the unity of Mahima Dharmis and their transcendence of caste restrictions. *Sanyasis* underlined their rejection of the traditional social structure by refusing to take food from Brahmans, princes, and some of the professional classes, on the grounds that this food may not have been acquired in a righteous manner.[23]

Expansion of Satya Mahima Dharma created a need for more centres of worship than Joranda. *Tungis* (small thatched huts) were built in those villages where a number of Mahima Dharmis resided. These places of worship contained sacred spaces and consequently the laity could join the services held there, but only *sanyasis* could reside in the *tungis*. A second type of religious centre, the *ashram*, was built. They were not as sanctified as the *tungis* and thus anyone could stay there as well as use them for various types of meetings. The distribution of *ashrams* provided an indication of the geographic spread of this movement. Orissa had the greatest number of *ashrams* (757), followed by Bengal (73), Andhra Pradesh (50) and Assam (33), with a total of 913.[24]

When Mahima Gosain passed away in 1876, a council was called at Joranda to consolidate the movement. Bhima Bhoi attended and was

[21] Anncharlott Eschmann, 'Spread, organization and cult of Mahima Dharma' in Panda (ed.), *Mahima Dharma O Darshana*, pp. 9–10; and Patra, 'Religious movement', p. 276.
[22] Eschmann, 'Cult of Mahima Dharma', pp. 10–11.
[23] Binayak Misra, 'Alekh religion in Orissa', *Modern Review*, 50 (1931), 529.
[24] Patra, 'Religious movement in modern Orissa', p. 280.

dissatisfied with the council's actions; he decided to found a monastery for his own version of Mahima Dharma. He chose the village of Khaliapali as the site for this new institution. Maharaja Niladhar Singh of Sonepure granted him land for the Khaliapali *āshram*. It was built in 1877 and quickly became the new centre of Mahima Dharma. Bhima Bhoi's main spiritual consort, Sri Ma Annapurna, supervised this *āshram*. She was a *sanyāsinī* who lived under strict moral vows. Bhima Bhoi had two other companions and in 1892 he fathered a daughter and a son from his two 'worldly' consorts.

Bhima Bhoi introduced the wearing of a rope made from Kumbhi bark to distinguish Mahima Dharmis from the general population. He also renamed the movement Kumbhipatras. Under Bhima Bhoi, Vaishnavism and the worship of Lord Jagannath came in for special criticism. The famous temple at Puri was seen as the centre of idolatry and responsible for many of the erroneous practices within contemporary Hinduism. On 9 March 1881, a group of Mahima Dharmis arrived in Puri to protest against the temple worship. They forced their way into the inner shrine and, according to some accounts, attempted to burn the wooden idols. The protesters were driven out, but tension between Satya Mahima Dharma and Hindu orthodoxy continued although not necessarily at this level.[25] In 1895 Bhima Bhoi died and was buried at the Khaliapali *āshram*.

Satya Mahima Dharma continued into the twentieth century. Scholarship on this movement is limited, and much of what has been written discusses the question of whether this was a Hindu or Buddhist movement. It is likely that the Satya Mahima Dharma was influenced by Buddhism, forms of *bhakti* developed in Orissa, plus some elements of tribal culture. The institution of confessions seems the most likely adaptation from Buddhist religious practices.[26]

As a transitional socio-religious movement in opposition to contemporary Hinduism, Satya Mahima Dharma drew support from the lower castes and partially assimilated tribal peoples who had little status and power within the society of Orissa. There is no evidence of influence from the colonial world of the British nor from cultural areas outside Orissa. Mahima Dharma bridged not only the pre-colonial and colonial worlds, but also the tribal and Hindu areas of Orissa and its surround-

---

[25] Eschmann, 'Cult of Mahima Dharma', p. 7; and Sahu, 'Bhima Bhoi', p. 18.
[26] Eschmann, 'Cult of Mahima Dharma', p. 8.

ing territories. Those who followed this movement were given forms of ritual, places of worship, assembly halls, their own priesthood, distinctive clothing, and customs that provided them with a separate identity at the edge of the Hindu religion.

THE CREATION OF THE COLONIAL MILIEU

The city of Bombay was the main centre of the new colonial milieu. From here it spread north towards Ahmadabad, slowly southwards along the narrow coast, and inland through Poona to the 'Desh', the territory of the Deccan. A second smaller centre of English influence was found in the city of Surat on the Gujarat coast. Bombay began with a settlement of merchants and officials of the East India Company. They were accompanied by Indian merchants, middlemen, and servants. The city attracted members of the commercial castes, especially Baniyas and Bhatias from Gujarat, who came to dominate much of the financial life of the city. Gujarati became the lingua franca of Bombay, but the Gujaratis themselves were sharply divided by subcastes that fragmented them into numerous social units. A few Nagar Brahmans of Gujarat, who knew Arabic and Persian, were attracted to the city, as were members of the Parsi or Zoroastrian community. Many Parsi merchants and traders of Surat moved south along with the English to become highly successful in the commerce of Bombay.

The bulk of Bombay's population were Maratha–Kunbis from the Deccan. They worked as unskilled labourers and accounted for 175,000 residents in 1881.[27] Chitpavan, Desharta and Saraswat Brahmans also settled in the city. By the mid-nineteenth century they had gained prominence in the professions, but did not dominate Bombay as they did the other areas of Maharashtra. Bombay was too heterogeneous for any one group to seize social, economic or religious control. By contrast Poona was a homogeneous city, Maratha in language and culture. It prospered during the reign of Baji Rao I (1720–40) as the capital of the Maratha Empire, and attracted considerable wealth, but suffered a decline in its economic status during the later part of the eighteenth century and the first two decades of the nineteenth. Poona was domi-

[27] Anil Seal, *The Emergence of Indian Nationalism: Competition and Collaboration in the Later Nineteenth Century* (Cambridge University Press, 1968), p. 83.

nated by Maratha Brahmans and was a centre of Hindu orthodoxy; a city rich in Maratha literature and culture with a strong sense of its recent political heritage. Influences from British culture passed from Bombay through Poona to the Desh, the lands beyond the coastal plain.[28]

Once the British were in control of the vast territories of the Maratha Empire, they began constructing their own system of administration. The first governor of the Bombay Presidency, Mountstuart Elphinstone (1819–27), adopted a cautious policy that used elements of the Maratha government and attempted to win the support of the Brahmans. An individual, peasant land settlement was introduced that fitted well with the society of the Desh. In acting thus, Elphinstone did not create an upheaval in the economy and society of Maharashtra similar to that which shook Bengal.[29] One institution he maintained was the *dakshinā*, a system of annual payments to Brahmans that supported teachers, temple and household priests, and *shāstrīs* (Brahman scholars). The extent of this institution can be seen from the fact that even under Baji Rao II, when the Maratha state had lost much of its wealth, 50,000 Brahmans received *dakshinā* payments in a single year.[30]

Within the realm of education the British maintained a similarly cautious programme. In 1820, the Native Education Society was founded in Bombay to improve existing schools and establish new ones. This was a direct descendant of the Bombay Education Society established in 1815 to educate European children of the city. English education was first accepted in Bombay, and more slowly in Poona. In 1821, Elphinstone opened the Poona Sanskrit College as a means to educate Brahmans. He hoped that they would eventually become interested in western thought. Initially this school taught purely Hindu subjects. Once again Elphinstone and the Bombay government started a long-term policy of hoped-for change, but in the short term acted to uphold the Brahminical establishment.

Another English school, the Elphinstone Institute, was founded in Bombay in 1825. In 1834, it became a college and began to produce the core of an English-educated elite. One of the first associations created

---

[28] Seal, *Emergence of Indian Nationalism*, pp. 70–1; and Ellen McDonald, 'City-hinterland relations and the development of a regional elite in nineteenth century Bombay', *Journal of Asian Studies* (Aug. 1974), 583–4.

[29] Ravinder Kumar, *Western India in the Nineteenth Century: A Study in Social History of Maharashtra* (London, Routledge & Kegan Paul, 1968), pp. 152–4.

[30] *Ibid.*, pp. 48–9.

by this educated group was the Scientific Society of Bombay established in 1848, partly through student initiative, and partly through the urgings of their English professors. One year later two branch societies were organized, one which conducted its meetings in Marathi, the other in Gujarati. All three associations became the centre of discussion and debate on social, religious, educational, and scientific issues, bringing to Bombay City criticism of society similar to that which developed in Calcutta, Delhi, and Lahore.[31]

A trend toward English education and the acceptance of western knowledge appeared in Poona. In 1832, the government founded an English high school and used *dakshinā* funds to do so. Four years later, in 1836, it was announced that the government would support only 'useful' knowledge. The local Sanskrit College dropped Vedic studies and an English principal was appointed for this institution. Changes were also made in the *dakshinā* system. Annual payments would, henceforth, be for the life of a particular recipient and could not be inherited. The amount spent on *dakshinā* payments gradually diminished as a more confident government slowly abandoned its tie to the Brahmans and to Hindu orthodoxy. In 1859, the *dakshinā* fund was shifted to the Department of Education and transformed into fellowships open to all castes in secular schools and colleges. In effect the *dakshinā* system came to an end as English education gained prominence in Poona. By the mid-nineteenth century, both Bombay and Poona acquired small-core groups of young men, primarily Brahmans, who had received or were studying for English education. During the same period a new force for change appeared first in Surat and Bombay City, and then in the Desh, as the colonial milieu expanded from the coast inland. As a result the first acculturative socio-religious movements arose in Surat.

ACCULTURATIVE MOVEMENTS AMONG THE
HINDUS OF GUJARAT AND MAHARASHTRA

The Manav Dharma Sabha

The British had been present in Surat since the second decade of the seventeenth century; however, it was not until the 1840s that tensions

[31] Richard Tucker, 'Hindu traditionalism and nationalist ideologies in 19th century Maharashtra', *Modern Asian Studies*, 10, no. 3 (July 1976), 234.

arose through the introduction of western education and missionary activities. Beginning in 1820, the Bombay government opened a school in Surat and another in Broach. Within a decade other schools were added throughout the cities of Gujarat. Their curriculum consisted of English texts translated into the vernaculars. The teaching staffs came from local communities, but were often educated in Bombay, as was illustrated by the career of Mehtaji Durgaram Manchharam (1809–78), a Nagar Brahman, born in Surat and trained in Bombay. In 1830 he became headmaster of the Government School in Surat, an institution founded in 1826. Four years later when the Surat English School was opened, Durgaram took the position of headmaster. He became a leading figure among the small group of educated Gujaratis who coalesced in the 1830s as critics of contemporary society. Participants in this group were Dadoba Panderung Tarkhad, Dinmani Shankar, Dalpatram Bhagubai, and Damodar Das. Durgaram spoke for the others when he rejected 'the existence of ghosts, their exorcism by means of incantations, the evils of early marriage and the bar against remarriage of high caste Hindu widows'.[32] By 1842, Durgaram had acquired a lithographic press that he and his friends used to disseminate their ideas, and the new knowledge being made available in the English schools. They did this through the Pustak Prasārak Mandalī (Book Propagation Society).

Advocates of cultural and religious change were spurred to action by the conversion of a Parsi student, Nasarwanji Manakji, and the resulting uproar in the Parsi and Hindu communities. After twenty days of pressure and debate the young Manakji recanted and was readmitted to the Parsi fold. This event led Durgaram, Dadoba, and a few friends to found the Manav Dharma Sabha on 22 June 1844. They held meetings every Sunday that were open to anyone who wished to attend. An article in the journal, *Prabhākar*, 5 January 1845, described their goals as being to 'select what is true of all religions, such as Christian, Muslim, Hindoo etc., to expose hypocritical arts ... [that various religious leaders] ... have put into practice, and the falsehoods they have inserted into the Shastras in order to secure superiority over others and to dispel ignorance which has led men to accept the stories of these

---

[32] Chavda, 'Social and religious reform in Gujarat', p. 210. This is the main source on the Manav Dharma Sabha and any other sources used will be cited.

deceivers as the word of God'.[33] As part of their programme of action, the Manav Dharma Sabha challenged magicians and the reciters of incantations to demonstrate their skills. If any could do so successfully, the Sabha would pay them Rs 27. They also criticized caste, but took no direct action against this institution. The Manav Dharma Sabha had only a short career as an active organization. It began to shatter in 1846 when Dadoba Panderung returned to Bombay, and ceased to function in 1852 when Durgaram Manchharam left for Rajkot. Although its life was severely limited, this Sabha was directly linked to later developments in Maharashtra and Gujarat as its members carried with them the ideals of the movement and became leaders in similar organizations.

The Manav Dharma Sabha appealed to the small, educated elite of Surat and began as a reaction to Christian conversions. For a brief period this society appeared to be the foundation of an acculturative socio-religious movement with an ideology that spoke of the need for significant change. Its ideas and programme, however, lacked the ability to generate strong commitment on the part of its followers, commitment of sufficient strength to directly challenge the leadership and domination of established religion. In spite of the short life span of this Sabha, the ideas generated here were passed on to two direct descendants, the first of which was the Paramahansa Mandali of Maharashtra.

The Paramahansa Mandali

The history of the Paramahansa Mandali was closely linked to the acculturative Manav Dharma Sabha and to the leadership of Dadoba Panderung (1814–82). Dadoba was born into a merchant family and received his final training in the Bombay Native School. In 1846 Bal Shastri Jambhekar, the headmaster of the Bombay Normal School, was replaced by Dadoba who returned carrying with him the ideas expressed by the Manav Dharma Sabha. He outlined his doctrines in *Dharma Vivechan* (A Discussion of the Unity of Man), a volume written in 1843, but not published until 1848. He listed seven principles that became the basis for the new association: that God alone should be worshipped, that real religion is based on love and moral conduct, that spiritual religion is one, that every individual should have freedom of thought, that our daily words should be consistent with reason, that mankind is one caste, and that the right kind of knowledge should be

---

[33] J. V. Naik, 'Early anti-caste movements in western India: the Paramahansa Sabha', *Journal of the Asiatic Society of Bombay*, 49–50–51 (1974–6, new series), 145.

given to all. These principles denied the polytheism of popular Hinduism, the caste system, and the Brahmanical monopoly of knowledge. Yet its promise of freedom of thought, and its insistence on reason as a base for moral conduct, meant that individuals who wished to follow Dadoba's ideas might do so without adherence to a single doctrine.[34]

In 1849, Dadoba and a small group of friends organized the Paramahansa Mandali, a radical socio-religious society that met in secret. All members were required to pledge that they would abandon caste restrictions. Each initiate had to take food and drink prepared by a member of the lower castes. Meetings were held at set times in the homes of various members and sympathizers. Most often they met in the home of Ram Bal Krishna Jayakar (1826–66), a Prabhu, who became president of the Mandali. These meetings opened and closed with *bhakti* hymns from the Marathi collection, the *Ratnamālā*, and were held in that language. At times prayers written by Dadoba were also recited as part of the worship service. They read papers and discussed a variety of social and religious topics. The group soon came to an agreement on two major principles. First, they would not attack any religion and, secondly, they rejected any religion which claimed that it had 'the infallible record of God's revelation to man'.[35] Thus the Paramahansa Mandali was limited to an intellectual rejection of religious revelations.

Those who joined this movement were largely young, educated Brahmans either from Bombay or drawn there in search of an advanced English education. As they completed their studies and left for employment elsewhere, they carried the Mandali and its ideas with them. Branches of this organization were established in Poona, Ahmadnagar, and Ratnagiri. The Poona Mandali was active and played a part in efforts to open the *dakshinā* system to non-Brahmans. Many of their members signed a petition to that effect and then had to struggle against orthodox attempts to excommunicate those whose names appeared on the memorial. The secret nature of the Mandali has made it difficult to trace its development and history during the 1850s. Rumours of its

[34] *Ibid.*, p. 146. This is the main source for the Paramahansa Mandali and if other sources are used they will be cited.

[35] The founding date of the Paramahansa Mandali is given differently by various sources. Naik implied it was in 1847, Zelliot gives the date as 1848 and Farquhar as 1849. See Naik, 'Early anti-caste movements', p. 144; Eleanor Zelliot, 'The Maharashtrian intellectual and social change: an historical view' in Yogindra K. Malik, *South Asian Intellectuals and Social Change* (New Delhi, Heritage Publishers, 1982), p. 38; and Farquhar, *Modern Religious Movements*, p. 75.

existence were prevalent as early as 1851–2. In 1860 the Mandali's records were stolen and made public. These documents contained the names of all members and a statement indicating that upon initiation each had eaten food forbidden to them by their caste. The Mandali collapsed immediately leaving behind outrage on the part of orthodoxy and humiliated radicals. In the aftermath two supporters of the Mandali converted to Christianity and one became a Theosophist.

The acculturative Paramahansa Mandali, following the path of the Manav Dharma Sabha with its attempts to reject the caste system, idols, orthodox rituals, and Brahmanical authority, left little behind it in concrete achievements. Its insistence on remaining a secret organization illustrated an unwillingness to openly challenge Hindu orthodoxy. The Mandali and its sympathizers drawn from the urban-educated Brahmans and merchants were isolated and had little base of support. Paralleling this absence of numerical and social strength was the lack of an ideology that provided its adherents with the emotional commitment needed to face the unwavering opposition of Hindu orthodoxy. Once their identities were known the Mandali disintegrated. Yet the ideas seen in the Manav Dharma Sabha and the Paramahansa Mandali appeared once more in the form of a new socio-religious movement.

The Prarthana Samaj

The establishment of a new society dedicated to changing the religious and social life of Maharashtra came from the internal heritage of the Paramahansa Sabha and from the external influences brought primarily by Keshab Chandra Sen (see pp. 34–9). Sen visited Bombay in 1864 and returned again in 1867. This second trip generated considerable enthusiasm among the English-educated elite of Maharashtra. That same year Dr Atmaram Panderung (1823–98), and a small circle of friends, created a new organization, the Prarthana Samaj (Prayer Society). Several of these individuals had been involved in the Paramahansa Mandali and thus both personnel and ideology were carried forth from the ruins of that organization.[36] With the exception of the Panderung brothers, the members of this organization were English-educated Chitpavan and Saraswat Brahmans.[37] In addition, the Samaj was aided by Gujarati merchants and members of the Parsi community, but

---

[36] Farquhar, *Modern Religious Movements*, p. 76.
[37] Christine Dobbin, *Urban Leadership in Western India: Politics and Communities in Bombay City, 1840–1885* (Oxford University Press, 1972), p. 251.

the actual membership was strictly Maharashtrian.[38] Bengalis continued to provide assistance to this new organization through visits by distinguished Brahmos. In 1872–3, Protap Chandra Majumdar spent six months in Bombay where he helped to organize night-schools for education among the working classes and aided in starting the journal, *Subodh Patrikā*; both were initiated in 1873. This journal was originally published in Marathi, but in 1877 English columns were added. In spite of the assistance and inspiration supplied by Bengali Brahmos, the Prarthana Samaj leaders refused to accept the label of 'Brahmos' or to formally link their own society with the Bengali Samaj.

Shortly after its founding, the members of the Prarthana Samaj agreed upon its rules and bye-laws. A managing committee was appointed and weekly meetings were scheduled for each Sunday. These gatherings consisted of *bhakti* hymns, lectures, and readings from various scriptures. The Prarthana Samaj showed a syncretistic acceptance of all religions. They drew upon Christian and Buddhist texts as well as different Hindu scriptures when compiling their weekly services.[39] Their Samaj was pledged to worship the one God and to seek the truth in all religions. They wished to avoid sectarian conflict in their pursuit of morality and truth. The Prarthana Samaj initially had a vague, undeveloped set of ideas. As Ranade, the Indian leader and politician, noted in 1872, 'our friends of the Prarthana Samaj seem to be perfectly satisfied with a creed which consists of only one positive belief in the unity of God, accompanied with a special protest against the existing corruption of Hindu religion, *viz.*, the article which denounces the prevalent idolatry to be a sin and an abomination'.[40] Later he wrote *A Theist's Confession of Faith* in which he attempted to create an ideological base for the Prarthana Samaj. In it he stressed the one compassionate, omnipotent God similar to the divine figure found in the writings of the Maratha *bhakti* saints. In 1874, a new meeting hall was opened and for this occasion Ranade, working with several other members of the Samaj, prepared a creed. It declared that: 'No carved or painted images, no external symbol which has been or may hereafter be

---

[38] Richard Tucker, *Ranade and the Roots of Indian Nationalism* (Bombay, Popular Prakashan, 1977), p. 58.
[39] Dobbin, *Urban Leadership*, pp. 250–1.
[40] Quoted in Tucker, *Ranade*, p. 59.

used by any sect for the purpose of worship or the remembrance of a particular event, shall be preserved here.'[41] From the first section of this statement the Samaj would seem to be directly condemning much of contemporary Hinduism. However, further on, they softened their attack considerably by a rejection of religious inflexibility: 'No created being or object that has been or may hereafter be worshipped by any sect shall be ridiculed or condemned ... No book shall be acknowledged or revered as the infallible word of God; yet no book which has been or may hereafter be acknowledged by any sect to be infallible shall be ridiculed or condemned.' The Prarthana Samaj retained its intellectualized vision of religious and social questions, and while it strove to change customs in both areas, it did not have the use of powerful emotional concepts and symbols to sustain its efforts and its followers.

The Samaj did attempt to provide education to all classes of the society and sought changes in four areas: they wished to end the ban on widow remarriage, to abandon all caste restrictions, to abolish child marriage, and to encourage the education of women.[42] They were, however, reluctant to act directly and were always careful not to break with Hindu society as had the Brahmos of Bengal. This led them to follow a cautious programme. For instance, some of the Samaj members worked openly for the acceptance of widow remarriage, but the Prarthana Samaj as an organization did not lead in this campaign.[43] The Prarthana Samaj managed to open branch societies in Poona, Surat, Ahmadabad and Karachi. The majority of new Prarthana Samajes were located to the East and the South-East, at Kirkee, Kolhapur, and Satara in the Desh, or in the towns of the Dravidian South. By the early twentieth century, eighteen Prarthana Samajes existed in the Madras Presidency.[44]

In 1875 the Prarthana Samaj faced its first crisis and a resulting schism among its members. Swami Dayananda Saraswati visited Gujarat and Maharashtra with the result that a new ideology of revealed truth, radical change, and open conflict provided a dramatically different species of religious movement. A section of the Prarthana Samaj

[41] This and the following quote are from *ibid.*, pp. 62–3.
[42] Farquhar, *Modern Religious Movements*, pp. 78–9.
[43] Tucker, 'Hindu traditionalism', p. 330.
[44] Farquhar, *Modern Religious Movements*, p. 77.

membership was attracted to Aryan ideology and were excited by Dayananda. They wanted to have the Prarthana Samaj openly reject all caste rules and restrictions. After considerable internal debate led by S. P. Kelkar, those who accepted Dayananda's message broke away and founded the Brahmo Samaj of Bombay. Kelkar's Brahmo Samaj failed after eight years, and in 1882 he returned to the Prarthana Samaj to become one of their few missionaries.

The Prarthana Samaj maintained various institutions: a free reading room, a library, night-schools for workers, an orphanage in Pandharpur and, after 1906, a Depressed Classes Mission of India under the leadership of Vithal Ramji Shinde. Such positive efforts did not lead to a direct attack on Hindu orthodoxy or Brahmanical power. By the late nineteenth century, the line of religious and social thinking exhibited by the Manav Dharma Sabha, the Paramahansa Mandali, and the Prarthana Samaj lost its strength and direction. Religion effectively remained in the hands of the Hindu orthodoxy. Only the widow remarriage debates of the 1860s, and the Age of Consent controversy of the 1880s and late 1890s, stirred orthodox leaders to organize. Both issues, however, were transitory and, consequently, so were the societies created by leaders on both sides of the issue.[45] In the 1880s and 1890s, Hinduism served as a vehicle of protest against the British and their culture and, in doing so, furnished symbols for political mobilization under the leadership of Bal Gangadhar Tilak. Social protest among non-Brahmans and untouchables move along secular lines rather than the theistic, syncretistic, nonaggressive and intellectualized protest of the Manav Dharma Sabha, the Paramahansa Mandali or the Prarthana Samaj. Brahmanical power was of such strength that it could not be openly challenged by an acculturative socio-religious movement. The Prarthana Samaj did succeed in creating various institutions, schools, reading rooms, places of worship, programmes for untouchable uplift, and exported its model of religious action inland to the Desh and to the peninsular South. Yet another example of such a movement existed in the Gujarat–Maratha areas, this from the minority community of Zoroastrians, the Parsis.

---

[45] Richard Tucker, 'From Dharmashtra to politics', *Indian Economic and Social History Review*, 7, no. 3 (Sept. 1970), 331–41.

AN ACCULTURATIVE MOVEMENT AMONG THE PARSIS

The Rahnumai Mazdayasnan Sabha

The Parsis, refugee Zoroastrians from Iran who, according to tradition, reached Gujarat in AD 936, spread along the western Gujarat coast living mainly in the ports and small towns of this area. Hereditary priests travelled with them ministering to small groups of families. In the thirteenth century Gujarat was divided into five *panths*. Each *panth* was governed by a council of priests and all five *panths* were tied together through links to Sanjan, the Iranian home of the Parsi emigrants. Thus the Parsis evolved a system of socio-religious orders not unlike the caste system that existed among Gujarati Hindus. The Parsis were a closed community as well. They did not convert and did not intermarry with non-Parsis. Their temples and *dokmas* (towers of silence), where the dead were exposed, were closed to non-Parsis. Access to their sacred literature was restricted to Parsi priests and discussed only within the community.[46]

Over the centuries of their diaspora the Parsis of India retained a limited contact with the Gabars, those followers of Zoroastrianism still living in Iran. In the 1720s, Dastur Jamasp 'Vilayati', a learned priest from Iran, visited Gujarat and brought with him a calendar, plus a number of manuscripts of the Zoroastrian scriptures. When he returned to Iran, he left behind him a divided community, unsure whether to adopt the Iranian calendar he had introduced or to retain their traditional one. In 1746 a group of Parsis decided to accept the Irani calendar on the grounds that it was the more ancient and thus the more correct of the two versions. They became known as the Kadmi or ancient section of the Parsi community as opposed to the Shahanshahis (royalists), who retained the calendar used in Gujarat. This produced a major division of the community, one that lasted into the twentieth century. A second division was created by the movement of Parsis into Bombay where many of them became wealthy as merchants, shipbuilders, and commercial middlemen. Thus a new group of prosperous Parsis contrasted with their more rural and small-town co-religionists

---

[46] Mary Boyce, *Zoroastrians, Their Religious Beliefs and Practices* (London, Routledge & Kegan Paul, 1979), pp. 167–8.

in Gujarat. The Bombay Parsis lived beyond the limits of the *panth* divisions and consequently were outside priestly control.[47]

As the Bombay Parsis prospered they began to construct religious buildings in the city, places of worship with a sacred fire and towers for exposing their dead. The money needed for construction and maintenance came from wealthy laymen who served as trustees to supervise the management of these new structures. Thus the laity of Bombay functioned beyond the authority of the hereditary priesthood. This community also posed questions for the East India Company in that they had little knowledge of its laws and customs. Consequently, the Company urged the Parsis to organize a council to oversee their fellow Zoroastrians. In 1728, the Parsi Panchayat was founded to manage the internal affairs of the community. It was composed of wealthy laymen and it too proved both a source of leadership and internal tension. The Panchayat's status and power fluctuated during the eighteenth and into the nineteenth centuries. From a low point of influence and social control the Panchayat was reconstructed in 1818 and issued a series of *bundobusts* (rules of conduct) in an attempt to create greater cohesion and uniformity within the Parsi community.[48] The Panchayat, however, continued to suffer from charges of nepotism arising from the fact that it was dominated by a handful of powerful merchant families.

In addition to internal tensions, the Parsi community faced a direct challenge from the Christian missionaries led by John Wilson, who held his first public discussion of Zoroastrianism in 1831. Wilson's attacks on this religion were disturbing, but in 1839 a far more serious danger arose when three Parsi students converted to Christianity. This shocked the Parsis as did Wilson's book, *The Parsi Religion*, published in 1843. Since the Parsis did not convert, Christian actions appeared difficult to understand and fearful in their impact. Perhaps as disturbing was the open discussion of their scriptures as they were examined by missionaries and European scholars. The Parsi priests were secretive, suffering from a degree of ignorance and a lack of the analytic techniques needed to end this ignorance. Nevertheless, the Parsis attempted to defend themselves against Wilson and his fellow missionaries. In the 1840s, Naoroji Furdunji edited *Fam-i-Famshīd*, a journal aimed at

---

[47] *Ibid.*, pp. 189–90.
[48] Dobbin, *Urban Leadership*, pp. 99–100.

defending the cause of Zoroastrianism. He also wrote a number of pamphlets and in 1850 published the book, *Tarīkha Farthost*, in which he 'proved' that Zoroaster pre-dated Christ and that his religion was superior to Christianity. The various forces challenging the Parsi community, and questions of its own self-identity within Bombay, stimulated the formation of a socio-religious movement designed to codify the Zoroastrian religion and reshape Parsi social life.[49]

In 1851, Naoroji Furdunji and a small group of educated Parsis from Bombay founded the Rahnumai Mazdayasnan Sabha (Parsis' Reform Society), with funds provided by K. N. Kama. Furdunji became president of the Sabha, an office he held until his death in 1885, and Sorabji Shapurji Bengali accepted the position of secretary. Bengali was an ardent writer, whose main subjects were the glories of ancient Iran and popularizing the new western knowledge. In 1850, he began publishing a monthly journal, *Jagat Mitra* (Friend of the World), to further the acceptance of his ideas among literate Parsis. The Sabha also issued its own journal, *Rast Goftar* (The Truth Teller), as the main voice of their movement. In 1851, S. S. Bengali started another journal, *Jagat Premī* (Lover of the World) with the purpose of disseminating knowledge of ancient Iran. It contained stories on Iran's cities, its sculpture and architecture, all as evidence of the greatness of the civilization that once existed in the Parsi homeland.

The broad purposes of the Sabha were to achieve 'the regeneration of the social condition of the Parsees and the restoration of the Zoroastrian religion in its pristine purity'.[50] To achieve this, Furdunji felt it was necessary 'to fight orthodoxy, yet with no rancour or malice ... to break through the thousand and one religious prejudices that tend to retard progress and civilization of the community'.[51] The leaders of the Sabha criticized elaborate ceremonies at betrothals, marriages, and funerals. They opposed both infant marriage and the use of astrology. The Sabha made known its opposition to orthodox beliefs and customs through lectures, pamphlets and the pages of their journal. It soon acquired a number of opponents among the priests and laity, even within Bombay where many of the older merchants still adhered to Parsi traditions.

The search of the purified and proper Zoroastrianism led those associated with the Rahnumai Mazdayasnan Sabha to introduce west-

[49] *Ibid.*, pp. 59–60.   [50] Farquhar, *Modern Religious Movements*, p. 84.
[51] Boyce, *Zoroastrians*, p. 200.

ern scholarship into the training of Zoroastrian priests. In 1854, K. N. Kama established the Mulla Firoz Madrassah to teach the languages of Zend, Pahlevi, and Persian to young priests. During the 1850s, he established a translation fund so that the findings of modern research on his religion could be made available to his fellow Parsis. In 1863, following his lead, Jijibhai's son, Rastamji, opened a seminary, the Sir Jamshedji Jijibhai Jarthosti Madrassah, under the headship of S. S. Bengali.[52] In 1864, Kharshedji Rastamji Kama, a cousin of K. N. Kama, established the Jarthosti Dini Khol Karnari Mandali to produce authoritative editions of the Zoroastrian scriptures, rituals and doctrines.[53] These efforts to discover proper beliefs and interpretations unsettled many of the literate and concerned Parsis. A further shock was generated with the visit of the German scholar, Martin Haug, in the 1860s. Haug declared that only the Gathas, a collection of ancient poems, could be considered as the words of the Prophet Zoroaster and thus should take precedence over all other texts. Haug went on to state that the Gathas taught a simple theism and not the elaborate ideology of contemporary Zoroastrianism. Once the initial shock passed, the critics of orthodoxy concluded that they had gained a new argument in their struggles with the religious establishment. They had in this theistic Zoroastrianism a doctrine that could be defended against attacks by Christian missionaries. European scholarship provided legitimization for those who wished to rediscover the 'pure' Zoroastrianism of antiquity.[54]

The definition of what was proper religion remained an issue that divided Parsis between those who advocated radical change, and those who wished only limited alterations in customs and rituals. The latter organized the Raherastnumai Mazdayasnan Sabha in opposition to the radicals. In 1863 Mancherji Hormasji Kama (1810–94) founded the orthodox journal, *Suryodaya* (Sunrise), edited by Manaji Barjorji Minocheer.[55] This division between radical and orthodox Parsis continued into the twentieth century. In 1909, a Parsi priest, Dr Dhala, returned from studying at Columbia University and announced the formation of an annual Zoroastrian conference, the goal of which was to inaugurate a

[52] Dobbin, *Urban Leadership*, pp. 63–4.
[53] *Ibid.*, p. 64; and Ervad Sheiarji Dadabhai Bharucha, *Zoroastrian Religion and Custom* (Bombay, D. B. Taraporevala, 1979, original edn, 1893), pp. 90–1.
[54] Boyce, *Zoroastrians*, p. 203.
[55] See Dobbin, *Urban Leadership*, p. 62; and Farquhar, *Modern Religious Movements*, p. 344, where he refers to the Rahe Rust (True Way). It is apparently the same society as the Raherastnumai Mazdayasnan Sabha.

movement for restoring Zoroastrian religion to its pristine sublimity and simplicity. The first conference was held in 1910 and explored a variety of religious, social, and educational questions. It paid particular attention to the need for a moral and religious education in their schools. The meeting was, however, rent by dissension and violence, as was the 1911 session. The 1912 and 1913 conferences proved far more successful and membership in the conference programme reached 500. A series of projects were organized including a revision of the ritual calendar, the education of Parsi priests, plans for industrial and technical education, a system of medical inspection for school children, the beginnings of a charitable organization, a dairy project, and an agricultural scheme.[56]

As the twentieth century progressed, a number of factors aided those who had demanded changes in Parsi customs and social behaviour. Many of the wealthy Parsis in Bombay were drawn into social contact with the English. Their wives began to appear at dinners, to change their habits of dress, and to adopt English customs and social forms. The age of marriage increased along with the amount of education given to their sons and daughters. The authority of traditional priests had not been transferred from Gujarat to Bombay, thus less resistance to change existed there than in many other Parsi communities.

The Rahnumai Mazdayasnan Sabha drew heavily on the colonial milieu and on western scholarship to construct its reinterpreted Zoroastrianism. The sacred texts, rituals and customs of the Parsis were studied by western scholars, and their knowledge became the foundation of religious change and for the instruction of a new generation of Parsi priests. The Sabha was the creation of an educated and urban class of Parsis in Bombay City, who became a highly succesful elite within that city and the broader world of British India. This acculturative socio-religious movement provided a reshaped heritage that anglicized Parsis could defend against Christian missionaries and that was compatible with their changed social, cultural, and economic environment. In so doing, the Parsi community was divided between this urban group and those who remained in Gujarat still under the authority of the traditional Parsi priests. Priestly power over the community as a whole was broken and authority among the rising elite shifted to prominent lay members who claimed their vision of Zoroastrianism

---

[56] Farquhar, *Modern Religious Movements*, pp. 88–9.

was the only true one. The wealth and status of these urbanized Parsis was thus extended into the sphere of religion, permanently altering the dynamics of the Parsi community. The Sabha was, as a result, highly successful in adjusting Parsi culture to the needs of the new urbanized Parsi elite, who in time became models of behaviour for younger Parsis. Orthodoxy was undermined by the loss of a monopoly of scriptural knowledge, by their low level of education, their ignorance of the Zoroastrian texts, and their inability to control the elite of Bombay. By 1947, the Parsi community had largely succeeded in adjusting to the colonial milieu with perhaps greater success than any other group in South Asia.

THE CENTRAL BELT AND MAHARASHTRA: A SUMMARY

This belt of hill tracts, river valleys, and the Kathiawar peninsula exists as a link and also a barrier between the northern plains and the Dravidian South, as was demonstrated by the transitional socio-religious movements that developed there. The Swami Narayana Sampradaya drew directly on the Gangetic basin for its leadership and ideology, while the Satnamis were indirectly linked to the area directly north. The Manav Dharma Sabha was Oriyan in its origins. The leadership and membership patterns of these movements also reflected the nature of this area, drawing supporters and leaders from high-caste Hindus, untouchables, and tribals. The Swami Narayana movement with its Brahman leadership, limited criticism of Hinduism, and emphasis on a re-enforced moral code belongs, in part, to past patterns of *bhakti* as well as the tradition of social protest. By contrast, the Satnamis began and ended as an untouchable movement with members of that community as both leaders and followers. The Satya Mahima Dharma were more complex in structure with leadership from Hindu Brahmans, and partly Hinduized tribals. This movement attempted to create a form of religion that bridged the gap from formal Hinduism and the tribal hill people at the edge of the Hindu world. Its customs and beliefs struck against the established Hindu society of the plains and attempted to replace that system with one that would integrate tribals, untouchables, and elements of the Hindu community into a new, equalitarian, socio-religious world. To accomplish this goal the Mahima Dharmis drew on a variety of past religious teachings.

This middle belt was slow to be incorporated into the colonial milieu. Its first acculturative movement was founded in Surat, one of the earliest areas to be integrated within the sphere of British cultural influence, but quickly shifted to Bombay, a major centre of colonial development. The ideology of religious criticism first crafted by the Manav Dharma Sabha was passed on and elaborated by the Paramahansa Mandali, and the Prarthana Samaj. In the process of transference, leadership was centred in the hands of Maharashtrian Brahmans among the English-educated elite. The entrenched power of Maharashtrian Brahmans limited the role and success of all three movements and made it impossible to challenge Hindu orthodoxy directly, or to call for dramatic change. By the end of the nineteenth century, the Prarthana Samaj, the last of these three, lost what little influence it possessed. This dominance of the Brahmans within Maharashtra marked a shift to a pattern of religious power found in the South, missing in Punjab and Bengal, but present in the Gangetic heartland.

Among the Parsis, the Rahnumai Mazdayasnan Sabha succeeded in challenging the domination of the Zoroastrian priesthood by building on a base of support among the urban Parsis of Bombay. They were beyond the territorial control of the priest, and their new sources of wealth and status freed them from priestly control. At the same time, success in the colonial milieu created for this new elite demands to reshape their religion, to defend it, and to legitimize their adjustment to the colonial world. This socio-religious movement succeeded but only at the price of dividing the Parsi community into two divergent wings, one still centred in the rural areas and small towns of Gujarat, the other with its base in the city of Bombay. Developments then among Hindus and Parsis of this region showed patterns drawn in part from the Gangetic plain to the North, but in Maharashtra far more characteristic of the Dravidian South.

CHAPTER SIX

THE DRAVIDIAN SOUTH

THE SETTING

The last regional chapter of this volume examines an area defined partly by geography, but more extensively by culture and language. The northern border of the Dravidian South begins on the east coast at the southern edge of Orissa, runs roughly along the northern lines of the Godavari River as it flows through the central Deccan, dipping south-west to Goa. The remainder of peninsular India extends to the southernmost tip of the mainland. Little exists in the way of geographically defined sub-areas within this region except for the thin western coast that continues from Maharashtra to the Cape. The rest of the peninsula is comprised of the Deccan plateau as it is narrowed by the convergence of the Western and Eastern Ghats to just above the Cape.

Each cultural and linguistic subdivision of the South radiates out from a core and blends into the others without clearly defined borders. The areas of each of the four languages – Telugu, Tamil, Kannada, and Malayalam – roughly correspond to the four southern states of India: Andhra Pradesh, Tamilnadu, Karnataka, and Kerala. Tamil is the oldest of the Dravidian languages with literature from the first century before Christ. The Tamil region was a second source of high culture pre-dated only by developments on the Indus and Gangetic plains.[1] The three other Dravidian languages are considerably younger. The literature of Kannada dates from the tenth century, Telugu from the eleventh, and Malayalam from the thirteenth to fourteenth centuries.[2] Each was influenced by Sanskrit and northern Brahmanical civilization, but still retained its own unique culture. A degree of unity exists between the four linguistic areas. All have a rough tripartite social structure consisting of Brahmans at the apex of their society, followed by non-Brahman

---

[1] Burton Stein, 'Circulation and the historical geography of Tamil country', *Journal of Asian Studies*, no. 1 (Nov. 1977), 7–8, 25.

[2] K. A. Nilakanta Shastri, *Development of Religion in South India* (Bombay, Orient Longmans, 1963), pp. 4–5.

5 The Dravidian South

castes, and below them untouchables. Their caste systems tend to be more extreme and rigid than the northern structures, with a greater degree of separation between Brahmans and all others. The untouchable members of society suffered from elaborate forms of discrimination enforced by both Brahmans and non-Brahmans.

The distribution of religions must be seen through the nineteenth- and twentieth-century political divisions of the South. The Madras Presidency directly administered by the British included the Tamil-speaking area, plus the eastern coastal plain, part of the Telugu linguistic sub-region, and a section of the Malabar coast where Kannada was the major language. Four major Princely States completed the Dravidian South. Hyderabad, in the south-central Deccan, was ruled by a small Muslim elite and populated by Telugu-speaking Hindus. Travancore and Cochin were Hindu states located in the Malayalam language area on the south-western coast. In the Kannada sub-region the state of Mysore held the largest percentage of Hindus among the four kingdoms. The percentages of the major religious communities are given in the table below. This illustrates the long involvement in overseas trade that characterized the western coast, and the differing communal pattern that emerged there as a result of this involvement.[3]

Ethnic and religious communities of the Dravidian South

Religious community	Travancore, Cochin	Hyderabad	Mysore	Madras Presidency
Hindu	66.67%	86.93%	91.00%	89%
Muslim	6.8%	10.32%	5.42%	6%
Christian	25.95%	0.40%	1.03%	3%

The Christians were significant only in Travancore and Cochin, while the Muslims had their highest percentage in Hyderabad. Otherwise the South was overwhelmingly Hindu. The Kerala Christians became known as 'Syrian-Christians', since they accepted the authority and rites of mid-eastern Christianity. Their community was affected by the Jesuits in the sixteenth and seventeenth centuries, and in the nineteenth and twentieth centuries by Protestant missionaries. The Christian com-

---

[3] Census, 1911, *Cochin Report*, p. 20; *Hyderabad Report*, p. 41; *Madras Report*, p. 38; *Mysore Report*, p. 50; and *Travancore Report*, p. 193.

munity was divided by schisms. In the sixteenth and seventeenth centuries those who accepted Jesuit teachings and Papal authority separated into their own subdivision, the Romo-Syrians. Converts made by Protestants were largely from the low castes and thus divided by theology and status from the Syrian-Christians who held a relatively higher position in the social structure.[4] The Muslims were descendants of merchants who, over time, created their own community, the Mopillas. They were known for their heritage of political revolts before and during the years of British rule.

The arrival of the British in south India began in 1620 when they established a small trading centre at Masulipatam. In 1639 the British acquired the site of Madras, but the East India Company did not annex significant tracts of territory until the second half of the eighteenth century. After the seizure of Bengal, they gained control of the Northern Circars in 1766. Under Lord Wellesley (1798–1805), the British seized the remainder of the east coast and in 1799 annexed half of Mysore's territory. At the close of the eighteenth and the early nineteenth centuries, a series of treaties brought one state after another under British indirect control: Hyderabad (1798), Travancore (1805), Cochin (1809) and Mysore (1831). The British had gained dominance of the South giving it a political structure that remained until 1947.

Once in control, the British adopted a conservative set of policies and refrained from any restructuring of the social or economic spheres of southern life. In land-owning and religion, the British largely accepted what was already in existence. Under Regulation VII of 1817, Hindu temples, monasteries, and in'ām lands donated to such institutions, fell under the supervision of the Board of Revenue. The Board was responsible for the finances, administration, maintenance, and operation of all Hindu religious institutions. This included supervising festivals, ceremonies, the health and welfare of pilgrims, and their hostels, along with the collection of pilgrim taxes. Thus the British government maintained the tie between religion and the state including support of the Brahman class. It is within this fusion of a new British elite and the older south Indian elites that the first of the transitional socio-religious movements appeared.

---

[4] Susan Bayly, 'Hindu kingship and the origin of community: religion, state and society in Kerala, 1750–1850', *Modern Asian Studies* (April 1984), 182–6, 210–11.

A TRANSITIONAL MOVEMENT AMONG HINDU
UNTOUCHABLES

The Nadars and Christianity

The Nadars were a caste associated with toddy, a liquor produced from the fermented sap of the Palmira tree. The production and sale of toddy were seen as polluting, thus the Nadars held a position in the social structure as untouchables. They could not enter Hindu temples, use public wells, approach members of the higher castes within a specific distance, were limited to the type of dress they could wear, and forced to live outside of the village proper. In spite of these disabilities, they ranked higher than the lowest untouchables. In addition, some Nadars had achieved a degree of wealth, control over land, and a resulting improvement in their social status. They were a small subdivision of the Nadar community, called Nadans, who functioned as landlords over others of their caste.[5]

The Nadars were centred in the Tinnevelly district of the Madras Presidency where they comprised the largest single caste. Nadars also existed in southern Travancore. Closely related castes were found as far north as the Billavas of Mysore.[6] Given the untouchable status of the Nadars, it is not surprising that they responded to a religion offering escape from their socio-religious disabilities; in this case that ideology was Christianity.

The Nadars first became acquainted with Christianity when Jesuit missionaries began proselytizing among the pearl fishers of the Tuticorin coast. In 1680 they organized a congregation at Vadakkankulam consisting largely of Nadars, and five years later erected a church. The Jesuits established a permanent mission in 1701 and by 1713 counted over 4,000 converts in the Vadakkankulam parish. During the remainder of the eighteenth century missionaries and south Indian catechists visited this community, but the influence of Catholic missionaries diminished, and in the late eighteenth century was replaced by that of the Protestants. In 1771, Anglican missionaries appeared from their bases in Tanjore and Trichinopoly. Along with Europeans, Indian converts carried on the work of proselytism. In 1784, a catechist named Rayappan made the first Nadar convert to Protestant Christianity. This

[5] Robert L. Hargrave, *The Nadars of Tamilnad: The Political Culture of a Community in Change* (Berkeley, University of California, 1969), pp. 12–42.
[6] M. S. A. Rao, *Social Movements and Social Transformation: A Study of Two Backward Caste Movements in India* (Delhi, Macmillan Company of India, 1979), pp. 22–7.

began a second wave of conversion during the 1790s. In 1797 a catechist with the Christian name of David succeeded in converting a group of Nadars. These new Christians were persecuted and consequently fled their home village for refuge on land purchased by David.

The pattern of conversion, persecution, and flight was repeated. The Nadan landlords and members of the upper castes attempted to halt conversions to Christianity by using their social and economic power over the Nadars. In response, David, with the help of an English merchant, organized a band of 'club men' who 'went about from place to place redressing the wrongs to the native Christians by force'.[7] By 1803, more than 5,000 Nadars had converted, but David died and the movement lost much of its momentum. Half of the converts had abandoned Christianity by 1815. The arrival of Charles T. E. Rhenius, however, revived the conversion movement among the Nadar community. Rhenius was a German, born in 1790, who reached India in 1820 under the sponsorship of the Church Missionary Society. Between 1820 and 1835 a new wave of conversion swept the Nadars of Tinnevelly. Group conversions took place, persecution followed, as did the establishment of Christian villages of refuge. In 1830 the Christians of Tinnevelly formed the Dharma Sangam (Religious Society). The Sangam raised funds for a permanent endowment to purchase land where converts could live together free of outside interference. In addition to the Dharma Sangam a Native Bible and Tract Society was established in 1822 with its own press. By 1831, they had published 45,000 tracts. Other funds were organized to aid the poor, to assist widows, and to pay the expenses of local missionaries.[8] By 1850, there were nearly 40,000 Christian converts in Tinnevelly district under the guidance of the Church Missionary Society and the Society for the Promotion of Christian Knowledge plus another 20,000 in southern Travancore.

The dramatic rise of the convert community in Tinnevelly district heightened animosity among upper-caste Hindus. Some time in the mid-1840s two organizations appeared. The first was the Vibuthi Sangam (Sacred Ash Society), a semi-secret association dedicated to ending

[7] Hargrave, *Nadars of Tamilnad*, pp. 43–5.
[8] Robert E. Frykenberg, 'The impact of conversion and social reform upon society in south India' in Philips and Wainwright, *Indian Society and the Beginnings of Modernization c. 1830–1850* (London, School of Oriental and African Studies, 1976), pp. 201–3.

Christian conversions. It was aided by a second association, the Madras-based Sadu Veda Siddhanta Sabha (Society for Spreading the Philosophy of the Four Vedas). The Sabha acquired a press of its own, published a paper, and numerous anti-Christian tracts. It also maintained contacts throughout the rural South. The Sadu Sabha appealed to wealthy men from various clean castes and attempted to hinder the missionaries through numerous charges sent to the Madras government. Associated with the rise of these organizations were attacks on Christian converts in November 1845. Hindu gangs converged on Christian villages, looted homes, and abused the converts. They challenged individuals to accept having ashes rubbed on their forehead, a symbol of Hinduism. If they refused they were considered Christians and treated appropriately.[9] Disturbances continued through the 1840s and into the 1850s. A final outburst of violence erupted in December 1858 in the town of Tinnevelly. Unrest declined as the Christian Nadars achieved a degree of acceptance and toleration, although tension remained between high-caste Hindus and the Christian community.[10]

Paralleling developments among the Nadars of the Madras Presidency were Christian conversions among their caste fellows in southern Travancore. Here the Nadars were largely toddy-tappers and tenants of the upper-caste Nayar and Vellala landlords. They held a similar position within the caste system. Nadars could not come closer to Nambudiri Brahmans than thirty-six paces or twelve paces to a Nayar. They could not carry an umbrella, wear shoes or gold ornaments, and Nadar women were forbidden to cover their breasts or to carry pots of water on their hips. These restrictions were open symbols of their untouchable status. The Nadars were also subject to heavy taxation and to the demands for corvée labour. They were at the same time aware of the conversions taking place among their fellow Nadars within British territory.[11]

Protestant missionaries first came to the Nadars of Travancore in 1819 when the London Missionary Society opened a church at Nagarcoil. By 1820, they had 3,000 Nadars under their care and instruction. Conversion quickly led to controversy as the Nadars attempted to defy some of the restrictions traditionally placed upon them. The form and direction of their demands were provided largely by Colonel Munro,

[9] *Ibid.*, pp. 207–8.   [10] *Ibid.*, p. 214.   [11] Hargrave, *Nadars of Tamilnad*, p. 57.

British Resident at the court of Travancore. In 1812 he issued an order permitting women converts 'to cover their bosoms as obtains among Christians among other countries'.[12] In May 1814 the government of Travancore issued a circular allowing lower-class women, who had converted, to wear a short bodice or jacket in the style of Syrian-Christian and Muslim–Mopilla women. In the mean time missionary women designed a jacket that would be satisfactory to their concepts of decency. The Nadars, however, were not satisfied, since their concerns were matters of caste status and not western prudery.

The conflict between Nadar converts and the Nayars intensified. By 1822 Nadar women wearing a breast cloth were abused, humiliated, and at times attacked by angry Hindus who stripped off their breast cloths. Hindus petitioned their government to stop the converts from adopting the dress and behaviour of the upper castes. Other issues began to appear along with the question of breast cloths. The Nadars were charged with avoiding the payment of rents and of refusing corvée labour. Tensions exploded in 1828 with a series of attacks on the converts and missions. The government of Travancore issued a ruling on 3 February 1829 that prohibited Nadar women from covering their breasts, confirmed the duty of Nadar men to perform forced labour, and chided them for seeking assistance from the missionaries. This diminished the violence for a while, but it did not dissuade the Nadar-Christians from continuing to push their demands. Tension rose once again in the 1850s and exploded in October 1858 with another series of attacks on Nadar women. Unrest continued into 1859, when troops were brought in to quell the disturbances. A royal proclamation was issued by the Travancore government on 26 July 1859 that returned to the earlier compromise allowing Nadar women to wear a jacket or cloth in the style of low-caste fisherwomen. This proclamation did not satisfy either of the parties, but gradually violence diminished as the Nadars continued their progress under the guidance of Christian missionaries.

The transitional movement of untouchable Nadars passed beyond the stage of criticizing Hinduism to the point where they rejected it entirely and sought caste uplift through conversion to Christianity, a religion that promised them equality and an end to their social disabilities. The Brahmanical dominance in southern society made it

---

[12] *Ibid.*, p. 59.

impossible for untouchables to openly criticize religious practice or their social position within Hindu society. Only by rejecting Hinduism could they hope to escape its socio-religious constraints. The Mahars of Maharashtra followed a similar path that led them to conversion to Buddhism in the 1950s. Other untouchable communities considered this option and historically have taken it. Christianity filled a role similar to that of other religions – Buddhism, Jainism, Sikhism, and Islam – that offered those at the lower end of the social structure a way to improve their status and escape from caste-based disabilities. Others would seek similar redress from social degradation within the sphere of the colonial milieu.[13]

Nadar involvement with Christianity pre-dated the British conquest and the creation of the colonial milieu. Although greatly aided by the arrival of European missionaries, the Nadar conversions belonged to the tensions of the pre-British world. This attempt by untouchables to seek relief through conversion contributed to religious tensions between Christians and Hindus, a situation that was accentuated by the activities of Christian missionaries throughout the nineteenth century. Hindu–Christian conflict created the one arena of major communal struggle in the South until the twentieth century, when northern forms of communal competition were exported to the South both against Christians and Muslims.

THE CREATION OF THE COLONIAL MILIEU IN THE SOUTH

The British presence in the South centred around Madras. Begun originally as Ft. St George, Madras grew into a city of 250,000 by 1800.[14] It was a hub of trade and commerce controlled almost totally by Englishmen and British-operated businesses. European economic dominance did not slow this expansion and the city reached 400,000 by 1881. Yet its composition was somewhat different from either Calcutta or Bombay. Fewer outsiders were attracted to it and nearly three-quarters of its inhabitants were born within the city. Overwhelmingly

---

[13] *Ibid.*, pp. 59–70.
[14] R. Suntharalingam, *Politics and Nationalist Awakening in South India* (The University of Arizona Press, 1974), p. 24.

Tamil-Hindus, Madras had only 12 per cent Muslims and 10 per cent Christians.[15] Its culture was that of Tamilnadu with the overlay of anglicization that grew from the introduction of English education.

In 1717 the East India Company established a school at Cuddalore.[16] That same year, missionaries of the Society for the Propagation of Christian Knowledge opened two charity schools in Madras City. The missionaries added to their educational efforts in 1784 with a school aimed at educating Anglo-Indian children. Yet progress was slow and English education was mainly in the hands of the missionaries. In 1819, the Madras Book Society was formed to provide books free of missionary influence and four years later, in 1823, the government formed the Committee of Public Instruction to plan for the opening of non-missionary schools. Throughout the 1820s and 1830s, however, the government did very little. Finally in 1834, the Hindu Literary Society opened its own English school to teach children of 'respectable families'.[17] This concern for education came within the context of heightened tensions between Hindus and missionaries stirred by the Charter Act of 1813, which allowed the missionaries to work freely within British-controlled territory, and by the controversy over Nadar conversions. The increased presence of missionaries stimulated criticism of the ties to Hindu religious institutions. In August 1838, the government announced a reversal of its policy supporting Hinduism and the Brahman caste.[18]

In November 1839, a petition asking for the establishment of an English college in Madras with 70,000 signatures was presented to the governor. This petition demonstrated the popular demand for English education and the opposition to missionary schools.[19] In 1841, the Madras High School was opened as part of a projected university system. The next year the government inaugurated four district schools in the major towns of the Presidency. The year 1841 also witnessed a concrete demonstration of what Hindu leaders had feared, when three students of a mission school converted to Christianity. The

[15] Anil Seal, *The Emergence of Indian Nationalism: Competition and Collaboration in the Later Nineteenth Century* (Cambridge University Press, 1968), p. 102.

[16] *History of Higher Education in South India: University of Madras, 1857–1957* (Madras, Associated Printers, 1957), vol. 1, p. 2.

[17] Suntharalingam, *Politics and Nationalism*, pp. 37–8.

[18] *Ibid.*, pp. 34–5.   [19] Seal, *Emergence of Indian Nationalism*, p. 107.

conversions stimulated the founding of the Pachaiyappa School in 'Black Town', an Indian section of Madras. This school, later Pachaiyappa College, was controlled by Hindu trustees with the goal of providing an education in English and through the regional languages.

In spite of the apparent demand for higher education, only a small number of students finished its four-year course. Between 1841–55, the number earning this degree was limited to thirty-six students. Enrolment in the Madras High School rose from sixty-seven to 221 in these same years, but many of the students quit after the first year or two. There was little need for such an education. Marathi remained the language of basic administration until 1854. Four years later, in November 1858, the government first held tests for positions earning more than Rs 50. At this time graduates of Arts and Law were exempted from these examinations. Thus an advanced English education became a direct path to administrative posts. A year earlier, the government acted to enhance education in English by opening the Madras University. The steps taken during the 1850s led to a rapid advance of English education during the second half of the nineteenth century. By the 1880s, university graduates exceeded the supply of government posts. Those who received an English education found themselves increasingly competing with Tamil and Telugu Brahmans. Between 1876–86, Brahmans accounted for 73 per cent of all successful candidates in Madras University. For the nineteenth century the English-educated elite was a Brahman elite centred in the city of Madras, and it was here that the colonial milieu made its first appearance.

The English language press had its beginnings with the *Carnatic Chronicle* in 1833. This journal carried articles in English, Tamil, and Telugu as it discussed local issues of general interest while attempting to remain clear of religious controversies. A similar policy lay behind the *Native Interpreter* founded in 1840; however, in October 1844 the *Interpreter* was purchased by Gajalu Lakshmanarasu Chetty and re-named the *Crescent*. Under the new name it became an advocate of Hinduism and a critic of government support for the missionaries. Friction between the two competing religious communities diminished during the 1850s only to be reawakened by a new round of conversions in the years after 1860, as missionaries returned once more to their scene of previous success in southern Madras Presidency and

Travancore.[20] They also entered new areas on the coast north of Madras City and inland to regions hitherto untouched.

Missionaries in Tamilnad found themselves facing a new type of opposition, this time by organized Hindu groups using many of the techniques introduced by the missionaries themselves. In Negapatam, Hindus held large processions and rival meetings to draw attention and hopefully audiences away from Christian gatherings. The anti-Christian forces were aided in 1887 by the establishment of the Hindu Tract Society. In 1889 they published eleven tracts, most in editions of 10,000. These tactics proved effective. Organized opposition remained strong through the 1890s and the missionaries made progress only slowly and largely among the poorest classes in the countryside.[21] As Christianity expanded into the rural areas and smaller towns, it became less a cause for the educated Hindus living in Madras City; their attention slowly turned to other issues.

During the 1850s, debates over social and religious customs began to appear among the small, educated Hindu class. In an effort to encourage change, Srinavasa Pillay, an educated Hindu who advocated social reform, organized the Hindu Progressive Improvement Society in November 1852. The Society advocated women's education, the betterment of the depressed classes, and widow remarriage. Those who joined Pillay tended to be Hindus who had worked with him in managing charities. Venkataroylu Naidu, another advocate of reform, founded the *Rising Sun* in July 1853. This journal discussed social issues among the Hindus. With the death of Srinavasa Pillay that same year, leadership of the Hindu Progressive Improvement Society passed to Venkataroylu Naidu who led this organization in founding schools for children of the depressed castes, providing scholarships to the needy, fighting for the Widow Remarriage Act of 1856, organizing a Hindu reading room, and the Hindu Debating Society in Madras City. There was, however, little acceptance of Naidu's ideas and, when he died in 1863, many of his projects, including the *Rising Sun*, died with him.[22] Impetus for changes in social and religious behaviour would next come from north-eastern India.

---

[20] Suntharalingam, *Politics and Nationalism*, pp. 38, 40–5, 143.
[21] Sundaraj Manickam, *The Social Setting of Christian Conversion in South India, 1820–1947* (Wiesbaden, Steiner, 1977), pp. 256–7.
[22] Suntharalingam, *Politics and Nationalism*, pp. 50–2.

ACCULTURATIVE MOVEMENTS AMONG
DRAVIDIAN HINDUS

The Brahmo Samaj, the Veda Samaj and the Prarthana Samaj

By the 1860s knowledge of the Brahmo Samaj had reached southern
India (see pp. 30–41). A Brahman of Cuddalore, Sridharalu Naidu,
learned of the Samaj and was sufficiently attracted to it that he sold his
property and left for Calcutta. He spent a year there studying Bengali
and Sanskrit as well as Brahmo ideology. Naidu then returned south
dedicated to spreading these new religious ideals. He did not, however,
attract widespread attention, but Keshab Chandra Sen did during his
visit to Madras in 1864. Sen gave numerous lectures, held meetings, and
stimulated many of the educated Hindus to rethink their social and
religious doctrines. Although his teachings were attractive and exciting,
Sen's outright rejection of idolatry went too far for Madras Hindus.[23]

A compromise resulted from Sen's visit that led to the founding of a
Veda Samaj at Madras City in 1864. This organization accepted the
theistic ideals of the Brahmo Samaj, but at the same time was careful to
remain within the borders of Hinduism. In its lengthy statement of
belief the members of the Veda Samaj considered marriage and funeral
rituals as 'matters of routine, destitute of all religious significance'.
Recruits spoke of 'discarding all sectarian views, of gradually abandoning caste distinctions, of tolerating the view of strangers and never
offending anyone's feelings'. They promised to abstain from polygamy, attendance or patronage of nautchs, child marriage, and to
campaign for widow remarriage. The Veda Samaj agreed to encourage
the use of the vernaculars, and assist in the publication of a journal
aimed at improving the 'social and moral condition of the community'.
Lastly, they would encourage the study and use of Sanskrit 'by means
not calculated to promote superstition'. This was then a restating of
Brahmo ideals and goals in a diluted manner that would not create
serious opposition from orthodox Hindus.[24]

By the end of the decade, Sridharalu Naidu reached Madras and
assumed the leadership of the Veda Samaj. Naidu reshaped this organization into a Brahmo Samaj in both name and content. The older rules
were removed and Naidu embarked on a Samaj programme. He sent a

[23] R. Srinivasan, 'The Brahmo Samaj in Tamilnadu', *Journal of the University of Bombay*
(1975–6), 216, 218–19, is the only source for this section; others will be cited.
[24] *Ibid.*, pp. 217–18.

memorial to the Viceroy championing the Brahmo Marriage Bill and in 1871 performed the first marriage in south India that followed Brahmo rituals. Naidu travelled throughout the South organizing new Brahmo Samajes. He also translated Brahmo literature into Tamil and Telugu, including Debendranath Tagore's *Brahma Dharma* and Keshab Chandra Sen's *Model Form of Divine Worship*. In addition he revived the nearly defunct journal, the *Tattvabodhinī Patrikā*, and began the *Indian Mirror*. Naidu both attracted new disciples and lost some of the members of the Veda Samaj through his stricter Brahmoism. One of Naidu's staunchest supporters, Doraiswami Iyengar, headed the Samaj of Purusawalkam. Iyengar may have been the only Tamil Brahman in the Brahmo Samaj. He was an excellent speaker, a writer, composer of hymns and editor of *Tattvabodhinī Patrikā*. Iyengar was the first Brahmo to openly abandon the sacred thread, an act for which he was condemned by orthodox Hindus. Iyengar travelled widely speaking to meetings in such cities as Bangalore, Tanjore, Trichinopoly, and Mangalore. When he died in 1887 the Brahmo Samaj lost one of its major figures. The movement had already suffered a grievous loss in 1874 when Sridharalu Naidu was killed in a carriage accident. These two deaths brought the Brahmo Samaj of Madras to the point of extinction when in 1879, Pandit Basanta Ram, a Brahmo from Lahore, helped to revive it.

Branches of the original Veda Samaj were founded in various towns of the South. Subbarayulu Chetty established one at Salem in 1866. After an initial period of enthusiasm, interest in this society waned and when Chetty died in 1868 it sank into a state of suspension. In 1871, S. P. Narasimalu revived the group changing it to a Brahmo Samaj. He was an enthusiastic and energetic leader who held fortnightly meetings in his home, launched a bilingual journal, the *Salem Patriot*, and started another Samaj at Coimbatore with a similar fortnightly journal, the *Coimbatore Patrikā*. Brahmo Samajes appeared in other towns, sometimes through local leadership and at other times through the arrival of a leader from outside the area.

The Brahmo Samaj of Bangalore was the result of British military policy. In 1872 a British regiment was moved from Burma to Bangalore. One of the regiment's clerks, O. M. Rajavelu Naidu, subscribed to the *Tattvabodhinī Patrikā*. Others in the office staff read this paper and together they founded a Brahmo Samaj within the regiment. They brought this Samaj with them to Bangalore where a number of educated

Hindus of the city began to attend its meetings. By 1872 a Brahman from Poona, Chandrasekhara Iyer, joined the Samaj and under his leadership it established schools, distributed prayer books and tracts, including one on female education, and started a Tamil monthly. If the Bangalore Samaj grew from an accidental combination of events, perhaps no other Samaj had as complex a history as the one founded in Mangalore.

The Brahmo Samaj of Mangalore emerged through the activities of Nireshvalya Arasappa, one of the few educated Billavas, a caste that held similar status to the Nadars further south. Arasappa had been in contact with Christian missionaries, exploring the possibility of conversion by the Billavas as a way to improve their social position. These negotiations failed and a friend of his, one Ullal Raghunathaya, suggested he might consider the Brahmo Samaj. As a result, in April of that year three Brahmo missionaries arrived from Bombay accompanied by a representative of the Prarthana Samaj. A meeting was held, but with little response from the Billava community. The Brahmos spoke English and appeared dressed in western clothes, a fact that left most of the Billavas confused and apprehensive. Raghunathaya and some Saraswati Brahman friends acted as translators with the result that a Brahmo Samaj was established with a membership of nineteen. Meetings were held at Arasappa's house until his death in 1876.

The Saraswat Brahmans who joined found it uncomfortable gathering at the home of a Billava. Consequently, on 11 June 1870 they organized a separate society, the Upasana Sabha (Worship Society). This new organization accepted Brahmo doctrine and began its own weekly meetings. The Upasana Samaj, however, did not openly condemn idolatry. In the meantime Raghunathaya remained loyal to his friend and continued to attend the meetings of the Brahmo Samaj. He was excommunicated in October 1871. Raghunathaya was later readmitted to the Saraswat caste, but as a result joined the Upasana Sabha. This organization later changed its name to the Brahmo Samaj of Mangalore, while the original organization founded by Arasappa disappeared. Thus the Brahmo Samaj was transformed from a broadly critical movement led by an untouchable, to one of limited goals under control of the Saraswat Brahmans of Mangalore.[25]

Branches of the Veda Samaj, the Brahmo Samaj, and the Prarthana

[25] Frank F. Conlon, *A Caste in a Changing World, the Chitrapur Saraswat Brahmans, 1700–1935* (Berkeley, University of California Press, 1977), pp. 101–3.

Samaj in south India depended on one or two dynamic and energetic leaders. When they died or left, these organizations tended to fade from view. All Brahmo Samajes faced consistent and strong opposition from Hindu orthodoxy and could survive only through the dedication of individuals willing to take great social risks and, in most cases, by carefully limiting their degree of radicalism. Even these societies, whether Brahmo Samaj, Veda Samaj, or Prarthana Samaj, tended to lose what little influence they were able to generate by the last two decades of the nineteenth century. The 1911 census lists only 374 Brahmos in the Madras report and by 1921 that figure had dropped to 171.[26]

Two of the three acculturative movements were imported from outside the Dravidian South and the third was but a pale echo of the Brahmo Samaj. Here, as in Maharashtra, Brahmanical dominance could not be successfully challenged. The urban-educated elite was neither strong enough to attack orthodoxy, nor sufficiently motivated to do so by an integrated ideology that could draw emotional commitment and provide legitimization for radical change. Ideas could be expressed, but it was not possible to put them into action except rarely and then only for short periods of time. Instead of the social and religious criticism of the Brahmo Samaj and related organizations, south Indian intellectuals were stirred by the Theosophical Society with its praise of all things Hindu and its criticism of orthodox Christianity.

Theosophists among Hindu orthodoxy

The origins of the Theosophical movement were rooted in one pattern of socio-religious dissent within western civilization. The term 'Theosophy' or divine wisdom, had become popular in the seventeenth century.[27] As Theosophy developed into a movement, it utilized ideas and symbols from Egyptian, Hindu, and Buddhist religions as legitimization for its criticism of contemporary life in Europe and America. Two unusual individuals, Helena Petrovna Blavatsky and Henry Steel Olcott, founded the Theosophical movement in 1875 after becoming acquainted through a shared interest in spiritualism. Madame Blavatsky was born on 12 August 1831 in Ekaterinoslav, Ukrainia. Evidently Blavatsky showed an interest in the occult when still young and later became a medium. In 1848 she was married to N. V. Blavatsky, a much

[26] Census, 1921, *Madras Report*, p. 63.
[27] Bruce F. Campbell, *Ancient Wisdom Revived, a History of the Theosophical Movement* (Berkeley, University of California Press, 1980), p. 28.

older man. She left him after three months, and in the years prior to 1872, when she appeared in Cairo earning her living as a medium, little was known about her. There she was befriended by a couple, the Coulombs, who were also involved in the occult. On 7 July 1873, Madame Blavatsky arrived in New York where she remained for the next five years. In the summer of 1874 she attended a gathering of spiritualists in Chittenden, Vermont, where she met Colonel Olcott. He was an ex-army officer who had become a journalist. Olcott and Blavatsky became colleagues and began to hold small, informal meetings at Madame Blavatsky's rooms. It was at one of these meetings, on 7 September 1875, that Olcott raised the idea of founding a Theosophical organization. The group readily agreed and created a temporary association with Olcott as chairman and William Quan Judge as secretary. They next framed their basic bye-laws and on 17 November 1875 formally inaugurated the Theosophical Society 'to collect and diffuse knowledge of the laws which govern the Universe'.[28] Initially the Society drew on such occult and spiritual concepts as existed in western civilization.

The ideology of the Theosophists progressed rapidly when, in 1877, Blavatsky published *Isis Unveiled*. This book appeared in two volumes, the first of which examined 'spiritualism, modern science, psychic phenomena, Mesmerism, the Kabal, the knowledge and achievements of ancient peoples, and psychic feats and wonders'. The second volume contained criticisms of Christianity, esoteric interpretations of it, and other religions, and a 'comparison of Christianity with Hinduism and Buddhism'.[29] *Isis Unveiled* created excitement and enthusiasm among those sympathetic with spiritualism, and devastating criticism from orthodox Christians. Blavatsky did not attempt to counter her critics, instead, in December 1877, she indicated her desire to leave the United States for India.[30]

Contact with India was first established by Colonel Olcott. An Indian friend, Mulji Thekersey, gave him the name of Harishchandra Chintamani, president of the Bombay Arya Samaj. Through Chintamani Colonel Olcott learned of Swami Dayananda Saraswati, and on 18 February 1878, he wrote to him. The letter arrived while Dayananda

---

[28] J. N. Farquhar, *Modern Religious Movements in India* (New York, Macmillan Company, 1919), pp. 213–15.
[29] Campbell, *Ancient Wisdom*, pp. 34–9.
[30] Farquhar, *Modern Religious Movements*, p. 226.

was staying at Lahore and was followed by a discussion of possible cooperation between the two organizations. On 22 May 1878, the New York group changed its name to the Theosophical Society of the Arya Samaj of India. The Society also recognized Swami Dayananda Saraswati as 'its lawful Director and Chief'. Letters continued to flow as both sides discussed their ideas and as the two Theosophical leaders prepared to leave for India.[31]

Olcott and Blavatsky sailed from New York on 17 December 1878, and arrived in Bombay on 16 February 1879. They were met by Chintamani and a few of his friends. Olcott delivered several public lectures in Bombay and caused something of a sensation with his criticisms of western culture and Christianity, plus his praise of Asian religions. Olcott and Blavatsky travelled from Bombay to Saharanpur to see Dayananda. They arrived there on 29 April and met Dayananda on 1 May. While waiting for Dayananda, Olcott lectured under the auspices of the local Arya Samaj. The meeting between Dayananda and his new allies was apparently cordial. When Dayananda travelled to Meerut, Olcott and Blavatsky accompanied him.[32] Next they returned to Bombay where they met with the governor in an effort to still the suspicions of the British-Indian government about their intentions. Numerous rumours, many of them characterizing Blavatsky as an immoral woman, floated about the English community and for months after their arrival in India they were followed by the police.[33] Government suspicions, however, did not impede the activities of the two leaders.

Olcott and Blavatsky joined Dayananda at Benares in December 1879. Blavatsky arrived accompanied by Alfred P. Sinnett, the editor of the Allahabad newspaper, the *Pioneer*. Sinnett was a respected figure in India and a valuable addition to their group. They met him while visiting Simla in 1880. Sinnett introduced them to leaders of the government and of society with the result that much of the suspicion generated on their arrival disappeared. Acceptance in Anglo–Indian society paralleled a growing tension between the Theosophists and Dayananda. Disagreements had arisen over various points of doctrine, particularly the Aryan concept of God and their sharp criticism of contemporary

[31] Har Bilas Sarda, *Dayanand Saraswati, World Teacher* (Ajmer, Vedic Yantralaya, 1946), pp. 524–8.
[32] *Ibid.*, pp. 536–7.
[33] Anonymous, *The Theosophical Movement, 1875–1925, A History and Survey* (New York, E. P. Dutton, 1925), pp. 51–2; Campbell, *Ancient Wisdom*, pp. 79–80.

Hinduism. An open break did not occur until Dayananda visited Bombay. He arrived on 30 December 1881 and attempted to reconcile their increasing differences. When this failed, he openly condemned both Blavatsky and Olcott, their ideas, leadership, and actions since arriving in India. After his lecture on 28 March 1882, Dayananda published a flyer entitled *Humbuggery of the Theosophists*. In July, Olcott responded in a special supplement to *The Theosophist*, a journal founded in October 1879. From this point on relations with the Arya Samaj were completely broken. For years afterwards each side continued to abuse and criticize the other.[34]

Following their break with the Arya Samaj, Blavatsky and Olcott restructured the Theosophical Society. They formalized three goals: 'to form a nucleus of the Universal Brotherhood of humanity, without distinction of race, creed, sex, caste, or colour; to encourage the study of comparative religion, philosophy, and science; and to investigate the unexplained laws of Nature and the powers latent in man.'[35] These goals were made public through numerous lectures by Colonel Olcott and in the pages of *The Theosophist*. From the beginning they drew both Europeans and Indians into the movement. A wide range of individuals joined including Allen Octavian Hume, Gopal Krishna Gokhale, and Major-General Morgan of the British-Indian army. Educated Hindus and Parsis became members and branch societies were established in different Indian cities. Sinnett organized one of the earliest branches at Allahabad. It was given a Hindu colouring under the name of the Prayaga Psychic Theosophical Society. It included Englishmen and educated Brahmans led by Gyanendra N. Chakravarti. Tensions arose between Englishmen and Indians over the question of caste distinction and the concept of a Universal Brotherhood. Difficulties also grew from the fact that Sinnett became a major link between Blavatsky and the 'Mahatmas' who sent messages to her through him and other Europeans. No messages passed through the Brahman Theosophists who considered it somewhat insulting that such revelations went only to 'beef-eating, wine-drinking Englishmen'.[36] The strains within this society, however, were not sufficient to divide it or to end its effectiveness, consequently the Allahabad branch remained active for many years.

[34] Sarda, *Life of Dayanand*, pp. 439–542, 555–9.
[35] Campbell, *Ancient Wisdom*, p. 78.
[36] Anonymous, *Theosophical Movement*, p. 625.

During 1880–1, Olcott and Blavatsky toured widely giving lectures from Lahore in the North to Ceylon in the South. In these early years the Theosophists had their headquarters in Bombay where in 1880 the Coulombs joined them. Madame Coulomb and her husband became assistants to Blavatsky in administrating the organization, and in maintaining its base of operations. In 1880, Blavatsky and Olcott began the institution of annual conventions designed to bring together Theosophists from throughout India. In addition, publications continued to appear. In 1881 Sinnett produced *The Occult World* and Olcott published his *Buddhist Catechisms*. In October of that year both Blavatsky and Olcott toured the South, visiting Tuticorin and Tinnevelly where there already was a branch society. They met with intense opposition from Christian missionaries and enthusiasm from Hindu leaders. In April 1882 they returned, this time for six weeks with even greater success. Societies were established in Madras City, Nellore, and Guntur. During this trip the idea of moving their headquarters to the Madras area was first discussed. Bombay had proved expensive and was less responsive to the Theosophists than Madras. The final decision to move was taken at the annual convention in December 1882.[37] They purchased an estate on the coast at Adyar, just south of Madras City, for their new headquarters.

Once settled at Adyar, Blavatsky and Olcott embarked on a new round of recruiting members and conducting an enlarged programme of activities. Blavatsky focused her attention on publishing *The Theosophist*, while Olcott travelled and lectured. In July and August 1883, he toured in the Tamil and Malayalam areas. New branches were opened in nearly all of the cities he visited. Olcott was greeted with considerable enthusiasm, particularly by the educated Hindus of the Brahman and higher non-Brahman castes. Funds came from merchants who had a tradition of supporting cultural and religious societies. Part of Olcott's message was the need for Sanskrit knowledge among young Hindus, and for a rediscovery of ancient Hindu accomplishments. A committee was established and chaired by Ganpati Rao and, in July, it announced plans to open Sanskrit schools in Triplicane, Mulapore, Black Town, and Madras City. Schools were also founded in Madurai, Bellary, Nellore, Vizianagram, Trichinopoly, and Guntur, and were managed by the local Theosophical Societies.[38] Colonel Olcott strove

---

[37] Suntharalingam, *Politics and Nationalism*, pp. 296–7.   [38] *Ibid.*, pp. 298–303.

to establish a library at Adyar that would bring together all the literature of the world's religions and become a place for scholarly study as well as the training of priests. In December 1886 the Adyar Oriental Library was opened with dignitaries representing Hinduism, Buddhism, and Zoroastrianism.[39] It marked an impressive achievement in Olcott's plans, but this success came in the wake of a crisis that struck the Theosophical movement at its very roots.

Olcott and Blavatsky left for Europe in February 1884 and, just before their departure, appointed a council to manage the Adyar headquarters during their absence. There had been a number of disagreements between the Coulombs and several leading members of the society. Before she left, Madame Blavatsky attempted to end these disputes by giving the Coulombs the task of caring for the buildings and also for her rooms while she was away. Tensions did not end, however, but erupted after Blavatsky and Olcott reached England. The Coulombs left Adyar for refuge among a group of Christian missionaries. They then proceeded to charge Blavatsky with fraud centring on a shrine room that was built into the Adyar headquarters. It supposedly had a fake back wall that opened into Blavatsky's bedroom enabling her to falsify a number of the spiritual phenomena that took place in seances she conducted.[40] The 'Shrine Room' controversy gained great publicity and tarnished Blavatsky's reputation. She returned to Madras in December 1884, and was met with a great welcome, but it was clear that if she stayed in India the entire matter would end in the courts. Olcott feared that a trial would become a test of Theosophy in general, and of 'the truth of the Esoteric Philosophy' and the 'existence of the Mahatmas' in particular. As a result Blavatsky left India after resigning as corresponding secretary. She did not return, and leadership in India fell completely into the hands of Colonel Olcott.[41]

By the end of 1884 Olcott was faced with holding together the Indian Theosophical movement that numbered over 100 branches throughout the subcontinent. During 1885 he returned to touring and lecturing. He visited thirty-one branch societies and gave fifty-six lectures. Meanwhile Blavatsky retained some degree of influence through her

[39] Ibid., pp. 303–4.
[40] Anonymous, Theosophical Movement, pp. 73–4; Farquhar, Modern Religious Movements, pp. 232–49.
[41] Campbell, Ancient Wisdom, pp. 88, 90–1.

writings. In 1888 she published *The Secret Doctrine*, a two-volume work running to 1,500 pages. In it she further developed her ideas on the nature of the universe, the unity of God, the identity of all souls with the over-soul, ultimate reality, and the cyclical nature of the universe.[42] For Indians she remained an absent, but inspiring figure, until her death in 1891.

The ideology of the Theosophists, as constructed during the joint leadership of Madame Blavatsky and Colonel Olcott, drew heavily on *Isis Unveiled* and *The Secret Doctrine* with its theme of ancient wisdom, known and retained by adepts or masters who had chosen Blavatsky to reveal this knowledge to mankind. After Blavatsky reached India, the term 'Mahatma' was increasingly used for these spirit beings. Supposedly Blavatsky spent seven years in Tibet studying with Master Morya, and later was in contact with Koot Humi, another of the Mahatmas. Together the Mahatmas constituted the Great White Brotherhood or the White Lodge, an organization that provided guidance for mankind in its evolutionary path towards spiritual fulfilment.

The Theosophists adopted a modified concept of rebirth and spiritual progress fused with the Hindu idea of karma. Hindu terms and concepts were added to the western spiritualists' tradition. Together they formed a system that placed each person in the world as the result of a descent of the ego from the universal soul down into the world of matter. Theosophy offered a path of evolution back to the universal soul. Each individual was composed of a physical body, an astral body, and a divine soul that passed from rebirth to rebirth. Such an ideology was sufficiently compatible with Hinduism that there was little difficulty in adjusting it to orthodox religious thought.

Colonel Olcott in his numerous lectures spoke glowingly of the glorious Hindu past, with its magnificent achievements in all areas of culture and science. Not only was the ancient civilization of India one of immense achievements, but it also was 'the cradle of European civilization, the Aryans [were] the progenitors of the Western peoples, and their literature the source and spring of all Western religions and philosophies'. Olcott maintained that sufficient research into the past would allow the world to know 'the whole truth about Aryan civilization'.[43] Educated Hindus enthusiastically welcomed this doctrinaire articulation by a representative of western civilization. Olcott and

[42] *Ibid.*, pp. 40–8. [43] Suntharalingam, *Politics and Nationalism*, p. 294.

the Theosophists offered self-respect and a series of arguments Hindus could use to protect themselves against western critics, especially the Christian missionaries. Through his lectures and travels, Colonel Olcott held the dominant position in the Indian Theosophical movement until the arrival in 1893 of a new convert, Annie Besant.

Born into an Irish family living in London, Annie Besant (1847–1933), grew up talented, rebellious, and deeply interested in religion. As a young adult, Annie Wood married an Anglican clergyman. She soon found the life of a pastor's wife limited and frustrating. She rebelled against both the marriage and orthodox Christianity. Annie Besant turned to writing pulp fiction and to investigating atheism and socialism. She became a journalist and it was in that role that she read *The Secret Doctrine* in 1888. Besant was so impressed with this work that she abandoned her previous beliefs and became an ardent Theosophist. She joined the household of Madame Blavatsky and began to edit the journal, *Lucifer*. Annie Besant rapidly gained a reputation among the Theosophists and when Blavatsky died she was one of the individuals considered for the presidency, as a possible replacement for Colonel Olcott, and as a successor to Blavatsky.[44] Olcott was facing widespread criticism at that time. In the *Report of the Proceedings of the Adyar Convention of 1892*, the Indian section listed 145 branches, but stated that only five lodges were doing satisfactory work. Olcott resigned as founder-president and then was reinstated, but critics still attacked him for supposedly poor leadership.

While this controversy continued, attention was drawn to the Parliament of Religions meeting in Chicago. In 1893 G. N. Chakravarti reached London on his way to the United States. He came as a representative of the Theosophical Society and of three Brahmanical organizations: the Hari Bhakti Prodayini of Cawnpore, the Varnashrama Dharma Sabha of Delhi, and the Sanatana Dharma Rakshani Sabha of Meerut.[45] Besant joined him when he departed for America and they returned to England together. Chakravarti then went on to India and Besant followed later. She reached Ceylon in November and arrived at Adyar for the annual convention. After the meeting was over, she and Olcott toured India. Besant proved to be a popular speaker who drew enthusiastic response from primarily Hindu audiences. Besant visited

[44] Anonymous, *Theosophical Movement*, pp. 294–5; Farquhar, *Modern Religious Movements*, p. 267; Campbell, *Ancient Wisdom*, p. 101.
[45] Anonymous, *Theosophical Movement*, p. 447.

numerous sacred sites, held meetings with Hindu priests, declared she was an Indian at heart, and adopted the sacred thread as a symbol of her union with the Hindu community.[46] During the years 1893–7, Besant travelled to lecture, attend meetings, and investigate the occult. She was often out of India and, when there, spent much of her time in Benares and only occasionally in Adyar. She founded the Central Hindu College at Benares in 1898 and made that city her personal headquarters.[47] In 1907 Colonel Olcott died and Annie Besant replaced him as president of the Theosophical Society. At this time she shifted to Adyar, where she was based until her death in 1933.

Annie Besant continued to lecture on the glories of ancient India and the role of spiritualism, but she also began to alter somewhat the ideological approach of Theosophy in India. Besant had been criticized by the Madras Social Reform Association for her uncritical praise of Hindu society. In 1908, she organized the Theosophic Order of Service with the goal of promoting practical, humanitarian work. It advocated brotherhood, national education, and an end to child marriage. The Order engaged in projects to abolish capital punishment, extend cooperatives, promote hospital visits, advocate prison reform, support child welfare, aid the blind, and oppose the 'white slave' trade. It became active in a number of countries.[48] There was nothing particularly Indian about their goals and projects, but through this new organization Besant introduced some of the social ideals that existed within Theosophy in its European and American settings.

By 1910 there were indications of another ideological departure as Besant began to talk of a need for national unity. In 1913 she delivered a series of political lectures under the title of 'Wake up India', a logical extension of Olcott's earlier discussions of ancient glory. Annie Besant's speeches were given within a much more politicized environment. In 1914, she joined the Indian National Congress. The following year she presented the concept of Home Rule Leagues and when the Congress failed to accept this she proceeded in 1916 to found them herself. The high point of Besant's involvement in Indian politics came in 1917 when she was elected president of the Indian National

---

[46] *Ibid.*, pp. 452–5.
[47] Eugene F. Irschick, *Politics and Social Conflict in South India; The Non-Brahman Movement and Tamil Separatism, 1916–1929* (Berkeley, University of California Press, 1969), pp. 27–8.
[48] *Ibid.*, p. 26.

Congress. Her career as a political leader, however, was short, for with the rise to prominence of Mohandas Karamchand (Mahatma) Gandhi, Besant dropped from the political centre. She could not accept Gandhi's leadership and so was left behind after 1919 as the nationalist movement entered a new period of activism.

Annie Besant's career as president of the Theosophical Society initially met with great success. In the first few years she increased membership by 50 per cent to a total of 23,000.[49] The Society reached its peak during the 1920s with approximately 45,000 members, but dropped sharply after 1930 to 35,000 or less. This rise and fall in membership was partly tied to the story of Jiddu Krishnamurti. In 1909, a long-time member of the society brought Krishnamurti's family to live at the Adyar headquarters. It included three boys, one of them the young Krishnamurti. Charles W. Leadbeater, an ex-Anglican curate who had joined the Theosophists in 1884, identified Krishnamurti as a vehicle of Lord Maitreya, and later of Christ. Krishnamurti was proclaimed the 'World-Teacher' who had come to impart true knowledge to mankind. Leadbeater and Blavatsky managed to obtain legal guardianship over Krishnamurti and his brother Nityananda. Gradually a cult centred on Krishnamurti. Besant founded the Order of the Star in the East with officers in various countries, its own periodicals, and badges. When students at the Central Hindu College began to wear badges with J. K. on them, Besant was forced out of that institution by prominent Hindus who feared a new type of conversion movement. During the 1920s Krishnamurti won increasing public attention. The Order of the Star in the East grew to some 30,000 members, many of whom also joined the Theosophical Society. As Krishnamurti matured he rejected the idea of a messianic role for himself. Finally in 1929, he dissolved the Order of the Star in the East and in 1930 he resigned from the Theosophical Society. Within a few years the membership dropped by nearly one-third. Annie Besant died in 1933 and George Arundale served as president for twelve years (1933–45). He was followed by the first Indian president, C. Jinarajadasa (1945–53).[50] Theosophy remained active in India, but with sharply diminished influence. During its earlier years, however, the Theosophists were nearly omnipresent throughout the subcontinent as they appeared in one region after another.

When still centred in Bombay, the Theosophists drew into their

[49] Campbell, *Ancient Wisdom*, p. 119.   [50] *Ibid.*, pp. 120–31.

circle Gujarati Hindus, such as Manilal Nabhubhai Dwivedi (1858–98), a scholar of Advaitavad philosophy, the Hindu mystic Nrisinhacharyaji (1848–98), who founded the Sri Shreya Sadhak Adhikari Varga in Baroda, and Shriman Natthuram Sharma (1858–1930) of Bilkha in Kathiawar. Olcott visited Gujarat in 1880 and helped to organize the Prajahitvardhak Sabha of Surat. He also assisted in opening a girls' school, a voluntary school-services organization, and a veterinary hospital. This Sabha later was affiliated with the Theosophical Society. Annie Besant visited Surat and Baroda in 1893 where she met the ruler, Sir Sayajirao. They discussed a variety of issues including questions of women's rights, education, and public welfare.[51]

In Bombay proper, the Theosophical Society drew Hindu and Parsi members. The Parsis produced a stream of tracts arguing that Zoroaster was divine and greater than the masters of Theosophy. He had introduced the ancient wisdom of Theosophical doctrine and so Parsi beliefs were fitted into this new ideology with a position of superiority. The Parsis also explained and justified their rituals according to scientific concepts along lines already established by Colonel Olcott. Theosophical teachings remained strong enough among the Parsis that in 1911 the Iranian Association was founded largely to curtail this influence. Educated Hindus also joined.[52] The most famous of these was Gopal Krishna Gokhale who remained a member from 1890–1905.

In Madras the Theosophists had their greatest impact on educated Hindus, largely among the Brahmans. They acted through their own societies and in alliance with other organizations. In 1880 A. Sankariah, Dewan-Peishkar of Trichur in Cochin State, established a Hindu Sabha based on 'the support of pundits and priests of social standing', that had as its goal the removal of 'dogmas, schisms and practices opposed to the consolidation of the Hindu nation'. The Hindu Sabha as part of its overall programme allied itself with the Theosophical Society.[53] Ragunatha Rao, president of the Madras Society, followed Olcott's arguments on the need to revive Hindu learning by founding, in 1886, his own organization, the Association for Propagation of True Religion. Rao hoped to restore Hindu society to its proper form when

---

[51] Vijay Singh Chavda, 'Social and religious reform movements in Gujarat in the nineteenth and twentieth centuries' in S. P. Sen (ed.), *Social and Religious Reform Movements* (Calcutta, Institute of Historical Studies, 1979), pp. 219–21.

[52] Mary Boyce, *Zoroastrians, Their Religious Beliefs and Practices* (London, Routledge & Kegan Paul, 1979), pp. 204–5; Farquhar, *Modern Religious Movements*, pp. 90, 345.

[53] Suntharalingam, *Politics and Nationalism*, p. 304.

all conduct was determined by the Shastras. Similarly, Sivasankara Pandiah, a Gujarati Brahman, through his involvement with the Theosophical Society, created the Hindu Tract Society in 1887 to defend Hinduism against all opponents. During the years 1887–9 branches were established in the smaller towns, tracts published, and Hindu preachers sent to tour throughout the South. He later organized the Hindu Theological College Fund with the help of educated Brahmans and the wealthy diamond merchant, Ramakrishnah Pantalu. In January 1889, they succeeded in opening the Hindu Theosophical High School with Pandiah as its headmaster.[54]

Theosophical lodges were established in the Telugu-speaking districts at Machilipatam, Guntur, Nellore, and Madanapalle, where they attracted aristocrats, officials, and members of the educated middle class. New institutions were opened including the Besant Theosophical College, the Besant Theosophical High School, and a night school at Madanapalle. This area became one of the centres of devotion to Jiddu Krishnamurti during the 1920s.[55] The influence of Theosophy was not limited to the western and southern regions of India, but reached as far north as Punjab. Here information points to a presence of Theosophical leaders and local organizations from the early 1880s. In 1881 *The Theosophist* contained an article in praise of Pandit Shraddha Ram Phillauri, the orthodox leader of Punjab.[56] Through the 1880s and 1890s, Theosophists lectured in Punjab and received considerable publicity. In 1895 Annie Besant drew the attention of educated Punjabis when she spoke at Lahore on 'The means of India's regeneration'. She argued for Sanskrit education and stated that it was imperative to teach children the meaning of Hindu symbols and rituals if they were to understand their own religion. This theme – the need and method of Hindu revival – ran through Theosophist writings and lectures wherever they appeared.

In 1887, when the Bharat Dharma Mahamandala was founded in Hardwar, the list of 'Gentlemen of special importance' was headed by Colonel Olcott. Through its history into the twentieth century, Theosophy appeared repeatedly in connection with the Mahamandala (see pp. 77–82). When Pandit Din Dayalu Sharma travelled to Hyderabad

[54] *Ibid.*, pp. 305, 309–10.
[55] V. Yasoda Devi, 'Social and religious reform movements in Andhra Pradesh in the nineteenth and twentieth centuries' in Sen, *Social and Religious Reform Movements*, pp. 365–6.
[56] Lahore, *Tribune* (13 August 1881), p. 10.

in 1897, he met with Shri Darabji Dosabai, president of the local Theosophical Society. This connection between the two organizations was publicly recognized in the Delhi meeting of 1900, when the Maha-mandala passed a resolution in praise of the Theosophists' work for Sanatana Dharma.[57] Theosophist involvement reappeared again in 1901–2, as control shifted to Swami Gyanananda. The Swami was allied with Theosophists one of whom, Dr Bal Krishna, led in attacking Din Dayalu. They were angered by Din Dayalu Sharma's criticisms of Annie Besant. Theosophical societies also existed in the North in Allahabad, Meerut, Benares, and Kanpur.[58]

A comprehensive picture of the Theosophical movement demands extensive research before it can be completed. However, there is enough information to indicate that this imported ideology attracted adherents in various regions of South Asia. Hindus responded to its criticisms of Christianity and western civilization, as well as to its praise of their own religion and culture. It strengthened Hindu conservatives and their attempts to revive orthodox Hinduism. In the nineteenth century, colonialism and new forms of travel made it possible for the Theosophists to trace the ideas they appropriated to their source, in this case India. Hindu–Buddhist concepts represented part of the legiti-mization necessary for their programme of social dissent within west-ern civilization. In turn they were compelled to defend orthodoxy and to refrain from social criticism in India. In this case the tradition of dissent and protest of one civilization, when transferred to the realm of another, lost its critical function and became a movement that defended religious and social orthodoxy. The Theosophists were thus a socio-religious movement of reverse acculturation, foreigners who adjusted to the realities of South Asia, and in the process reoriented belief, behaviour, and social goals. Other movements in the South developed opposing ideologies that struck against the socio-religious system then in existence.

Swami Narayana Guru and the untouchables of Kerala

This socio-religious movement originated from the position of the Izhavas in the caste system of Kerala. The Izhavas, like the Nadars, were considered untouchables, but had higher status than the lowest

---

[57] Pandit Harihar Swarup Sharma, an untitled, unfinished and unpublished Hindi biog-raphy of Pandit Din Dayalu Sharma, pp. 32, 104, 117.

[58] *Ibid.*, pp. 186–90.

castes, the Nayadis, Puluyas, and Cherumas. The Izhavas controlled coconut cultivation and toddy-tapping. Many were tenant-farmers to Nayar landlords, but some had served the military and had been rewarded by gifts of land. There was a small number of educated Izhavas trained in Sanskrit, and the traditional Hindu medical system of Ayurveda. As an untouchable caste they faced numerous restrictions on their dress, customs, and religious practices, not unlike those placed on the Nadars. They could not attend schools with high-caste children, take jobs in government service, enter Hindu temples or have idols of the higher gods in their own temples. Yet they were the largest caste in Kerala, accounting for 26 per cent of the population.[59]

By the mid-nineteenth century attempts to improve the status of the Izhavas made their appearance. The Izhavas had their own temples where priests, Izhavattis, conducted the necessary rituals.[60] In 1852, Velayudha Panicker travelled to Goa where he learned the Brahmanical rites used in high-caste worship. In 1854 he established the first Izhava temple for the worship of Lord Shiva, a type of worship hitherto forbidden to the Izhavas. This form of agitation for change was transformed by Swami Narayana Guru into a socio-religious movement.[61]

Swami Narayana was born into an Izhava family on 20 August 1854 in the village of Chembazhanti near Trivandrum. His father, Matan Asan, conducted a traditional school. The young Narayana studied Sanskrit, Malayalam, Tamil, and astrology with his father. He learned Ayurveda from an uncle and received a more advanced education from a well-known scholar, Kumanpalli Raman Pillai. After completing his education he returned to Chembazhanti to direct his own school. The young Swami did not stay with this for long, but left for periods of meditation and penance. He was married, but refused to settle into a householder's life. Sometime in the mid-1880s, Swami Narayana began to preach his own doctrine of socio-religious change, primarily to the Izhavas and then to the broader community.

In 1887–8, Swami Narayana founded a temple and monastery at Aruvipuram. By consecrating this temple to Lord Shiva in 1888, he defied the religious restrictions traditionally placed on the Izhava community. In order to maintain and manage these institutions, Swami

[59] Rao, *Social Movements and Social Transformation*, pp. 22–4, 27.

[60] Valiyaveetil Thomas Samuel, 'One caste, one religion and one God for man: a study of Sri Narayana Guru (1854–1938) of Kerala, India', thesis submitted to the Hartford Seminary Foundation (1973), p. 46.

[61] Rao, *Social Movements and Social Transformation*, pp. 45–6.

Narayana created the core of an organization that later became known as the Sri Narayana Dharma Paripalana Yogam (the Society for the Propagation of the Religion of Sri Narayana Guru). By 1890 Swami Narayana had acquired an extensive following among the Izhavas, and by 1901 a general acceptance by the Hindus of his scholarly abilities.[62]

Swami Narayana Guru succeeded in articulating a doctrine aimed at improving the social position of the Izhavas. He urged them to abandon the occupation of toddy-tapping and to abstain from drinking liquor. In a single slogan he linked status, custom, and occupation: 'Drink not, serve not, and produce not liquor!' He admonished them, instead, to enter into trade and commerce as more acceptable occupations. Swami Narayana also condemned all forms of animal sacrifice, the worship of the goddess, the use of obscene songs, all marks of low-caste status and forms of behaviour unacceptable to the clean castes. Swami Narayana developed simplified and less expensive ceremonies to replace the traditional ones. He advocated a marriage ceremony to be performed at an Izhava temple using hymns in Sanskrit and Malayalam.[63] His message of social change was carried by groups of volunteers who travelled from village to village and town to town, asking their caste fellows to abandon the old unacceptable customs.

Initially, Swami Narayana acted to make Izhava behaviour compatible with the norms of Brahmanical and Sanskritic society. As this movement passed into the twentieth century, it began to condemn the caste system as the basis of Hindu social structure. The broadening of this movement came as two new leaders, Dr Palpu and Kumaran Asan, the writer and poet, joined Swami Narayana. Dr Palpu was the first Izhava to receive an education in western medicine. He achieved this by attending the University of Madras, but, after acquiring an MD degree, he was refused a position with the Travancore government. Afterwards he became active in agitating against the restriction on Izhavas in the educational and administrative systems. In 1885 he organized a memorial to the Diwan of Travancore that condemned the present caste system, but he received no response from the government. In 1892, he tried again with the Malayalee memorial signed by 10,000 Izhavas, Christians, and Muslims. In 1896 he made a third attempt, this time

[62] *Ibid.*, p. 40.   [63] *Ibid.*, pp. 38–9, 55.

with 13,000 Izhava signatures.[64] All three memorials made the same demands and all three failed. Dr Palpu's efforts tended to be limited to the elite and had no roots in the mass of the Izhava society. He discussed this with Swami Narayana Guru and Kumaran Asan, with the result that all three joined together under the banner of Swami Narayana's ideology. It was a fusion of these separate streams – one an evolving, socio-religious stream with growing acceptance within the Izhava caste, and a second more elitist, secular and political movement led by educated Izhavas and appealing to that community – which constituted the Swami Narayana movement of the twentieth century.

THE DRAVIDIAN SOUTH: A SUMMARY

The peninsular South was predominantly a Hindu world with the one exception of a significant Christian community on the west coast. The Muslims, by contrast, were limited to 10 per cent or less of the population, with one compact community, again on the west coast. The Hindus dominated non-Hindus in nearly all aspects of life and the Brahmans dominated the Hindus. As in Maharashtra, this led to tensions between Brahmans and non-Brahmans, as well as to socio-religious movements, one transitional and one acculturative, among the most depressed members of society, the untouchables.

Christianity's long presence in the South and its encouragement by missionaries, even prior to the establishment of the colonial milieu, produced sharp religious tensions. The Nadars found Christianity an attractive ideology that provided them with an avenue of social mobility through the rejection of Hinduism and the caste system that it supported. Three areas of Christian-Hindu strife emerged. First, among the Nadars of Tinnevelly within British-controlled territory, then with members of the same caste in the Princely State of Travancore, and finally in the latter half of the nineteenth century in Telugu-speaking districts north of Madras, where Protestant missionaries achieved considerable success. In each of these areas Hindu orthodoxy reacted sharply to Christian challenges. Within this region the most widespread form of communal conflict arose between the Christian and Hindu communities. Unlike the northern regions, accultur-

[64] P. M. Mammen, *Communalism Versus Communism: A Study of the Socio-Religious Communities and Political Parties in Kerala, 1892–1970* (Columbia, Missouri, South Asia Books, 1981), pp. 34, 53.

ative movements such as the Brahmo Samaj or the Arya Samaj did not lead in this struggle with the missionaries.

The ideologies and organizational structures of acculturative movements, the Brahmo Samaj, the Arya Samaj, and the Prarthana Samaj, reached the South, but neither they nor the Veda Samaj, managed to construct and maintain significant organizational activity. This type of socio-religious movement appeared and disappeared sporadically. It was dependent on individual leadership that in turn often proved unstable. Social critics could not openly oppose orthodoxy on issues of belief, custom or ritual. What religious organizations appeared and survived were largely orthodox and dedicated to reviving elements of existing Hindu religion. The most dramatic and unusual of the religious movements found in the South during the nineteenth century, Theosophy, came from the West rather than from a region of South Asia.

The Theosophists drew on centuries of socio-religious dissent and protest within western civilization. They borrowed non-western symbols and ideas as part of their ideology and followed them back to their sources in Egypt and South Asia. The Hindu–Buddhist symbols that they employed were needed to legitimize their doctrine of protest in the West and thus could not be criticized in South Asia. There, the Theosophists found it necessary to argue for the superiority of contemporary Hinduism and Buddhism. The transformation from one civilization to another brought the Theosophists from a position of critics and dissenters to one of champions of orthodoxy and the status quo. In this, they were at opposite poles from Swami Narayana Guru of Kerala with his socio-religious movement of uplift for the Izhavas that sought initially to incorporate within this untouchable community the values and practices of Brahmanical Hindus. In the twentieth century, Sri Narayana Guru and his followers rejected that system. With the new century, the socio-religious movements of South Asia existed within an increasingly politicized world that contained dimensions of competing nationalism and heightened religious conflict. Five movements that survived and prospered in the new century will provide examples of religious action within a changed context.

CHAPTER SEVEN

THE TWENTIETH CENTURY:
SOCIO-RELIGIOUS MOVEMENTS IN A POLITICIZED WORLD

THE SETTING

The twentieth century brought a number of crucial alterations to the context within which socio-religious movements functioned, succeeded, or failed. The most important of these changes was the rise to prominence of secular nationalism expressed by the Indian National Congress. Nationalist fervour peaked four times before 1947: first in the years 1905–7, then during the three Gandhian campaigns of 1919–22, 1930–4, and 1942. This wave-like pattern was contrasted by periods of severe religious conflict that emerged in a counter-design following the nationalist peaks. Both waves, nationalist and communalist, produced political action, but with conflicting goals and opposing organizations.

A third pattern of modifications arose from the constitutional reforms. The most significant came in 1909 when separate electorates were granted to the Muslims of British India. This method of reserving seats in the regional and central legislative bodies was basic to the concept of religion as a community, that is, a collection of individuals defined through their adherence to a particular set of doctrines. The concept of religion as a community grew from the introduction of a decennial census in 1871. The census defined religious communities, counted them, and examined their characteristics as social and economic units. The granting of separate electorates linked religion, the census reports, political power, and political patronage. The later constitutional reforms of 1919 and 1935 extended the number of religious and social groups who were given a share of political power.[1] In turn, these 'reforms' stimulated and reinforced a new form of political institution.

[1] Kenneth W. Jones, 'Religious identity and the Indian census' in N. Gerald Barrier (ed.), *The Census of British India: New Perspectives* (Delhi, Manohar Publications, 1981), pp. 73–101.

Within three religious communities – the Muslim, Hindu, and Sikh – an organization emerged that attempted to speak for the interests of each. The first of these was the Muslim League founded in 1906 by politicized Muslims, many of whom were active in the Muhammadan Educational Conference established by Sayyid Ahmad Khan (see pp. 63–70). The Muslim League saw itself as the spokesman for all Muslims of British India. By the 1930s, it began to articulate a Muslim nationalism expressed through the concept of Pakistan, a separate Muslim state. A similar line of development among politically conscious Hindus began with the founding of the Punjab Hindu Conference in 1909. In 1915 this annual meeting was reorganized into the Sarvadeshik Hindu Sabha, and in 1921 it was renamed the Akhil Bharat Hindu Mahasabha. By the mid-1930s, the Mahasabha, under the leadership of Vinayal Dhananjay Savarkar, began to expound a Hindu nationalism opposed both to the secular nationalism of the Indian National Congress and the religious nationalism of the Muslim League. A third such organization arose out of the struggles over control of Sikh shrines and *gurdwārās*. On 15 November 1920, 175 Sikhs established the Shiromani Gurdwara Prabandhak Committee. By 1925 they had succeeded in gaining control over all Sikh *gurdwārās* and the revenue they generated. The Shiromani Prabhandhak Committee became a semi-parliamentary body for the Sikhs. Associated with it was the Akali Dal (Army of the Immortals), an activist wing of the same movement. By the 1940s, radicals among the two groups talked of a separate state for Sikhs as they too moved toward religious nationalism. Socio-religious movements continued to develop within this politicized world, but were less visible than in the nineteenth century and were challenged by new secular types of dissent and protest.

As the twentieth century wore on, new ideologies reached India from the West, particularly in the years after World War I. Democratic socialism from England and various types of Marxist–Leninist thought gained adherents among young, educated Indians, and by the 1930s so did the fascism of Italy and Germany. This rapidly expanding pool of ideas and symbols provided a variety of non-religious vehicles for dissent that in the nineteenth century would have turned to one or another form of religion. Within this increasingly complex world we shall examine the fate of five socio-religious movements that extended from the nineteenth into the twentieth century.

The Ramakrishna Math and Mission

In the first decade following the death of Vivekananda (see pp. 41–6), the Ramakrishna movement expanded its activities both in India and the United States. Theoretically it was unified under the presidency of Swami Brahmananda and the Board of Trustees of the Belur Math. In fact, it was rather decentralized and chaotic because it was led by both monks and members of the laity. Supposedly, there was a clear differentiation between the functions of the *maths* and the missions, but in reality *math* and mission engaged in various overlapping activities. Projects were founded often on local initiative without either the approval or supervision of the centre. One example of unplanned growth can be seen in the monastery built at Puri. This began with the acquisition of a small piece of land in 1911. It was used as a retreat for monks, but in 1920–1, due to a local fire, the monks entered into relief work and added a small dispensary. By 1932, when a permanent monastery was built medical relief work had become a permanent function of the *math*.[2] The mission centres suffered from less of a contradiction of purpose, but still evolved in various directions without any overall planning.

The first General Report, issued in 1912, recorded the growth of this movement. It listed seven monasteries, and six mission centres. These were all affiliated with the Belur headquarters and came under the Board of Trustees. In addition there were many experimental programmes, centres, and schools, effectively outside control of the headquarters. Beyond India existed chapters of the Vedanta Society in the United States founded by Vivekananda and led by monks dispatched from Belur. Various societies were opened only to disappear later. The most successful ones were in New York, Boston, Washington, DC and San Francisco, plus a retreat in the Berkshire mountains. By the 1930s, others performed well in Chicago and Los Angeles. The role of the Ramakrishna Math and Missions in the United States was more limited than in India, since there was no dimension of social service. They concentrated on teaching Vedanta doctrine through lectures and publications. Vedanta societies maintained temples, quarters for their monks and retreats for both clergy and laity.

The Indian mixture of religion and social service was exported to a

---

[2] Swami Gambirananda, *A History of the Ramakrishna Math and Mission* (Calcutta, Advaita Ashram, 1957), p. 242.

number of other countries, primarily those with Hindu immigrants. The Ramakrishna movement organized institutions in Malaya (1903), Burma (1910), and Ceylon (1924). By the 1930s they either had, or were about to have, permanent centres in Argentina, England, the Fiji Islands, France, Germany, Singapore, and South Africa. Through the 1920s and 1930s, however, this expanding movement was beset with internal tensions. In 1920, Brahmachari Ganendranath took over the management of the Sister Navedita School in Benares. He soon came into conflict with the officials at Belur by defying their authority. Through the 1920s Brahmachari Ganendranath acquired a following among the monks and laity as a struggle developed between his faction and the Board of Trustees over who had legal rights to the property and institutions. It was partially settled in 1929 when Belur officials called upon the police for help. The Brahmachari and a number of his disciples then left the Ramakrishna order. Next tensions shifted to the South where Swami Nirmalanda claimed that the Belur Math had no legal authority over *maths* and missions in the South. This controversy was finally brought to an end when the courts ruled in a civil suit that the Bangalore centre and all other property in the South were legally in the hands of the Belur group. Swami Nirmalanda and his disciples then left the order.

Another controversy broke out following the death of Swami Brahmananda on 10 April 1922. At a Trustees' meeting held on 2 May 1922, Swami Shivananda was chosen as president. He was then the oldest member of the organization, a deeply religious man, but not interested in administration. This choice met with disapproval among many of the younger monks. As tensions rose, an extraordinary general meeting of the Ramakrishna Mission was held on 2 June 1925. It in turn decided to call a convention of all members to bring order and, it was hoped, a degree of tranquillity to the movement. The young reformers, led by Swami Bhumananda, demanded that the older monks who held the position of Trustees or officers should resign, including Swami Shivananda, and that henceforth all Trustees would be within the ages of thirty-five to forty-five. They contended that many of the monks were too old to hold power and should turn it over to the next generation.

The convention met from 1–8 April 1926. Over 100 institutions were represented by 350 monks and guests. They passed a number of resolutions in roughly three categories. First, there were declarations of goals for the organization and here educational work received particular emphasis. A second set of resolutions attempted to meet some of the criticisms of the younger monks, by discussing ways of improving communications between officers and members of the movement. The main thrust of this conference, however, was embedded in a series of steps taken to ensure greater central control. New centres would only be opened when approved by the Trustees and were to be inspected annually. All monastic preachers would be properly trained and the heads of each monastery limited to tenures of four to six years. Centres could not be directed by a local, monastic worker. The duties of the two leading centre officials, the chief supervisor and secretary, were to be defined by bye-laws written at the Belur headquarters. These resolutions were not given constitutional sanction, but remained guidelines for greater centralization and professionalization of the movement.

As expansion continued, so did efforts to strengthen the power of the Belur headquarters. Difficulties with Brahmachari Ganendranath continued until the Convention of 1926 and spurred the meeting of 29 March 1929, when the Board of Trustees further amended its regulations and procedures. They limited the total number of members in the Mission to 700. New monks were required to have recommendations from two members of the Governing Board and to declare their allegiance to the movement. All meetings needed a quorum of fifty and had to be announced at least fifteen days in advance. Further, all decisions or resolutions could only be passed with a two-thirds majority. Additional steps were taken in a conference held at Belur in April 1935, and at a monks' conference convened in March 1937. At this latter meeting all monastery rules were standardized. The struggles of the 1920s and 1930s led to a much more uniformly governed movement, one that continued to expand as new institutions and programmes were added.

The report of 1946–7 gives a picture of the Ramakrishna movement just prior to Independence. At that time there were ninety-one permanent centres in India, forty missions, thirty-one monasteries, and twenty combined mission–monastery programmes. In addition, a number of sub-centres existed with a variety of different goals and purposes. Beyond India, the Ramakrishna movement was strongest in the United States with twelve centres; Burma contained two and the others, Argentina, Ceylon, England, the Fiji Islands, France, Mauritius, and the Straits Settlements (Malaya), had one centre each. This collection of religious and service institutions embarked on a variety of relief campaigns, including responses to natural disasters: earthquakes, floods, cyclones, plague, and famines. They also aided refugees and fire victims.

By 1947 the pieces of an acculturative socio-religious movement left by Vivekananda at his death had been fashioned into an effective blending of the Hindu monastic tradition, and contemporary professionalism that managed a wide range of institutions. Vivekananda's concepts of *karma yoga* and self-help generated a combination of religion and social service new to Hinduism while defending many of the rituals and beliefs of orthodoxy. In the process Vivekananda himself became one of the most popular figures in the Hindu world. To many he represented a revived Hinduism that met the challenges of western critics and succeeded against them in their own home territory. The figure of Ramakrishna, as seen through the writings of Swami Vivekananda, attracted young men whose abilities created this system of *maths* and missions that spread throughout South Asia and then to various regions of the world. Theirs was a doctrine of religious piety and social service that is the most dramatic expression of a Hindu social gospel. Other movements added a dimension of social service to their religious activity, but no group made it as central to their doctrines as did the Ramakrishna disciples. Thus this acculturative movement brought to Hinduism organizational skills, concepts of social action, and western science, that gave them an effective role in the colonial milieu and beyond to the West that created that milieu. A more restricted impact can be found in the Radhasoami Satsang of the United Provinces and Punjab.

The Radhasoami Satsang

In the twentieth century the divided Radhasoami Satsangis (see pp. 72–7) became focused around three associations, one in Punjab and two in Agra. The Beas Satsang rested on the foundation laid by Jaimal Singh who in the twelve years before his death on 29 December 1903 had initiated 2,345 individuals.[3] He was succeeded by Baba Sawan Singh Grewal, who remained head of the Beas Satsang until his death in 1948. Grewal was an effective leader on both the level of religious

[3] Om Parkash, 'Origins and growth of the Radha Soami movement in the Punjab under Baba Jaimal Singhji Maharaj, Beas, (1884–1903)', *Punjab History Conference: 12th Proceedings* (1978), 227–8.

thought and of practical daily life. As with Jaimal Singh, he served in the military, specifically as a senior engineer in the Military Engineering Service. Grewal too attracted former soldiers to the movement and during his career initiated 124,000 devotees into the Satsang. Under his guidance, the *āshram* on the Beas was transformed into a modern town called 'Dera Baba Jaimal Singh'. He designed many of its buildings, including the *satsang ghar*, a community meeting house. Dera Beas became the organizational headquarters for the Beas Radhasoamis. Outside this town the Satsang held considerable agricultural land used to assist in maintaining their community.[4]

The teachings of the Beas Satsang were based on the belief that Shiv Dayal passed gnostic knowledge to his disciple, Jaimal Singh.[5] There were, however, few theological differences between the doctrines of the Beas group and those taught by the two other Radhasoami branches. The Beas Satsangis were given five sacred names upon initiation instead of the single name used by the Agra societies. The Beas vision of Shiv Dayal was somewhat more limited, for they saw him as one of a long line of religious saints, while the Agra branches claimed that Shiv Dayal was a *paramātmā satguru* (supreme saint), unique in human history. Personality and devotion to a particular *guru* accounted for this division within the Radhasoami movement, as it would in another schism.

A major crisis evolved following the death of Brahm Shankar Misra in 1907, since there was no immediate successor to him in the Soamji Bagh line of *gurus*. Brahm Shankar had named his sister, Buaji Saheba, as the next in line; however, since she was a *pardah nīshīn* woman (one who followed the institution of female seclusion), her effective leadership was limited to an inner circle of spiritually advanced disciples.[6] During this period two new contenders for leadership emerged; one was Sri Kamta Prasad Sinha, later known as Sarkar Sahib. He gathered a group of disciples who met together at his Satsang held in Ghazipur. Tensions developed between the Ghazipur Satsang and the Central Administrative Council. On 26 March 1910, Kamta Prasad declared his

---

[4] Mark Jurgensmeyer, 'The Radhasoami revival of the Sant tradition', an unpublished manuscript, pp. 4–5. Also see Jurgensmeyer, *Religion as Social Vision: The Movement Against Untouchability in 20th-Century Punjab* (Berkeley, University of California Press, 1982), pp. 211–12.

[5] Philip M. Ashby, *Modern Trends in Hinduism* (New York, Columbia University Press, 1974), p. 77.

[6] S. D. Maheshwari, *Radhasoami Faith, History and Tenets* (Agra, Radhasoami Satsang, 1954), p. 67.

Satsang independent of the Council.[7] He remained a contestant for leadership of the Radhasoami movement along with Madhava Prasad Sahib, later known as Babuji Maharaj. Madhava Prasad was employed as chief superintendent in the Accountant-General's office at Allahabad. He was an associate of Brahm Shankar and a long-time devotee of the Radhasoami movement. He often visited Agra and assisted Buaji Saheba in her efforts to administer the Radhasoami organization. Through these efforts he won considerable support among the Satsangis. In 1913 the stalemate broke. First Buaji Saheba died on 21 May, and then in December, Sri Kamta Prasad Sinha passed away. The result of these deaths was not a reunion of the Radhasoamis, but an immediate crisis among the Ghazipur Satsang. They had shifted their headquarters to the town of Morar and there a struggle erupted between Sri Anand Swarup, 'Sahibji Maharaj', who became the new head of this faction, and the relatives of the late *guru*, Kamta Prasad Sinha. Anand Swarup moved his Satsang to Ambala and established its permanent headquarters at Dayal Bagh, outside Agra.

While the Ghazipur faction was being transformed into the Dayal Bagh Satsang, Madhava Prasad became the next *guru* of the Soamji Bagh Radhasoamis and took the title of 'Babuji Maharaj'. He held this office until his death in October 1949. The creation of two rival *satsangs*, located next to each other in Agra, led to a lengthy battle of lawsuits, and occasional violence that lasted into the decade of the 1940s. This was primarily a struggle over control of property and access to certain sacred shrines in and around Soamji Bagh. During the years of conflict, Dayal Bagh was transformed into a religious community, the headquarters of an expanding movement and a thriving colony. In 1937, Gursarandas Mehta succeeded to the *guru*ship of the Dayal Bagh Satsang following the death of Anand Swarup. As for Sawan Singh of Beas, this new leader was a trained engineer. His training helped to expand Dayal Bagh into an economically successful community with an emphasis on the development of small industries.[8] By 1947, the Radhasoamis of Dayal Bagh had created a self-contained community with industries, schools, and modern farms, all held collectively by the Satsang.

The central role of the *guru* in this acculturative movement provided flexibility and religious authority, but also schisms from competing religious leaders. The Radhasoamis were unable to create a structure

[7] *Ibid.*, pp. 379–80.   [8] Jurgensmeyer, 'Radhasoami revival', p. 5.

strong enough to retain unity in the movement. Attempts to adopt imported organizational forms only partially succeeded and were repeatedly defeated as one group after another followed its own spiritual master and created new Satsangs. The major subdivisions, however, prospered as they moved along different social and cultural lines. The Beas Satsang drew much of its support from Punjabi Sikhs, while the Dayal Singh wing retained the original base among upper-caste Hindus from the western third of the Gangetic basin. The composition of their membership was not rigid and individuals joined from both the Hindu and Sikh religions. Leadership, however, was more clearly divided between the Sikhs of the Beas Satsang and the Hindu Brahmans of the Dayal and Soami Satsangs. All three wings appealed to English and vernacular literates, who comprised the majority of their members, and all drew upon the religious traditions of Hinduism and Sikhism. Theirs was a successful and inwardly focused religious movement. Both the Dayal Bagh and Beas communities had blended the tradition of the *sants* with contemporary technology and science. The Radhasoamis survived and prospered in the twentieth century by remaining aloof from many of the controversies of that period; a somewhat different path was followed by the Arya Samaj.

The Arya Samaj

The twentieth century began as the Arya Samaj (see pp. 95–103) was demonstrating sustained growth. During the years 1891–1901, the Samaj increased by 131 per cent from 39,952 to 92,419. This expansion took place primarily in two states, the Punjab with 25,000 Aryas, and the United Provinces with 65,268.[9] As the Samaj entered new territories, the need for a central organization became increasingly apparent. After several years of discussion, a subcommittee was selected, at the 1908 anniversary celebration of the Gurukula Kangri, with the task of drafting a set of regulations and a proposed structure for a Sarvadeshik Sabha, an all-India representative association. The Sarvadeshik Arya Pratinidhi Sabha held its first meeting in Delhi on 31 August 1909. Twenty-seven delegates were elected to this body from six provincial Pratinidhi Sabhas. All provincial *sabhās* were represented, save one, the Arya Pradeshik Pratinidhi Sabha of Punjab, the organizational spokes-

[9] Kenneth W. Jones, 'The Arya Samaj in British India, 1875–1947' in Robert D. Baird (ed.), *Religion in Modern India* (Delhi, Manohar Publications, 1981), pp. 27–54. This is the basic source for the Arya Samaj in the twentieth century and if others are used they will be cited.

man for the moderate 'College' Aryas. In spite of their formal separation, the Punjabi moderates cooperated with the Sarvadeshik Sabha on numerous occasions.

The new Sarvadeshik Sabha presided over a steadily expanding movement. The Arya Samaj had already followed the flow of Hindu immigrants abroad. In 1896 the *Satyārth Prakāsh* (see p. 96) was carried to Mauritius by members of the Bengal Infantry. Within the next two decades Arya Samaj branches were established there in what became the first major centre of the Samaj outside British India. The Samaj travelled further west in 1904, when Pandit Purnanandji, an Arya Samaj missionary, visited Nairobi. In the next year Bhai Parmanand, another missionary, reached Durban and then went on an extensive tour of South Africa. Diffusion abroad moved in waves, as the Samaj entered areas settled by Indian immigrants. During the 1920s and 1930s overseas Aryas organized their own representative *sabhās* and affiliated them with the Sarvadeshik Sabha: British East Africa (1922), South Africa (1927), Fiji (1928), Mauritius (1930), and Dutch Guyana (1937). Expansion within India brought additional representative *sabhās* into the central organization. Bihar joined as a separate body in 1930 and in 1935 a provincial *sabhā* was established for the Princely State of Hyderabad.

The decennial census reported continued growth for the Samaj in British India. In 1931, they reached the total of 990,233. By 1947 the Samaj should have had between one and a half to two million members. The *Arya Directory* of 1941 indicated 2,000 Arya Samajes affiliated with the provincial *sabhās*. In the 1940s the educational world of the Samaj stretched as far south as Sholapur in Maharashtra, and Hyderabad in the Deccan. There were 179 schools and ten colleges in India and Burma. These included regular arts schools, industrial training institutions, girls' schools, Sanskrit schools and religious training centres. In addition, the Gurukula Kangri had become the model for an alternative system of education, different from the Dayananda Anglo-Vedic schools and their imitators. A number of Gurukula-style institutions were founded, some affiliated with the Arya Pratinidhi Sabha, Punjab, and others administered locally. In 1921 the original Gurukula became a university, and by the 1940s there were seven major institutions in the Gurukula system. The *Arya Directory* listed a total of thirty-three institutions labelled as 'Gurukulas'.

By 1947 the Arya Samaj had grown into a complex world of associations at the local, provincial and central levels. They maintained numerous institutions – schools, orphanages, student hostels, widows' homes, reading rooms, libraries, publishing houses that issued tracts, newspapers, and journals, missionary societies, and various organizations dedicated to social reform. Clearly the most fundamental task of the Samaj lay in administering and funding these organizations. Institutional maintenance led the Samaj to declare itself as non-political, and to refrain from direct participation in the nationalist campaigns. During the years 1905–10, they were, however, labelled as seditious, particularly the College Aryas, and suspicions remained in the minds of many English officials until Independence, and not without reason.

Many Aryas supported Mahatma Gandhi's first non-cooperation campaign. At its height, in August 1921, the Mopillas of Kerala rose against the British and their Hindu neighbours. The Aryas were shocked and horrified, since the Mopillas not only attacked Hindus and their property, but also conducted forced conversions to Islam. At a meeting of the Arya Pradeshik Pratinidhi Sabha in Lahore it was decided to send assistance to the Hindus of Kerala. The primary aid they provided was the institution of *shuddhi*, used by Arya missionaries to reconvert Hindus to their religion and to readmit them into Hindu society. The Samaj also sent financial aid and assisted in rebuilding damaged Hindu temples. The Mopilla uprising led to the introduction into the South of ideas and tactics developed in the northern areas of acute religious competition.

After the cessation of the non-cooperation campaign in February 1922, north India sank into a morass of religious strife. Within this context the Malkana Rajputs appealed to the All-India Kshatriya Mahasabha, a caste association, to be readmitted into Hindu society. The Kshatriya Mahasabha accepted their proposal at their annual meeting on 31 December 1923. At the same time approximately eighty representatives from Hindu, Jain, and Sikh caste associations agreed to form a new organization, the Bharatiya Hindu Shuddhi Sabha. It had as its goal a reconversion campaign among the Malkanas. The Sabha was headed by two Aryas, Swami Shraddhanand, president, and Lala Hans Raj, vice-president. The Shuddhi Sabha raised funds, supported missionaries, and conducted an extensive campaign among the Malkana. Both wings of the Samaj joined in this programme providing leadership, resources, and manpower. Muslims of north India responded almost immediately with a counter movement that sent missionaries to persuade the Malkanas to remain within Islam. In turn the Arya Samaj was encouraged to further its own programmes of communal defences.

The section of the Hindu community most subject to conversion were untouchables. At the Lahore anniversary celebration of 1922, Bhai Parmanand presented a vigorous condemnation of the caste system, particularly its persistence among members of the Samaj. Shortly afterwards came the founding of the Jat Pat Todak Mandal (the Society for the Abolition of Caste). The Mandal decided to work first among Aryas, since it was necessary to remove caste distinctions within the Samaj in order to facilitate the incorporation of new members brought in through *shuddhi*. Samaj efforts to remove caste distinctions, as well as its earlier attempts to transform untouchables into clean-caste Hindus through *shuddhi*, stimulated a new movement within the Chamars of Punjab.

In 1925 Mangoo Ram, an Arya school teacher who had travelled abroad, became the outspoken leader of the Ad Dharm (original religion) society. The organization sought to establish a separate religious identity among Punjabi untouchables, who, according to Mangoo Ram, comprised their own *qaum* or religiously defined community, neither Muslim, Hindu, nor Sikh. The Ad Dharmis modelled their own organization after the Samaj. Many of the untouchable leaders had been educated at Arya schools and were once adherents of the Samaj. Mangoo Ram called upon his followers to list themselves in the 1931 census as members of a separate religion. In so doing they were withdrawing from the Hindu community and also entering into competition with the Arya Samaj. The Ad Dharm movement lost strength during the 1940s, and in June 1946, Mangoo Ram closed the Jullundur office of the Ad Dharm. The Ad Dharmis reappeared in the 1960s and 1970s, this time in the context of an independent India.[10]

Within an environment of communal conflict and untouchable uplift, a new *samāj* institution began to evolve. Plans were made to celebrate the centenary of Dayananda's birth and a grand conference resulted. It met from 15–21 February 1925, in Mathura, and was attended by representatives of all Arya Samajes. The two wings of the Samaj had cooperated on the Mopilla and Malkana *shuddhi* campaigns and once again they worked together. This meeting offered a new method for assessing the opinions of leading Aryas and expressing

[10] Jurgensmeyer, *Religion as Social Vision*, pp. 35–80.

them in a series of statements, but while this conference articulated various ideas and demands it lacked an organizational structure to transform these suggestions into concrete programmes. The 1925 gathering set a precedent that was followed in 1927, although this next conference was stimulated by a set of different causes.

Religious violence grew bitter in 1926 and 1927. The murder of Swami Shraddhanand at the close of 1926 was followed in early 1927, by riots in the Bareilly area on the occasion of Muharram. Arya Samaj individuals and buildings were attacked with the alleged assistance of the local police. On 24 July 1927, the Sarvadeshik Sabha called for a series of meetings to take place in north India on 7 August 1927. At these assemblies, Hindus, Sikhs, Parsis, and Jains, as well as Aryas, were asked to pass resolutions expressing their anger over the apparent police hostility toward Hindus and the violence that resulted. They were then requested to send copies of these resolutions to all levels of government. In September, a managing committee was appointed to organize the first Arya Mahasammelan (great conference), scheduled for early in November in Delhi. Unlike the centenary conference, this gathering was called specifically to deal with the question of religious violence. The Delhi Mahasammelan became the first of four such conferences held prior to Independence.

The Delhi Mahasammelan followed in organization and function the model of the 1925 centenary celebration. It passed a series of eighteen resolutions, beginning with a tribute to Swami Shraddhanand. The conference then went on to elaborate statements that accused the government of failing to protect the Hindu community, condemned Muslim violence, called for more extensive *shuddhi* campaigns, continued work among the depressed castes, and asked for an end to caste distinctions among all Aryas. These resolutions had a common theme of communal defence and solidarity. Two new institutions were created, the Arya Raksha (Defences) Committee and the Arya Vir Dal (the Aryan Army). Branches of the Vir Dal were founded, funds raised, and volunteers recruited. This militant arm of the Samaj served on a variety of occasions from the *satyāgraha* struggle in Hyderabad to the upheavals of Partition in Punjab.

The Bareilly Mahasammelan of 1931 considered a wide range of issues centring on the need of the community for self-protection. The Arya Vir Dal was praised, and all Aryas urged to support it, to found local branches, and to raise both funds and recruits for the Dal. The main task of the Dal was to protect Aryan culture, assist the oppressed, and provide social service. Educational developments, the system of Arya preachers, and internal social reform among members, drew attention and resolutions. By now the Samaj saw *satyāgraha* as an important tool for itself. The Mahasammelan also turned its attention to restrictions on various Arya Samaj activities in the major Muslim states, specifically Hyderabad, Bhopal, Bahawalpur, and Rampur. This last concern grew rapidly during the 1930s, and finally culminated in the Arya Samaj's first *satyāgraha* campaign. Unlike the Delhi and Bareilly Mahasammelans, the third one was focused on the fifty-year anniversary of Swami Dayananda's death, planned for 14–20 October 1933, and held in Ajmer. The lack of a major overriding problem behind this conference meant that resolutions, nine in all, tended to be relatively general, covering major themes of the movement. Meanwhile religious conflict in the North had abated somewhat and Arya Samaj attention began to be increasingly focused on the Muslim-dominated state of Hyderabad.

The Arya Samaj had been in the Hyderabad state since the nineteenth century, but only in the late 1920s and early 1930s did the Samaj begin an active expansion of its role. In response the Nizam of Hyderabad's government grew steadily more suspicious of the Samaj. Both sides distrusted each other and saw the other as motivated primarily by religious fanaticism. A struggle between the two proved inevitable. The Samajists started a *satyāgraha* campaign with the state in October 1938, but the formal Arya Samaj *satyāgraha* did not begin until 31 January 1939. With the backing of the Sarvadeshik Sabha other Arya groups, such as the Arya Vir Dal, joined this campaign as did students from the Gurukulas and Arya leaders throughout British India. The Hindu Mahasabha also sent parties of its members to perform *satyāgraha*. This struggle ended when the Nizam's government announced a set of political reforms on 17 July 1939. By this time approximately 8,000 Hindus had been jailed. On 17 August all political prisoners were released and the *satyāgraha* campaign was discontinued. This marked the first successful *satyāgraha* campaign for the Arya Samaj and the Hindu Mahasabha. Only in areas of communal conflict did the Arya Samaj find an acceptance of their ideology and techniques below the Vindhya mountains. In the rest of south India barriers of language and culture made it extremely difficult for the Samaj to gain adherents.

After the Hyderabad *satyāgraha*, the Arya Samaj again became involved in Hindu–Muslim conflicts in the North. As in the Muslim Princely States, tensions developed between Muslim-dominated governments and the Arya Samaj. In Sind, the Hindus were a small minority located primarily in the cities and towns. By 1943 the Sind provincial government found itself under pressure by various Islamic groups to ban the *Satyārth Prakāsh* of Swami Dayananda Saraswati. Muslims objected to chapter fourteen in which Dayananda attacked Islam. In 1946, after months of indecision the Sind government restored an earlier, unenforced ban.

The Aryas responded with a *satyāgraha* campaign on 14 January 1947, and it was over by 20 January. The Sind government simply ignored the *satyāgrahīs* and refused to arrest them even when they publicly defied the ban. The Aryas interpreted this as a capitulation by the Sind government and so terminated their campaign as another 'victory' in the struggle to protect their rights. Following the Sind campaign, the Arya Samaj was soon engulfed by the Partition and Independence. The Samaj was driven from the newly created state of Pakistan and, in the aftermath, it went through a period of re-establishing lost institutions and reorganizing itself.

An aggressive acculturative movement, the Arya Samaj expanded from its base in the North-West to as far south as southern Maharashtra, and carried its own form of communal competition to Kerala and Hyderabad. Nonetheless, the Samaj failed to strike deep roots in the territory below the Vindhya mountains. With the twentieth century, it spread across the seas following the path of Indian emigration. The Samaj institutions carried by them included social programmes of education, untouchable uplift, orphanages, as well as a network of temples, reading rooms and meeting halls, all supported by an elaborate system of fundraising. Samaj publications aided both missionary work and the devotion of its adherents. The Arya Samaj was not, however, primarily focused on social service, but on the propagation of their own religious truth and its defence against all who did not accept it. The addition to Hinduism of a conversion ritual backed by paid missionaries propelled the Samaj into religious conflict. In the twentieth century Aryas continued to oppose Christian missionaries and the proponents of Islam. In the latter case Samaj efforts paralleled the rising clash between Hindu and secular nationalism with those who demanded a political expression of Muslims' religious consciousness.

The aggressive defence of Aryan doctrine also brought them under suspicion of the British-Indian government and to near clashes with that power. In independent India the Arya Samaj prospered; it also entered into new religious struggles, this time with the Sikh community. For the Ahmadiyahs, Independence meant a sharply different fate than its old opponents in the Arya Samaj.

The Ahmadiyahs

The fourteen years from 1900 until the outbreak of World War I were marked by a series of important developments within the Ahmadiyah movement (see pp. 115–19). The century began with new leaders gaining prominence around the central figure of an aging Mirza Ghulam Ahmad. Two young Ahmadis, Muhammad 'Ali and Khawaja Kamal ud-Din, founded and edited the *Review of Religions* published simultaneously in Urdu and English.[11] Both men would later play a role in the development of a separate Ahmadiyah branch in Lahore. Mirza Ghulam apparently was aware of a contest for leadership that might arise upon his death. In 1906 he organized the Sadr Anjuman-i-Ahmadiyah (Central Ahmadiyah Association), to serve as an executive body until his death when it would choose his successor. Mawlawi Nur ud-Din was appointed president of the new council and through this office became the leading figure in an inner circle of Ahmadis.[12]

Mirza Ghulam Ahmad died on 26 May 1908. He was replaced by Nur ud-Din, who became Khalifah Masih I. He retained the office of president of the Sadr Anjuman as well. Quarrels arose over this dual role and confusion as to the powers of each officer. Khawaja Kamal ud-Din claimed that supremacy lay with the Sadr Anjuman, while others maintained that it rested with the Khalifah. Debates over this issue and challenges to the leadership of Nur ud-Din led him to resign from the Sadr Anjuman in 1910. Mirza Ghulam's son, Mahmud Ahmad, replaced him, but the internal tensions did not disappear. The situation was further complicated in November 1911 when Nur ud-Din was injured by a fall from his horse.[13] He continued as Khalifah,

---

[11] Spencer Lavan, *The Ahmadiyah Movement, A History and Perspective* (Delhi, Manohar Book Service, 1974), p. 96.

[12] *Ibid.*, pp. 97, 99; Muhammad Zafarulla Khan, *Ahmadiyyat, The Renaissance of Islam* (London, Tabshir Publications, 1978), p. 195.

[13] Khan, *Ahmadiyyat*, pp. 195–202.

but physically weakened was even less effective than he had been before this accident. Once more the issue of a new leader surfaced. Mahmud Ahmad appeared the most logical choice and discussion between the Qadiyani Ahmadiyahs and a new faction formed at Lahore seemed to agree, but Nur ud-Din did not die so that the question remained unanswered.[14] During this period of uncertainty the Ahmadiyahs took an important step. In April 1911, Mahmud Ahmad published an article in which he declared that all Muslims outside their movement should be considered kāfirs, that is, heathens beyond the borders of Islam. This statement led to intense friction between the Ahmadis and various Islamic leaders.[15]

By 1913 the Lahore Ahmadis led by Muhammad 'Ali and Khawaja Kamal ud-Din began to compete openly with the Qadiyanis. On 19 June 1913 the first issue of the paper, al-Fazl (The Grace of God), was published in Qadiyan. On 10 July, its rival, Paighām-i-Sulh (Message of Peace), was issued in Lahore.[16] Tracts appeared criticizing the leadership of Mahmud Ahmad as the Lahoris articulated their own interpretation of Mirza Ghulam Ahmad and his teachings. The Ahmadis of Lahore considered Mirza Ghulam as a mujaddid, a renewer of Islam rather than a prophet. They stressed unity of all Muslims and even criticized the government for its handling of the Kanpur mosque controversy of 1913. The Qadiyanis stayed with their interpretation of the Mirza as a nabī (prophet), and continued to maintain their loyalty to the British government.[17]

The final split came after the death of Nur ud-Din on 13 March 1914. Mahmud Ahmad was chosen to become Khalifah Masih II and in response Maulawi Muhammad 'Ali, who had been in Qadiyan, left permanently for Lahore. The movement divided into two centres, as the Lahoris held reformist doctrines that led them back in the direction of the broader Islamic community. They turned their attention to missionary work, inspired by Khawaja Kamal ud-Din's trip to England in 1912–13. In 1914 they founded the Ahmadiyah Anjuman Isha-'at-i-Islam (Ahmadiyah Association for the Propagation of Islam) as the vehicle for proselytism abroad.[18]

Mahmud Ahmad, the new Khalifah Masih, solidified his hold over the Ahmadis loyal to him. At a meeting held on 12 April 1914, a

---

[14] Lavan, Ahmadiyah Movement, p. 106.   [15] Ibid., p. 176.
[16] Khan, Ahmadiyyat, p. 209.   [17] Lavan, Ahmadiyah Movement, pp. 57, 122–3.
[18] Khan, Ahmadiyyat, p. 228.

resolution was passed that gave all power within the organization to the Khalifah who stood supreme in relation to the Sadr Anjuman.[19] In 1915 he established the Anjuman-i-Taraqqi-Islam (the Committee for the Propagation of Islam) in which he outlined a plan of action whose goals were to: (1) found primary schools in the Punjab; (2) establish a training college for Muslim missionaries and (3) translate the Qur'an with explanatory notes in Urdu and English. In addition they expected to publish tracts and perform social service among the criminal tribes of the province.[20] In May of the same year, they published the *Conditions of Bai'at*, a basic creed for the Ahmadiyah. In it the lines dividing Ahmadis from other Muslims were clearly drawn: Ahmadis were to pray only when led by an Ahmadi *imām* and, if none was available, they should pray alone; they were forbidden to marry their daughters to non-Ahmadis or to attend a non-Ahmadi funeral. This statement of Ahmadi separateness created another wave of struggles between them and other Muslims. Persecution of Ahmadis by Muslims continued from 1916 onwards. In 1917 conflict with the Ahl-i-Hadith erupted once again and lasted until the communal strife of the 1920s reversed Ahmadi policy toward the Islamic community.[21] The shift towards a pro-Islamic stance was paralleled with a growing willingness to criticize the British-Indian government.

This new Ahmadiyah orientation was clearly demonstrated in the early 1930s. A series of riots broke out in 1930 as Kashmiri Muslims came into open conflict with the Hindu Maharaja and his government. Muhammad Ahmad supported the Kashmiri Muslims. His views were articulated in several articles that appeared in the April, June, and July issues of *al-Fazl*. As tensions in Kashmir continued, an All-India Kashmir Committee was formed with Muhammad Ahmad as its president. This shift of Ahmadi policy was challenged by the Majlis-i-Ahrar-i-Islam, an organization of Muslims who were allied with the Indian National Congress. During the years 1934–6, a bitter struggle ensued between the Ahmadiyahs and the Ahrars, one which finally forced the Ahmadis to withdraw from the political clash in Kashmir. With the failure of this political venture, they returned once again to missionary activities and to further restructuring of the community.[22]

In three addresses, delivered on 23, 30 November and 7 December

---

[19] Lavan, *Ahmadiyah Movement*, pp. 112–3.   [20] *Ibid.*, p. 113.
[21] *Ibid.*, pp. 113–14, 125.   [22] *Ibid.*, pp. 145–82; Khan, *Ahmadiyyat*, pp. 159–275.

1934, Mahmud Ahmad introduced a programme called *Tahrīk-i-Jadīd* (New Scheme). He listed nineteen rules for living a simple, austere and moral life. A wide variety of topics were covered on such subjects as food, dress, and housing. Mahmud Ahmad prohibited his followers from attending the cinema, theatre, circuses, and most places of amusement. Instead he extolled manual labour and requested volunteers for service and missionary work. This initial statement of nineteen rules was expanded to twenty-four. Also the voluntary aspect of the programme was changed to a compulsory demand. Much of the manpower and financial resources generated by the *Tahrīk-i-Jadīd* went to aid Ahmadi missionary programmes, as this Punjabi movement became truly international. By 1970, the Ahmadiyahs had constructed 352 mosques outside South Asia. The distribution was as follows:

West Africa	235	Europe	5
Far East	72	United States	4
East Africa	24	England	2
Indian Ocean	8	Israel	1
		South America	1

Four major centres were Ghana (166 mosques), Sierra Leone (43), Nigeria (22), and Indonesia (70).[23] The Ahmadis also maintained 135 missions in forty different countries with 143 professional missionaries and thirty-five others who staffed schools and dispensaries. They published nineteen newspapers and staffed seventy-one educational institutions outside South Asia, as well as conducting an active programme of translation. The Ahmadis had published the Qur'an in eleven foreign languages.[24] Qadiyan remained the headquarters of this expanding network of institutions until the partition of British India.

With the creation of India and Pakistan, the Ahmadis resident in India left and resettled in Pakistan. Mahmud Ahmad decided, however, that 313 Ahmadis should stay in Qadiyan to act as caretakers of the shrines and sacred places of that town. This group survived and prospered in India, while on 19 September 1949 a new headquarters was

---

[23] Khan, *Ahmadiyyat*, p. 48.
[24] Bharakat Ahmad Rajeke, *Ahmadiyya Movement in India* (Qadiyan, Mirza Wasim Ahmad, 1968), pp. 54–6.

established in Pakistan at Rabwah.[25] The Ahmadis carried with them all the conflicts and ambiguities of their relationship with other Muslims, as well as their own strengths as a religious movement that opened the way for social mobility to many members of the lower and middle classes. Their position in Pakistan was made ambiguous when, on 7 September 1974, the Ahmadis were declared non-Muslims, even as sixty-three years earlier they had declared all non-Ahmadis *kāfirs*.

This acculturative Muslim movement was beset by struggles for leadership that produced a division over its relation to the broader community of Islam expressed by the organizations centred on Qadiyan and Lahore. The Qadiyanis were more openly opposed to Islamic orthodoxy than the more moderate Lahori faction. After a brief period during the 1930s when they were involved in political conflict, the Qadiyanis turned their energies to proselytism in South Asia and increasingly outside the subcontinent. In this they were highly successful, particularly in Africa and south-east Asia. By 1947 the Ahmadis had built an impressive network of mosques, schools, and organizations that reached throughout the world with the exception of the communist countries. They were not, however, as successful in Pakistan where they clashed with the government and, as a result, lost their recognized status as Muslims. Thus, the Ahmadiyah movement appears to have a more assured future beyond South Asia than within the subcontinent. Swami Narayana Guru's socio-religious movement evolved quite differently as it entered the new century.

Swami Narayana Guru of Kerala

On 15 May 1903, the combined efforts of Swami Narayana (see pp. 179–82), Dr Palpu, and Kumaran Asan led to the founding of the Sri Narayana Dharma Paripala Yogam (the Union for the Protection of the Way of Life of Sri Narayana). This organization was informally founded in 1888, but now it was registered with the government. The Yogam linked socio-religious concerns with socio-political issues. Swami Narayana Guru appealed to the mass of the Izhava community, while Palpu and Asan found greater acceptance among the educated and intellectual elite. In the years after the establishment of the Yogam, Swami Narayana continued his emphasis on religion. In 1904 he opened a new headquarters, the Sivagiri Math at Varkala in southern

---

[25] Khan, *Ahmadiyyat*, pp. 318–22.

Travancore.[26] In 1912, two more temples were consecrated at Sivagiri where Swami Narayana was eventually buried. Gradually the Swami created a network of temples and monasteries. He built another temple at Palghat in 1907, and in 1913 founded an association, the Vijnanodaya Sabha, to manage it. In 1914 he established the monastery at Alwaye, and later added a Sanskrit school. New institutions were also located in Cochin, Malabar, Madras, Kanchi, Madurai, and in Ceylon. Numerous associations appeared dedicated to the dissemination of Swami Narayana's ideals and to various forms of improvement for the Izhavas.[27]

In the early twentieth century Swami Narayana broadened his vision into a general condemnation of Hindu society. He wrote *Jāti Mīmāmsā* (Critique of Caste) that claimed the caste system was wrong and that it should be abolished. He urged his followers 'not to ask another person's caste and not to even think about caste'. He called upon the lower castes to end all barriers to interdining. In the schools and temples he founded, all members of the lower castes were welcome. The Swami also argued that the sacred books of Hinduism should be available to everyone regardless of their status.[28] In order to further demonstrate his determination to end caste discrimination, he hired Pulayas, who were considered untouchable by the Izhavas, as cooks for the monasteries under his control.[29]

The Swami's uncompromising doctrines on caste ran into opposition from within the Izhava community. Still, he persisted using arguments from the sages, Vyasa and Parasara, on the irrelevance of birth and the importance of action. Swami Narayana asserted that 'Caste degrades men and so is not wanted'.[30] His judgment on caste, fused with his interpretation of religion in general, produced the slogan, 'One God, one religion and one caste'. Swami Narayana articulated his ideas in hymns, philosophical works, and short essays. They were written mostly in Malayalam, a few in Sanskrit, and one in Tamil. He drew on a

---

[26] Valiyaveetil T. Samuel, 'One caste, one religion and one God for man: a study of Sree Narayana Guru (1854–1928) of Kerala, India', a doctoral dissertation submitted to Hartford Seminary Foundation (1973), p. 72.

[27] M. S. A. Rao, *Social Movements and Social Transformation, A Study of Two Backward Caste Movements in India* (Delhi, Macmillan Company, 1979), pp. 46–7.

[28] Samuel, 'One caste, one religion, one God', p. 94.

[29] Rao, *Social Movements*, p. 212.

[30] Samuel, 'One caste, one religion, one God', p. 150.

combination of sources to justify and explain his teachings. These included Advaitavedanta, drawn from the *bhakti* saints, Tamil Shaivites, and the Tirukural. He may also have been influenced by Buddhist, Jain and even Christian thought.[31]

In addition Swami Narayana attempted to remove a series of what he considered were 'bad customs'. These included festivals at the time of a girl's marriage, another when a daughter reached puberty, and one when women became pregnant for the first time. He felt these were expensive and unnecessary.[32] Through Swami Narayana's restructuring of religion, his changes in social behaviour and his strong emphasis on education, he wished to create a new Izhava community. He also began to move beyond the limits of a single caste through his religious reinterpretations. During the first two decades of the twentieth century, Kumaran Asan, and Dr Palpu continued their struggle to gain admission for Izhavas into government schools and the ranks of government employees. To this they added a search for political representation and for access to all public roads and public buildings.[33] Pressure from the Izhavas created opposition within the Nayar community that resented what they saw as Izhava pretentiousness. In 1919, under the leadership of a young Izhava, T. K. Madhavan (b. 1886), untouchables and non-Hindus (both Muslim and Christian) demanded *paura sāmatwam* (complete citizenship rights). By 1920, they had achieved a few minor victories, but frustration and expectation far outstripped achievements.

In February 1924, Swami Narayana held a two-day conference of all religions at Alwaye. Representatives from Christianity, Buddhism, Islam, the Brahmo Samaj, and the Arya Samaj attended as the Izhavas turned to a discussion of possible conversion to another religion as one way to escape their untouchable status. Swami Narayana and Madhavan argued against conversion. They were aided by the Vykom *satyāgraha*, since this struggle drew away the attention and enthusiasm of many Izhavas. Mahatma Gandhi also joined in this campaign. At issue here was the use by untouchables of the main village road that passed a local Hindu temple. The Vykom *satyāgraha* campaign was followed by the removal of restrictions in 1928 on use of such roads. With this success, talk of conversion ceased and the Izhavas looked for

---

[31] *Ibid.*, pp. 100, 157, 193.   [32] *Ibid.*, p. 91.   [33] Rao, *Social Movements*, pp. 49, 52.

relief within the boundaries of Hinduism.[34] Under the leadership of Madhavan, the Izhavas were granted access to educational institutions and the reservation of certain government positions.

These victories drew the Yogam into political action as an organization of Izhava advancement. Swami Narayana was disturbed by the emphasis on politics and withdrew from the Yogam. He founded a purely religious organization, the Narayana Dharma Sangha Trust, in January 1928. The Sangha was an order of monks, priests, and lay disciples. In his will, Swami Narayana left all property, 'temples, mutts, schools and factories', to the Trust.[35] After Swami Narayana's death on 20 September 1928, the Sangha and the Yogam entered a lengthy and bitter fight over control of this property. The Yogam retained its earlier developmental pattern, becoming a largely political movement grounded in the Izhava caste. Religion played a declining role, although the question of conversion was once more seriously debated in the mid-1930s, but the issue died as the Izhavas again achieved some of their goals. Afterwards, members of the Yogam were attracted to new secular ideas of socialism and Marxism, in their continuing campaign for equality.[36]

The teachings of Swami Narayana were maintained by the Sangha, which remained an essentially religious organization. It trained monks at the Brahma Vidyalaya at Sivagiri, published literature on the Swami's ideals and republished his writings, managed educational institutions, and officiated at numerous religious rituals. The Sangha also operated medical centres and homes for the destitute. Annual conferences that brought together representatives of all religions were held at Alwaye, which had also become a centre of pilgrimage. The two organizations, the Yogam and Sangha, differed, undoing the political and religious union created in 1903.

A third organization, the Sri Narayana Gurukula, carried on the concept of personal spiritual leadership begun by Swami Narayana. Sri Nataraja Guru, the son of Dr Palpu and a leading disciple of Swami Narayana, founded this organization in 1923. Little was done with it until Nataraja Guru returned from Europe after earning his doctorate in philosophy. He considered himself, as did others, to be Swami Narayana's 'true' successor. Nataraja Guru soon discovered, however,

---

[34] *Ibid.*, pp. 58, 66–7.   [35] Samuel, 'One caste, one religion, one God', p. 140.
[36] Rao, *Social Movements*, pp. 75–6, 225–6.

that both the Yogam and Sangha were firmly in the hands of other leaders unwilling to relinquish their authority. He then turned his attention to the Gurukula, a separate organization with its own temples, *āshrams*, and overseas branches in the United States, Europe, and the Middle East.[37] The three organizations – the Yogam, the Sangha, and the Gurukula – followed different paths in the post-Independence period, each drawing on the career of Swami Narayana Guru.

As it entered the twentieth century, Swami Narayana Guru's movement expanded its institutions to include numerous new temples, monasteries, schools, and a supporting structure to finance and manage them. He also led his followers from efforts to uplift the Izahavas towards a general condemnation of the caste system and to clashes with Hindu orthodoxy defended by the Brahmans and Nayars of Kerala. Following the death of Swami Narayana Guru his followers split in three groups: a political wing, the Yogam, that accepted secular ideas in its search for an end to the discrimination suffered by the Izhavas; a society, the Sangha, that followed the original teachings of Swami Narayana Guru; and the Gurukula that centred on a 'legitimate' successor of Sri Narayana. All three movements were led by educated Izhavas and largely supported by members of that caste, with the exception of the Gurukula that gained a broader following, including foreigners from outside the subcontinent.

THE TWENTIETH CENTURY: A SUMMARY

The Hindu movements that survived and prospered in the new century expanded both within South Asia and beyond, with the result that Hinduism became an international religion for the first time in modern history. This new dimension of Hinduism came through the emigration of Hindus throughout the British Empire and eventually to countries beyond it. Socio-religious movements travelled with these emigrants. Among Hindus, the Arya Samaj demonstrated this type of expansion to its widest extent, while the Swami Narayana Guru society, and the Radhasoami Satsang were more limited in their overseas expansion, at least within the years before Independence. Two socio-religious movements, one Hindu, the Ramakrishna Math and Mission,

[37] *Ibid.*, pp. 97–8, 228.

and the other Islamic, the Ahmadiyahs, expanded both through emigration and the conversion of individuals from outside South Asia. For the Ahmadiyahs this was a successful continuation of Islamic proselytism. For the Ramakrishna monks it marked a new dimension of Hinduism. They and the Aryas grafted an institution of conversion on to the Hindu religion.

The socio-religious movements of the nineteenth century added a dimension of social service to Hinduism that had not been present previously. The Ramakrishna movement had created a permanent system of social service through its monks who practised medicine, taught in schools, and administered a variety of relief measures. For the Ramakrishna monks and nuns, this type of action was the main expression of their religious convictions. Other societies, however, conducted similar types of social service as an adjunct to their overall religious programme. During the twentieth century, religious movements continued to conduct and expand their social service, as new secular organizations entered this field, including the various sections of national, state and local government.

Each of these movements faced difficulties and strains from their growth, and each suffered from schisms as a result. The Aryas came first with the division of the 1890s, and the others followed during the first two decades of the twentieth century. Growth led to tensions within each, as internal debates erupted over the nature of religious authority, the meaning of ideology, the degree of local control that would be permitted, the fields of action to be undertaken, and from personal rivalry between strong leaders. Socio-religious movements also needed to adjust to the emergence of communal conflict and the clash of competing nationalisms.

Socio-religious movements did not openly identify with nationalism, but instead, maintained that they were strictly religious organizations. Any other stance would have placed them in direct conflict with the British government and threatened the destruction of all they had built. The Ramakrishna monks remained largely outside politics as did the Radhasoami Satsangs, but the Arya Samaj found itself increasingly drawn into political action in defence of the Hindu community. Its *shuddhi* campaigns, anti-Muslim *satyāgrahas*, and organizational developments, such as the Arya Vir Dal, placed the Samaj along a path parallel, at times, to the Hindu Mahasabha and, at other times, to the Indian National Congress. The Ahmadiyahs, with their struggles against the Ahrars and Ahl-i-Hadith, and later with the independent state of Pakistan, were drawn not so much into rival nationalisms, but into conflicts within the Islamic community. Politics in the twentieth century was not solely focused on nationalist competition, but encompassed numerous forms of caste, communal, regional, and class struggles. The Swami Narayana Guru movement, for example, was divided between its religious aspect and its concern for untouchable uplift.

By Independence, socio-religious movements inhabited a complex ideological world as secular motifs of nationalism, socialism, communism, and fascism were available to justify social change. Secular ideologies provided new forms of legitimization for dissent, even as religion added new dimensions to its own sphere of action. The overall impact of this change, however, was to weaken the role of religious movements. Once they had provided the only form of legitimization for protest, a situation that was permanently altered. Religious and secular movements competed for the attention of those who dissented from the norms of society. Yet, there also remained a powerful political appeal of religion as a basis for nationalism. South Asia contained a religious state, Sikh nationalists, and a body of Hindus who rejected the secular foundations of independent India. Within this world, socio-religious movements continued to appear and to demand new forms of social behaviour, customs, and belief.

CHAPTER EIGHT

CONCLUSION: RELIGION IN HISTORY

TRANSITIONAL MOVEMENTS WITHIN THE HISTORICAL CONTEXT

Within nearly a century of British rule over the South Asian sub-continent, socio-religious movements reshaped much of the social, cultural, religious, and political life of this area. Three civilizations provided models for movements of dissent and protest that sought to 'purify' and restructure contemporary society. New associations, techniques, and forms of group consciousness came into being during these years as religious change encountered increased politicization and competing nationalism. The historic process of internal dissent and cultural adjustment was dynamic as the traditions of the past flowed into the colonial milieu, and were increasingly altered by that environment. There was no clear point of beginning or end of the transitional movements of pre-British history, as they reached forward into the colonial milieu linking that era with what went before.

Leadership of the transitional movements followed a pattern that extended back for many centuries. Professional religious practitioners, Brahmans, and the 'ulamā accounted for the largest percentage of leaders, but they also came from merchant, peasant, untouchable and tribal segments of society. This diversity of leadership was parallelled by support from differing social groups as was illustrated by the Namdharis, who found their adherents primarily among the non-Jats, and the Nirankaris, whose members were drawn mainly from Sikh Jats. The variation in groups to which these movements appealed also followed well-established paths. Islamic movements, with the 'ulamā as leaders, either attempted to reach all Muslims or focused almost exclusively on the 'ulamā class of the religiously educated. Some movements were concentrated on a specific level of society, such as those of the Christian Nadars or Satnamis; both aimed at Hindu untouchables. Similarly, Satya Mahima Dharma flourished among the lower castes and tribals of Orissa.

All transitional movements advocated some degrees of change and consequently generated discord in one or more areas of life. Often associated with this conflict was a clarifying and hardening of boundaries between religious communities and the defining of sectarian positions within a given religion. All but one of these movements declared their aims as a 'return to past purity'. The Nadars, who converted to Christianity, abandoned Hinduism rather than attempt to restructure it. For them Christianity provided an alternate religion that would, they hoped, enable them to escape from their social classification as untouchables. This movement, however, set one section of the Nadar group against another. It also created conflict between Christians and Hindus.

The three traditions of protest present in South Asia manifested themselves in both transitional and acculturative movements. Among Hindus the power of Brahman priests, the rituals they conducted, idol worship, the limited and subordinate role of women, polytheism, and the caste system were condemned repeatedly as they had been over many centuries. Muslim leaders arose who called for a return to purity and the rejection of erroneous customs and innovations, much as the Khawarijites and the followers of al-Wahhab had done. Sikhs too sought to remove various 'false' customs and forms of worship as shown by the Nirankaris' return to the Sikhism of Guru Nanak or the attempts of the Namdharis to revive the *panth*. Acculturative socio-religious movements in each religious community demanded such changes and, consequently, many elements of their programmes were in no way new or 'modern', nor were they the creation of interaction with Christianity and western civilization. Instead they were contemporary expressions of centuries-old dissent. What was new, however, were different elements of the acculturative movements of the nineteenth century.

ACCULTURATIVE MOVEMENTS WITHIN THE
HISTORICAL CONTEXT

The emergence of acculturative movements within the colonial milieu was both a continuation of socio-religious dissent, and a modification of this tradition. The context was new as South Asians, who came into direct contact with the English, and their version of western civilization, adjusted to the realities of British dominance. Those, who could not ignore these new rulers but who depended on them for their social and economic position, found ways to restructure their own cultural heritage in order to retain a place within that heritage. They could neither ignore the English nor could they join British society and find acceptance within it.

The English brought a new civilization, but one that was itself undergoing rapid and escalating change. English culture contained tensions between older patterns of life and 'new' forms of social, political, and economic expression undergirded by developments in science and technology. Within western thought this new knowledge, and all that accompanied it, was understandable by the concept of 'progress', an idea foreign to South Asia. Members of the educated elite accepted this concept readily as they strove to possess the 'progress' and 'modernity' owned by the British. These movements supplied a way in which 'progress' could be achieved and legitimized. The path to a better future lay in a return to a pure and proper past; to the 'fundamentals' of religion as presented in ancient texts once those texts were properly understood and comprehended. Individuals needed the guidance of inspired men and their disciples, but once the path was given and the signposts erected, then a new and better world could be achieved by turning back to the righteous past.

Science and technology posed few problems for South Asian religious thinkers. If all truth rested in the scriptures or in the teachings of an inspired master, and if science was itself true, then no contradiction could possibly exist. Unlike in the West, science was not perceived as possessing an alternative authority to religion; thus it was simply incorporated into the greater religious truth. It was more difficult to answer the challenges of western superiority and the allied threat of Christian conversion. Military and technological dominance were linked in British imperialist ideology to claims of racial and religious superiority. By the second half of the nineteenth century, Christianity was fused with the Raj and had become an integral part of the imperial English culture.

South Asian religious leaders articulated three different positions in response to Christian insistence that they alone possessed religious truth, and were compelled to convert all non-Christians to that truth. Rammohun Roy argued for an equivalence between Christianity and Hinduism based on the ethical core of each religion. Both were encrusted with superstition, error, and mistaken forms of ritual, but once these were removed, the two religions stood on an equal footing.

Others, such as Ramakrishna, Keshab Chandra Sen, and Swami Vive-kananda, insisted that all religions were true and, like the spokes of a wheel, led by different paths to the same ultimate reality. This doctrine justified remaining in the religion of one's birth and made conversion unnecessary. Both arguments denied the superiority of Christianity. By far the largest group of religious leaders – Muslim, Hindu, Parsi, and Sikh – maintained that their particular brand of religion was superior to Christianity. This they could 'prove' by using their own set of religious beliefs as the normative measure for all religions. The controversies generated by opposing religious groups took new forms and intensity when South Asian religions successfully adopted the technology of printing.

Protestantization

The printing press arrived in South Asia as part of a mature technology and thus did not take centuries to develop, as it had in Europe. The one necessary addition, the casting of type fonts for South Asian languages, was accomplished in the late eighteenth century, along with the first dictionaries and grammars needed to standardize languages for the process of setting them in type. The production of inexpensive printed texts accelerated the translation of scriptures and commentaries into the vernacular languages to make them available to a wider audience than could respond to material written in Sanskrit, Arabic, or Persian. English was also used, but this could only reach a small elite of English literates. The vernaculars offered a wider audience, but still an audience limited to those who were literate. Consequently, education became an increasing necessity driven by a dependence on the printed word. Socio-religious movements, both transitional and acculturative, uti-lized printing and translation. They also produced a stream of didactic and polemical literature that explained the newly translated texts, elab-orated on their ideologies, and defended them from critics within and without their own religious community. Members of these movements learned proper behaviour, customs, and beliefs through oral instruc-tion and, for many, through reading. The availability of a printed text encouraged the creation of creeds that summarized a complex set of teachings, and furnished a basic statement of belief for the disciples of a particular movement.

The patterns of religious authority were modified by printing since texts became available to anyone who was literate, as did the 'right' to speak out on religious issues through inexpensive pamphlets and tracts. Neither Brahmans, Parsi priests, nor the 'ulamā had a monopoly of religious authority. Challenges to these groups had appeared in centuries past, but with printing those who acted in opposition could do so far more effectively. Printing, translation, and literacy combined to create a framework, in many ways parallel to the Protestant Reformation in Europe with its abandonment of classical Latin, its proliferation of translations and religious writings, and its insistence that the devout read scriptures as an essential part of their search for salvation. As in Protestantism, many of the socio-religious movements of South Asia taught that truth lay in the text, and that it was the duty of their adherents to study these writings in order to find within them a key to a proper, moral and spiritual life.

The leaders of acculturative movements lived and worked within the new context of colonial domination, of intrusive western civilization, and of technological change. Several of the founders of these movements showed limited influence from the colonial milieu. Swami Dayananda, Mirza Ghulam Ahmad, and Ramakrishna Paramahansa were not educated in English schools or employed in jobs that brought them into contact with the British elite. However, they were aware of Christian missionary activities and thus of a new historical situation that surrounded them. Those who came to follow such leaders and became, in the process, leaders themselves, were drawn almost exclusively from the English-speaking elite. They were individuals caught between their heritage and British colonial society. The socio-religious movements they led created a cultural and psychological world in which they could find a place for themselves, one that was acceptable to them and one they could defend against the attacks of western critics, both secular and religious. Those who acted to defend their own religion also entered into a struggle with orthodox leaders who found enemies more unacceptable than the Christians. Many members of the pre-British, indigenous elite sided with orthodoxy, and were opposed by new elites among the English literates and also regional vernacular elites. This division into opposing groups was clearly demonstrated by the two Singh Sabhas; the Amritsar society with its establishment leadership, and the more radical Lahore Sabha with its aggressive educated elite drawn from various social strata. Similar divisions appeared in all religious communities.

FORM AND FUNCTION

Along with printing, the Christian missionaries introduced new forms of religious organization and action. Voluntary associations were not new to South Asia in that religious movements had for many centuries drawn individuals to them on the basis of belief rather than birth. The Christians, however, carried with them the concepts and forms of weekly congregational meetings held by structured societies with formal membership and sets of written rules. The British–Indian government also strengthened this type of organization through laws granting legal recognition to associations that registered with it, which, in turn, gave them legal rights to own property and to conduct business. *Sabhās*, *anjumans*, and *samājes* sprang up in all religious communities with officers, constitutions, bye-laws, and annual reports – in short the organizational structure adopted from the British. These societies purchased property, built places of worship, schools, orphanages, widows' homes, reading rooms, homes for aged cows, dispensaries, hospitals, and their own mission stations. They bought printing presses and issued their own newspapers, journals, tracts, and books. These organizations also created impressive financial systems that enabled them to maintain and expand the variety of institutions they founded. They employed sophisticated forms of fundraising, such as triple receipting, publishing lists of donations and regular financial reports. Funds were collected on numerous occasions including gifts on long-established holy days, newly created holidays, at conferences, religious fairs, and festivals. Once money was obtained, organizations placed it in bank accounts and even invested it in government notes or through loans. Imported financial forms contributed to the vigour of these socio-religious movements and to their ability to engage in religious competition as well as social service.

Formal religious societies, patterned on Protestant associations and based on the technology of printing, became an established part of South Asian life and even during times of internal crises, they tended to struggle within the bounds of elections, parliamentary manoeuvres, and all the rituals of British organizational life. Even those movements that retained the authority of a spiritual master adopted many of the elements of imported, organizational and legal procedures. As a result, religion in South Asia began to flow into new forms of expression. The content, however, remained more South Asian than western.

DIFFERING GOALS AND PROGRAMMES

The socio-religious movements of the British period added new dimensions to the existing religions of South Asia. All religions gained a greater degree of social service as movements undertook such tasks as forms of disaster relief, the construction of schools, orphanages, and hospitals. The Ramakrishna Math and Mission, with its system of hospitals and dispensaries, and its extensive relief projects, added to Hinduism a dogma of social service and a successful programme based on that dogma. The Arya Samaj brought to Hinduism not only a system of proselytism with professional missionaries, but a ritual of conversion by which anyone could become a Hindu. Thus their redefined Hinduism could compete openly with conversion religions. The Ahmadiyahs and Radhasoami Satsangis transformed the traditional religious centres into model religious cities at Beas, Agra, and Qadiyan with industrialization and commerce as well as religious teachings.

Socio-religious movements among untouchables, whether transitional or acculturative, followed a pattern that began with attempts to improve the status of a particular caste, went through a period of aggressive attacks on the overall structure of society, and then, having failed to change the world around them, sank back to the more limited goals of caste improvement. The Satnamis demonstrated this ending as a permanent, low-caste, sectarian division of Hinduism. The Sri Narayana Guru movement went through a similar cycle, but then divided into three streams, one a political caste association, another a sectarian society largely among the Izhavas, and the third a religious society centred on one leader with branches in Kerala and abroad. The Nadars demonstrated a more radical pattern by breaking off from Hinduism in favour of conversion to Christianity. In the post-Independence period, the Mahars choose the same strategy when they converted to Buddhism. Untouchable movements by and large failed to change the social system or to alter dramatically the status of their supporters. At the opposite end of the spectrum stood orthodox attempts to defend the status quo.

Orthodox movements attempted to maintain existing religion and drew their support mainly from pre-British elites. They might have called for limited change, and a few adjustments to British culture, but largely acted to protect contemporary religion. They tended to appear in reaction to challenges by religious leaders, who demanded radical change and who directly attacked the content of existent religion, as well as those who were within the religious establishment. Orthodox societies often proved transitory and ineffective, as was demonstrated by the Hindu Dharma Sabha of Bengal or the Sanatana Dharma Sabhas of the Punjab. The Bharat Dharma Mahamandala, by contrast, constructed an effective subcontinental organization that successfully functioned into the post-Independence period. The Barelwi *'ulamā* among Muslims also had a lasting impact. On occasion, societies emerged through specific struggles, such as the Hindu defence Vibuthi Sangam Sabha and the Sadhu Siddhanta Sabha that attempted to meet the challenge of Christian conversion in Tamilnadu. Nevertheless, orthodox defence movements were rarely able to build sustained organizational and institutional structures as effectively as many of the acculturative socio-religious movements with their more radical attempts to reshape religion and society.

All socio-religious movements, transitional, acculturative or orthodox–defensive, were fundamentalist, i.e. they sought a return to what each considered the 'fundamentals' of their religion. This process can be envisioned as one with a series of concentric circles. The outermost circle contains various rituals and customs that, while practised, were not basic to religious belief. The greater degree of radical criticism plunged religious leaders from the outer circles towards the core of belief and practice. Often these were relatively technical issues of modes of prayer, rituals of cleansing, and various types of religious authority based on saints either living or dead. The Muslim movements of return demonstrated this process of searching for fundamentals. The Barelwi *'ulamā* accepted a wide range of rituals and authority figures such as *pīrs* and saints. Others rejected these as erroneous innovations. The Ta'ayunis found them unacceptable, but did not condemn Shi'iahs and their concept of an *imām*. The Tariqah-i-Muhammadiyah, and most of the groups that followed afterwards, rejected elements of popular Islam and debated just what was acceptable. The more radical moved steadily inwards turning away from a greater percent of contemporary Islamic practice. The most extreme, the Ahl-i-Qur'an, maintained that only the sacred Qur'an was valid as a religious authority and all else was to be rejected, thus reaching the core of Islam. Similarly, in Hinduism the Brahmos rejected much of Hinduism and saw the Upanishads as the legitimate source of religious authority. The Aryas went one step further to the Vedas as their ultimate container of religious truth and, in the process, condemned almost the whole of popular Hinduism. Fundamentalism then referred to a process of winnowing down religious authority and practice as group after group defined what was true and used those authorities to justify their doctrines of return to the 'truth'. Within South Asia the function of religions changed, the forms of legitimization were altered, and during this process these religions moved overseas.

BEYOND THE SUBCONTINENT

From the late nineteenth century to the twentieth, there was an increased internationalization of South Asian socio-religious movements. Emigration and the conversion of individuals outside the subcontinent accounted for the extension of South Asian socio-religious movements into the rest of the world. For Islamic groups, such as the Ahmadiyahs, success abroad did not add a new dimension to the parent religion since Islam was already present throughout much of the world. Hinduism, by contrast, was limited by its lack of proselytism and conversion to the subcontinent. The conversion of non-Hindus brought new opportunities and problems to Hinduism, especially when it came to integrating converts into the Hindu social structure. Emigration rather than conversion accounted for the majority of Hindus who resided outside the subcontinent. Theosophy with its blend of European dissent and Hindu orthodoxy added a transitory fusion of the two civilizations, but little in the way of a lasting change to either. The post-Independence period has seen a continuation of this internationalizing of religions as emigration has carried orthodox Hinduism, Islam, and Sikhism abroad, as well as socio-religious movements from all three communities.

COMMUNALISM AND RELIGIOUS NATIONALISM

The British-Indian government exacerbated religious conflict through various actions of its own, although in numerous instances it is doubtful that they had any idea what might result from those actions. The initiation of the decennial census in 1871 set about a process that redefined religion. It became in the minds of the census officials a formally defined group of people with quantified characteristics, the most important of which was their numerical size and rate of growth.

Each census defined, counted, and described the major religious communities, and the 'recognized' socio-religious movements, that is, those important enough to have been listed in the census. To be discussed in the census reports gave an official recognition of a movement's existence and importance; but, above all else, the comparative rates of growth measures whether or not a religion was succeeding or failing.

Administrative and political acts by the government often heightened religious competition and the identification of individuals with a particular set of religious beliefs. For instance, in 1882–3 the Hunter Commission travelled throughout India holding hearings on which language should be used in education. It is open to question whether the British officials cared deeply as to which of the languages were finally used in the schools. For them, this was primarily an administrative problem, but the Commission, by its presence and the question that it was investigating, invited agitation by leaders of various religious communities.

The creation of municipal councils during this same period brought into existence a new arena of religious competition as individuals on these bodies acted as representatives of their respective religious communities, rather than of themselves or of secular interests. It was, however, the constitutional reforms of 1909 that fused, once and for all, religion, the census, and political patronage into a single system. The granting of separate electorates to Muslims necessitated the definition of that religious community and its enumeration, an act that could only be done by the Indian census. The extension of these separate electorates in 1919 and 1935 to religious, social, racial, and various interest groups further tied religion to the political system.

The religious upheavals of the nineteenth century, with their debates, creeds, and various forms of competition, led to a growing sense of belonging to a particular sectarian movement and, beyond that, to membership in a broader religious community. This sense of communal identity grew in intensity and came from a variety of sources as the century progressed. Most fundamentally the desire to find and resurrect a past purity, when conducted in a multi-religious society, meant that, inevitably, the practices and beliefs of other religions were seen as intrusive influences responsible for contemporary decadence and error. Ideologies that gave psychological satisfaction to one movement had to be protected from others, both within and without the community.

Public debates and printed tracts, pamphlets, journals, and books all added fuel to controversies and provided a form of entertainment to those who attended these verbal and literary contests. Proselytism with missionaries, street preachers, and public meetings added further impetus as South Asia entered an era of religious competition greater than any in previous centuries. A form of group identity, communalism, that rested on a primary loyalty to the religiously defined community, became a force within South Asian society. Communalism, a base for religious nationalism, was the product of existing divisions within South Asia, exacerbated and given institutional form through the dynamics of socio-religious movements and British colonial policy.

The years of British domination in South Asia were particularly dynamic and entailed a multiplicity of changes as the existing cultures of the subcontinent interacted with the new, imported culture. This period can only be understood in terms of a continuum of action and change. South Asian civilizations were never static, never without motion in all spheres, and especially in the area of religion for it repeatedly acted as a motive and vehicle for change. The role played by religion can only be comprehended by viewing it in terms of time and place, and in terms of its function within an historical context. The socio-religious movements examined in this study acted as vehicles of protest and dissent that expressed tensions within the pre-British world and within the colonial milieu. Once founded, they evolved along lines of their own dynamics as each movement drew together human energies and, through their ideology, focused them in particular directions. Although expressed in religious terms the motivation behind a movement often contained a variety of sources – social, economic, and cultural. Regardless of the non-religious origins that lay beneath the surface, it was forms of religions that gave concrete reality to these subsurface tensions. Religion then, like society and culture, was in a continual motion, only the speed changed, at times increasing and at times decreasing due to the variations in the situation of a particular time and place, that is, the historical context.

With the fusion of religion and politics, each of the major communities developed their own political organizations that spoke for the religious group and competed with other political bodies. Feeding into this process of the politicization of religion was the intensification of religious identity and loyalty to the religious group. This consciousness rested on a sense of belonging to one body of people and of being different from all others. In it existed a potential for nationalism, that is a political expression of separate identity. Muslim, Hindu, and Sikh communities did generate such religious nationalism. With the coining of the word Pakistan, and the adoption of the Lahore Resolution of 1940 that made a separate Muslim state the goal of the Muslim League, Islamic nationalism matured as did Hindu nationalism in the 1930s with the writing of Bhai Parmananda and Vinayak Dhananjay Sarvarkar. A few Sikhs spoke of a Sikhistan in the period just before Partition, and this has since resurfaced again during the third decade of India's Independence. Politicized religion developed as one dimension of the greater world of religion and involved only a small part of that world, except for times of communal violence.

Within the context of nation states, technological development, urbanization, and a vast variety of changes in many elements of daily life, the tradition of protest and dissent persists. Those who seek to restructure society now do so in terms of religious symbols and authority, as they have done for centuries. Religious dissent has been modified and at times blended with various secular ideas to produce new ideologies of protest. Yet religion in itself remains a powerful vehicle for the mobilization of human resources. It is within this increasingly complex world that the many forms of religious protest, drawn from three different civilizations, will continue to make themselves felt within the South Asian subcontinent.

GLOSSARY OF INDIAN TERMS

āchārya: a Hindu religious preceptor.

Adi Granth: see the Granth Sahib.

Advaitavad: monism, the Hindu belief that all things are made of one thing, namely Brahmā; the ultimate reality and cosmic deity.

Advaitavedanta: end of the Vedas, the doctrine of philosophical monism expounded by the Hindu sage, Shankara (AD 788–820), that has become the basis of orthodox Hinduism in much of South Asia.

anjuman: a society or assembly.

ardas: a Sikh prayer.

ārsha: derived from divinely inspired sages, thus an authoritative Hindu text.

ārya: noble, of descent from the ancient Aryans, associated with the *rishis* and the Vedas.

ashrāf: respectable gentlemen of good birth in Islamic society.

āshram: (1) a Hindu religious retreat; (2) the four stages of Hindu life.

bai'at: initiation as a disciple of a Muslim *pīr* or *shaikh*.

bhairāgī: Hindu recluse, mendicant.

bhakti: devotionalism, with a highly emotional and personal focus on a Hindu deity.

bid'ah: innovations to Islamic doctrine or practice, thus errors or sinful accretions.

bīra: a Sikh congregation.

bīredār: leader of a Sikh congregation.

brahmachārī: a student; a Hindu in the first, the *brahmacharya* stage, of four stages of the Hindu life cycle, a celibate.

Brahman: priestly class, first in the *varna* system.

caste: an endogamous social unit that is ranked hierarchically and associated with a particular occupation or occupations; membership is by birth, for life, and according to an individual's karma; violations of caste customs are punished by a caste council, *panchāyat*; the most severe punishment is outcasting, in which a person is totally expelled from his or her caste.

dakshinā: a financial gift given to a Brahman priest for his support, generally donated by Hindu kings.

dār ul-harb: the house of war, that area of the world ruled by non-Muslims.

dār ul-Islām: the House of Islam, that area of the world ruled by Muslims.

dār ul-'ulūm: schools of advanced training for Islamic scholars and theologians.

Dassam Granth: a collection of writings attributed to Guru Gobind Singh.

dharma: duty in the broadest sense, includes a Hindu's religious, social and occupational obligations as defined by his place in the social system. The term is also used to mean 'religion'.

dharmshālā: free lodging for Hindu pilgrims located at temples and places of pilgrimage.

Divali: the 'Festival of Lights', marks the New Year according to the Hindu Vikrami era, also the return of Lord Rama to his capital of Ayodhiya and his coronation.

dokmas: towers of silence, used by the Parsis for the exposure of the dead.

durbār: royal audience, holding a court, occasionally used as an organizational title.

fara'īz: the obligatory duties of all Muslims.

fatwa (sing.), *fatwā* (pl.): ruling of a *muftī* on Islamic doctrine and law.

fiqh: jurisprudence, Islamic law as interpreted by generations of scholars.

Ganga: the Ganges River, sacred to Hindus.

Gathas: a collection of ancient poems attributed by Parsis to Zoroaster, the founder of Zoroastrianism.

gāyatrī mantra: a sacred verse and short Hindu prayer addressed to the Sun god.

giānī: one possessing knowledge, wisdom, intelligence; a Sikh theologian.

gopī: milkmaid, companion of Lord Krishna.

goshālā: cowshed, a home for cattle, often built by pious Hindus or Hindu organizations.

Granth Sahib: the collected works of the first five Sikh gurus, also referred to as the Adi Granth.

granthī: one who reads the Granth; a Sikh priest.

grihastha: householder, one who has an occupation and family; the second stage of life in the Hindu *āshram* system.

gurbānī: hymns from the Granth Sahib.

gurdwārā: a Sikh centre of worship.

guru: a spiritual preceptor, the title used primarily by Hindus and Sikhs.

gurukula: residential teaching institution conducted by one or more religious masters.

hadīth: the sayings of the Prophet Muhammad validated through chains of evidence.

hajj: annual pilgrimage to Mecca, a duty of all Muslims.

Holi: a spring festival of the Hindus.

hukamnāmā: a Sikh ruling on religious doctrine or practice.

ijmā: practice or doctrine validated by a consensus of the Muslim community.

ijtihād: the concept of individual inquiry and reasoning within Islamic theology, to be conducted only by those who have a religious education and are thus qualified.

imām: (1) religious leaders who possess authority as successors to the Prophet Muhammad, a Shi'ite doctrine; (2) the leader of prayer or of a Muslim community.

in'ām: gift of rent-free land.

jihād: (1) a holy war against non-Muslims; (2) the internal struggle for religious perfection.

kāfir: a heathen, those who do not believe in Islam.

kalām: Muslim theology.

Kali: female deity, one of the wives of Shiva, a goddess of birth, destruction, death, and salvation; an embodiment of *shakti*.

kalimah: the Islamic profession of the faith.

karma: the totality of one's past actions determines the place into which one is born in the Hindu social structure.

karma yoga: the Hindu doctrine of selfless action for the fulfilment of *dharma*.

keshadhāri: a Sikh who has not had his hair cut or shaven, thus a follower of Guru Gobind Singh's concept of Sikhism.

khalifāh: a successor to the Prophet Muhammad as head of the Islamic community.

khalsa: the society of the pure, founded by Guru Gobind Singh.

kirpān: a short sword or dagger worn by orthodox Sikhs who follow Guru Gobind Singh's teachings.

Krishna: a manifestation of Lord Vishnu on earth, one of the most popular deities of Hinduism.

Kshatriya: a warrior class, second in the *varna* system.

lāthī: a wooden stave, the traditional weapon of the peasants.

madhī: the rightly guided one who descends to earth to destroy those who hold erroneous beliefs and to establish a period of religious perfection.

madrassah: a school that prepares *'ulamā*.

mahant: a Sikh who administers the *gurdwārā*.

mahimā: exaltations, greatness, dignity, majesty.

majlis: an assembly.

maktab: a primary school.

mānav: of men, humanity, mankind.

mandala: a circle, zone, territory, subdivision.

mandalī: a circle, party, team, band.

mandap: an assembly hall.

mantra: a verbal formula that possesses sacred power.

masih mau'ūd: Christ returned, messiah.

masjid: a Muslim place of worship.

math: a Hindu monastery.

maulawī: a learned man, a scholar.

muftī: a scholar of Islamic law, of the *sharī'at*.

mujaddid: a renewer of Islamic law who turns Muslims back to the true revelations of God.

mujāhidīn: Islamic warriors fighting for the faith.

muridī: a disciple of either a *pīr* or *shaikh*.

mūrti pūjā: idol worship.

namāz: five daily prayers, a duty of all Muslims.

nechārī: a version of the word 'nature' used as a negative name for the followers of Sayyid Ahmad Khan.

nirguna: without form, attributes or qualities, an epithet of God used by some Hindus and Sikhs.

niyog: an ancient Hindu custom that permitted a widow to bear children.

pālā: a Hindu ascetic, an order of the Swami Narayana Sampradaya.

panchāyat: a council of five, a village court used to judge crimes and disputes, and to give the appropriate punishment.

pandit: a Hindu priest, a learned man.

panditā: female pandit.

panth: the religious path, term primarily used by Sikhs and Hindus, can refer to the Sikh community; a subdivision of the Parsi community.

paramahānsa: the most advanced stage of achievement by Hindu ascetics in search of perfection and liberation from the cycle of rebirth.

pardah: seclusion of women, primarily Muslim, adopted by some non-Muslims.

patrikā: newspaper, journal, magazine.

pīr: the religious preceptor who leads a Sufi order, same as *shaikh*.

pīr-muridī: a disciple-master system used in Islam, mainly by the Sufis.

prabandhak: manager, director, executive.

prachār: preaching.

prarthānā: prayer.

pratinidhi: representative, delegate.

pujārī: a Brahman priest who conducts rituals.

qaum: a tribe, community, people.

qāzī: a judge who administers Islamic law.

qiyās: analogical reasoning and consensus in Islamic law.

Qur'an: the sacred text of Muslims as revealed by God to the Prophet Muhammad.

Ram Navami: the birthday of Lord Rama.

Ras Dhari: a participant in a circle of dance of the *gopīs* that honours Lord Krishna; a custom among many of Krishna's Hindu devotees.

rishi: a divinely inspired Hindu sage.

sabhā: a society or association.

sādhu: a Hindu religious mendicant.

sahajdhārī: name for those Sikhs who did not accept the teachings of Guru Gobind Singh.

sāhib, sāhab: master, lord, a term of respect for males.

samādhi: trance, meditation, a tomb.

samāj: society, association.

sampradāya: community, sect, religious movement.

sanātana dharma: the eternal religion, in the nineteenth century this term came to stand for orthodox Hindus.

sandhya: morning and evening prayers using hymns from the Vedas.

sankyāyoginī: a female Hindu ascetic.

sant: a Hindu saint, one who controls all emotions.

sanyās: (1) the formal stage of renunciation; (2) the last of the four stages of the Hindu life cycle.

sanyāsī: a Hindu who has entered the stage of renunciation, an ascetic.

sanyāsinī: a female Hindu ascetic.

sat: truth, essence, life.

satī: the Hindu custom of burning a widow on the funeral pyre of her husband.

satsang: group, community, fellowship of true believers.

satya: truth, veracity.

satyāgraha: grasping or holding truth, term used by Mahatma Gandhi for his ideology of non-violence.

satyāgrahī: a follower of *satyāgraha*.

sayyid: a descendant of the Prophet Muhammad.

shabad: 'word' in Punjabi, can refer to divine revelation or divine communication.

shabd: 'word' in Hindi, can refer to divine revelation or divine communication.

shaikh: (1) when used by Sufis this is a religious preceptor who leads a Sufi order; (2) used by individuals who claim descent from the Companions of the Prophet Muhammad.

shakti: female power.

shaktism: the worship of female deities.

sharī'at: the law based on Islamic scriptures and religious knowledge.

shāstra: a Hindu religious or secular treatise.

shāstrī: Hindu scholar learned in the Shastras.

Shi'ah: Muslims who believe that religious authority was passed to Muhammad's son-in-law, 'Ali, and then through his descendants; such authority is later held by *imāms*, living religious leaders.

shirk: polytheistic religious beliefs.

shuddhi: a Hindu purification ritual used by the Arya Samaj as a ritual of conversion for Hindus who joined other religions, then as an uplift ceremony for untouchables, and later as a conversion ritual for non-Hindus.

Shudra: peasant class, fourth in the *varna* system.

siddhi: an enlightened religious teacher, primarily Hindu.

silsilah: a chain of authority descending from a Sufi *pīr* or *shaikh*.

Sufi: Islamic mystics who seek God directly.

sunnah: customs and traditions associated with the Prophet Muhammad.

Sunni: followers of *sunnah*, the majority of Muslims who do not accept the passage of authority through 'Ali.

sūtra: manual on the teachings and practices in any one of a wide range of subjects.

tafsīr: commentaries on the Qur'an.

taluqdār: holder of a landed estate.

Tantras: texts of the Tantric cults that worship through magical, esoteric, and mystical rituals many of which use erotic and forbidden practices. They are thus often considered as heterodox Hindu sects.

tarīqah: path, way, a Sufi order headed by a *pīr* or *shaikh*.

tawhīd: monotheism, expresses the unity of God in Islamic thought.

Tulsi beads: a Hindu rosary made of seed from the holy tulsi (basil) plant.

'ulamā: Islamic theologians, learned men.

untouchable: member of a caste whose very presence pollutes, usually because of their occupation.

updeshak: a Hindu preacher or missionary.

'urs: festivals commemorating the death of an Islamic saint.

ustād: master, teacher, preceptor.

Vaishnavism: a major division of Hinduism that centres on Lord Vishnu and deities associated with him, especially his ten manifestations on earth. Two of the most popular of these manifestations are Lord Rama and Lord Krishna.

Vaishnavite: a follower of Vaishnavism.

Vaishya: the merchant class, third in the *varna* system.

varna: an ancient Aryan class system, with four levels: Brahman, Kshatriya, Vaishya and Shudra.

varnāshramadharma: a combination of three words, *varna*, *āshram*, and *dharma*. The entire term expresses the ideal Hindu religious order; in the nineteenth century this word came to stand for orthodox Hinduism.

Ved prachār: preaching the Vedas.

Vedas: most ancient and sacred of the Hindu texts, four collections of hymns, prayers, and magic formulae: the Rig, Sama, Yajur, and Atharva Veda.

vidyārthī: student, learner, scholar.

yoga: religious disciplines for achieving unity of mind and body, for gaining *moksha*.

BIBLIOGRAPHICAL ESSAY

The sources used in this study were diverse and scattered through a variety of forms: monographs, articles in edited volumes, scholarly journals, unpublished manuscripts, dissertations, encyclopaedias, and government documents that included census reports, district gazetteers, and various reports. This diversity grew partly from the attempt to place socio-religious movements in their historic context, and partly from the fragmented nature of scholarly writing on religious subjects. Individuals who write about religion do so from various points of perspective, as scholars of diverse disciplines, as members of particular movements, as casual observers, and ardent missionaries. Consequently, the literature varies in its sophistication, biases, factual reliability, styles of writing, and in technical issues such as the transliterations of non-English words.

Of all the literature utilized here, the one volume that proved the most comprehensive and that entailed the most similar aims to my own was J. N. Farquhar's *Modern Religious Movements in India* (New York, 1919). This study viewed religious movements from a sympathetic Christian perspective that judged all groups in terms of whether or not they appeared to be moving towards English Protestant Christianity, or away from it. Nevertheless, Farquhar's book contains a vast amount of reliable data and has thus stood as the single authoritative source on socio-religious movements since its publication. Material from Farquhar's study was cited in numerous places throughout this volume. Beyond Farquhar, however, exists a vast pool of data. Information on Christian dissent and its accompanying socio-religious movements came from two studies: *Pursuit of the Millennium* by Norman Cohn (Fairlawn, New Jersey, 1957), and Jeffrey B. Russell, *Dissent and Reform in the Early Middle Ages* (Berkeley, 1965). For the background on Islam and its development, two studies provided effective reference: Philip K. Hitti, *The Near East in History: A 5000 Year Story* (Princeton, New Jersey, 1961), and Fazlur Rahman, *Islam*, 2nd edn (Chicago, 1979).

To construct the framework for the two major religions of South Asia – Islam and Hinduism – a number of books furnished an overall view of historical developments. Those dealing with Islam since its arrival in South Asia included Aziz Ahmad, *Studies in Islamic Culture in the Indian Environment* (Oxford, 1964), M. Mujeeb, *The Indian Muslims* (London, 1967), and Ishtiaq H. Qureshi, *The Muslim Community of the Indo-Pakistani Subcontinent* (New York, 1960). Among the studies that focused on the more recent past were Aziz Ahmad, *Islamic Modernism in India and Pakistan, 1857–1964* (London, 1967), M. A. Kharandikar, *Islam in India's Transition to Modernity* (Bombay, 1968), and Tauriq Ahmad Nizami, *Muslim Political Thought and*

Activity in India during the First Half of the 19th Century (Aligarh, 1969). General studies of Hinduism are many, but only two were used here: Thomas J. Hopkins, *The Hindu Religious Tradition* (North Scituate, Massachusetts, 1971), and the collection of translated materials, William Theodore DeBary (ed.), *Sources of Indian Tradition* (New York, 1959). Also useful were three encyclopaedias: James Hastings (ed.), *Encyclopedia of Religions* (New York, 1908–27) – twelve volumes that covered a large number of religions – Benjamin Walker, *The Hindu World, an Encyclopedic Survey of Hinduism* (New York, 1968), and Margaret and James Stutley, *Harper's Dictionary of Hinduism, Its Mythology, Folklore, Philosophy, and History* (San Francisco, 1977). Maureen Patterson aided this project by making available her card files that were later published in *South Asia Civilization: A Bibliographic Synthesis* (Chicago, 1981). Finally, a valuable source was Barron Holland, *Popular Hinduism and Hindu Mythology: An Annotated Bibliography* (Westport, Connecticut, 1979).

In constructing the historical context of the different regions, Anil Seal, *The Emergence of Indian Nationalism: Competition and Collaboration in the Later Nineteenth Century* (Cambridge, 1968) proved valuable. Charles H. Heimsath, *Indian Nationalism and Hindu Social Reform* (Princeton, 1964), also supplied data for more than a single chapter. A variety of government documents including decennial census reports, district gazetteers, and reports on the development of printing and publication, contributed significantly to each chapter. The census report volumes are one of the richest pools of data on socio-religious movements of the late nineteenth and twentiety centuries. They often provided a starting point of research as to a particular movement and also supplied data on the social and cultural environment from which movements emerged.

Much of the material was found in edited collections on a variety of different topics, some religious and others not. The more general collections included: Robert I. Crane and Bradford Spagenberg (eds.), *Language and Society in Modern India* (Columbia, Missouri, 1981), Michael J. Mahar (ed.), *The Untouchables in Contemporary India* (Tucson, 1978), C. H. Philips and Mary Doreen Wainwright (eds.), *Indian Society and the Beginnings of Modernization, c. 1830–1850* (London, 1976), S. G. Malik (ed.), *Dissent, Protest, and Reform in Indian Civilization* (Simla, 1977). Volumes that focused on religion were: Robert D. Baird, *Religion in Modern India* (Delhi, 1981), G. A. Oddie (ed.), *Religion in South Asia* (New Delhi, 1977), S. P. Sen (ed.), *Social and Religious Reform Movements* (Calcutta, 1979), Bardwell Smith (ed.), *Religion and Social Conflict in South Asia* (Leiden, 1979), and his *Hinduism, New Essays in the History of Religions* (Leiden, 1982). Information for specific regions was drawn from studies that either examined the region or specific movements within it.

The discussion of Bengal and the North-East rested on Sufia Ahmad, *Muslim Community in Bengal, 1884–1912* (Dacca, 1974), Salahuddin A. F. Ahmed, *Social Ideas and Social Change in Bengal, 1818–1835* (Leiden, 1965), David Kopf, *British Orientalism and the Bengal Renaissance, The Dynamics of*

Indian Modernization, 1773–1835 (Berkeley, 1969), and Pradip Sinha, *Nineteenth-Century Bengal, Aspects of Social History* (Calcutta, 1965). These studies examined various aspects of Bengal society and the cultural impact of the British as seen from divergent perspectives. For the discussion of the Fara'izi movement there was one main publication, Mu'in-ud-din Ahmad Khan, *History of the Fara'idi Movement in Bengal, 1818–1906* (Karachi, 1965). Other sources helped to complete the picture of this group: Blair B. Kling, *The Blue Mutiny, The Indigo Disturbance of 1859–1862* (Philadelphia, 1966), Kalyan Kumar Sengupta, 'Agrarian disturbances in 19th century rural Bengal' in the *Indian Economic and Social History Review* (June 1971), Rafiuddin Ahmed, 'Islamization in Nineteenth century Bengal' in Gopal Krishna (ed.), *Contributions to South Asian Studies*, no. 1 (Delhi, Oxford University Press, 1979), and Abdus Subhan, 'Social and religious reform movements in the nineteenth century among the Muslims – a Bengali reaction to the Wahhabi movement' in Sen, *Social and Religious Reform Movements*.

The amount of material on each socio-religious movement varied dramatically depending on scholarly production and interest. For the Brahmo Samaj, the scholarly literature included two histories of the movement, Sivanatha Sastri, *History of the Brahmo Samaj* (Calcutta, 1911), vols. 1, 2, and David Kopf, *The Brahmo Samaj and the Shaping of the Modern Indian Mind* (Princeton, 1979). In addition the articles by John Morearty, 'The two-edged word: the treacherousness of symbolic trnsformation: Rammohun Roy, Debendranath, Vivekananda and "the Indian golden age"' in Warren Gunderson (ed.), *Studies on Bengal* (East Lansing, Michigan, 1976), Warren M. Gunderson, 'The fate of religion in Modern India: the cases of Rammohun Ray and Debendranath Tagore' in the same volume, James N. Pankratz, 'Rammohun Roy' in Baird, *Modern Religion*, D. H. Killingley, 'Vedanta and modernity' in Philips and Wainwright, *Indian Society*, and Alalendu Guha, 'Impact of Bengal renaissance on Assam: 1825–1875' in *Indian Economic and Social History Review* (Sept. 1972), supplied a number of interpretations and data.

The section on the Vaishnava revival was constructed from two articles by Alexander Lipski, 'Vijay Krsna Goswami: reformer and traditionalist' in the *Journal of Indian History* (University of Kerala, 1974), and 'Bipanchandra Pal and reform Hinduism' in *History and Politics* (Nov. 1971). For the Ramakrishna Math and Mission a single organizational history by Swami Gambhirananda, *History of the Ramakrishna Math and Mission* (Calcutta, 1957), covered events within this movement, particularly in the post-Vivekananda period. It was also the only extensive source on the organizational aspects of this movement in contrast to the numerous articles that examined Vivekananda as a religious leader. Excerpts of Vivekananda's writings and speeches came from Eknath Ranade (compiler), *Swami Vivekananda's Rousing Call to the Hindu Nation* (Calcutta, 1963). Articles on Vivekananda included Cyrus R. Pangborn, 'The Ramakrishna Math and Mission: a case study of a revitalization movement' in Smith, *Hinduism, New Essays*, Leo Schneiderman, 'Ramakrishna: personality and social factors in the growth of a religious movement' in *Journal for the Scientific Study of Religion* (Washington DC, Spring 1969), and

Prabha Dixit, 'The political and social dimensions of Vivekananda's ideology' in *Indian Economic and Social History Review* (New Delhi, July–Sept. 1975). The literature on Bengali-Hindu movements was far more extensive than the existing sources on the Muslims of this region or on many other regions.

A general background on the Gangetic core came from C. A. Bayly, *The Local Roots of Indian Politics, Allahabad, 1880–1920* (Oxford, 1975), the introduction and first chapter of Paul R. Brass, *Factional Politics in an Indian State, the Congress Party in Uttar Pradesh* (Berkeley, 1965), Francis Robinson, 'Municipal government and Muslim separatism in the United Provinces, 1883 to 1916' in *Modern Asian Studies* pt. 3 (1973), A. A. Powell, 'Muslim reactions to missionary activity in Agra' in Philips and Wainwright, *Indian Society*, Jurgen Lutt, *Hindu Nationalismus in Uttar Prades, 1867–1900* (Stuttgart, 1970), and G. R. Thursby, *Hindu-Muslim Relations in British India, A Study of Controversy, Conflict, and Communal Movements in Northern India* (Leiden, 1975). The literature on Muslim movements in this region included Qeyamuddin Ahmad, *The Wahabi Movement in India* (Calcutta, 1966), Harlan Otto Pearson, 'Islamic reform and revival in nineteenth century India: the Tariqah-i-Muhammadiyah', a doctoral dissertation in History at Duke University (1979), Zia ul-Hasan Faruqi, *The Deoband School and the Demand for Pakistan* (Bombay, 1963), Barbara Daly Metcalf, *Islamic Revival in British India* (Princeton University Press, 1982), and David Lelyveld, *Aligarh's First Generation, Muslim Solidarity in British India* (Princeton, 1978). Metcalf's work was particularly valuable for its extensive discussion of both the creation of the Deoband school and other Islamic socio-religious movements of the same period. Zia ul-Hasan Faruqi's monograph was much more limited in its usefulness.

The sources for information on the Radhasoami Satsang varied significantly in their points of view. For instance, S. D. Maheshwari, *Radhasoami Faith, History and Tenets* (Agra, 1954) was an internal study that saw all events from the perspective of a single faction within the Satsang. More objective in their treatment were Philip A. Ashby, *Modern Trends in Hinduism* (New York, 1974), the unpublished manuscript by Mark Juergensmeyer, 'Radhasoami reality: the logic of a modern faith', and the article by Om Parkash, 'Origins and growth of the Radha Soami movement in the Punjab under Baba Jaimal Singh ji Maharaj, Beas (1884–1903)' in the *Punjab History Conference: 12th Proceedings* (1978). The picture of the Bharat Dharma Mahamandala came primarily from a single source, the unpublished and unfinished Hindi biography of Pandit Din Dayalu Sharma, written by his eldest son, Pandit Hari Har Swarup Sharma, and an annual publication, the *Sri Bharat Mahamandala Directory, 1930*, published in Benares.

The diversity of the sources for the Gangetic core, although extensive, was less than those for Punjab and the North-West, where socio-religious movements among Hindus, Sikhs and Muslims presented an even more complex picture of religious interaction. As with all regional chapters this one began with data drawn from the Census reports, and several overall studies of the region including G. S. Chhabra, *Advanced History of the Punjab* (Ludhiana,

1962), John C. B. Webster, *The Christian Community and Change in 19th Century India* (Delhi, 1976), and the two volumes of Khushwant Singh's *History of the Sikhs* (Princeton, 1966). The prime source for the Nirankari movement was John C. B. Webster, *The Nirankari Sikhs* (Delhi, 1979), and the article by Man Singh Nirankari, 'The Nirankaris' in *Punjab Past and Present* (April 1973). Information on the Namdharis came primarily from Fauja Singh Bajwa, *The Kuka Movement: An Important Phase in Punjab's Role in India's Struggle for Freedom* (Delhi, 1965). Discussion of the Singh Sabhas rested on the introduction in N. Gerald Barrier, *The Sikhs and Their Literature (A Guide to Tracts, Books, and Periodicals, 1849–1919)* (Delhi, 1970), articles by Ganda Singh, Gurdarshan Singh, Harbans Singh, and Teja Singh in a special edition of *Punjab Past and Present* (April 1973), edited by Ganda Singh and titled, 'The Singh Sabha and other socio-religious movements in the Punjab, 1850–1925'.

Literature on the Arya Samaj is fairly extensive. Two books dealt with Swami Dayananda's life: Har Bilas Sarda, *Life of Dayananda Saraswati, World Teacher* (Ajmer, 1946), and the excellent biography by J. T. F. Jordens, *Dayananda Saraswati, His Life and Ideas* (Delhi, 1978). Organizational activities of the Samaj were drawn from Kenneth W. Jones, *Arya Dharm, Hindu Consciousness in 19th Century Punjab* (Berkeley, 1976), his articles, 'The Arya Samaj in British India, 1875–1947' in Baird, *Religion in Modern India*, 'Ham Hindu Nahin: Arya-Sikh relations, 1877–1905', *Journal of Asian Studies* (May 1973), and 'Religious identity and the Indian census' in N. G. Barrier (ed.), *The Census in British India: New Perspectives* (Delhi, 1981). Movements related to or derived in part from the Arya Samaj were discussed in Mark Juergensmeyer, *Religion as Social Vision: The Movement Against Untouchability in 20th-Century Punjab* (Berkeley, 1982), in P. V. Kanal, *Bhagwan Dev Atma* (Lahore, 1942), a history of the Dev Samaj, and in Tulsi Deva, *Shraddha Prakash, Pratham Bhag, Shri Pandit Shraddha Ram Ji Ka Jivan* (Lahore, 1896), the only available biography of the first Hindu orthodox leader in this region.

Sources for the Ahmadiyahs of Punjab were two books, one by an American scholar, Spencer Lavan, *The Ahmadiyah Movement, a History and Perspective* (Delhi, 1974), and a second by a prominent member of the movement, Muhammad Zafarulla Khan, *Ahmadiyyat, The Renaissance of Islam* (London, 1978). Three short tracts also contained valuable data: Barakat Ahmad Rajeke, *Ahmadiyya Movement in India* (Qadiyan, 1968), Muhammad Zafarulla Khan, *The Message of Ahmadiyyat* (Qadiyan, 1970), and Mirza Mahmud Ahmad, *What is Ahmadiyyat?* (Jullundur City, 1963). The literature related to developments in Maharashtra and the Central Belt showed a similar diversity.

A variety of studies aided in constructing the general picture of this region. The historic context was drawn from three books: Ravinder Kumar, *Western India in the Nineteenth Century: A Study in Social History of Maharashtra* (London, 1968), Christine Dobbin, *Urban Leadership in Western India: Politics and Communities in Bombay City, 1840–1885* (London, 1972), and Richard P. Tucker, *Ranade and the Roots of Indian Nationalism* (Bombay, 1977). Tucker's articles, 'Hindu traditionalism and nationalist ideologies in 19th century Maharashtra', *Modern Asian Studies* (July 1976), and 'From Dharmashatra to politics', *Indian Economic and Social History Review* (New Delhi, Sept. 1970) along with Ellen McDonald, 'City-hinterland relations and the development of a regional elite in nineteenth-century Bombay', *Journal of Asian Studies* (Aug. 1974), and Eleanor Zelliot, 'The Maharashtrian intellectual and social change: an historical view' in Yogindra Malik, *South Asian Intellectuals and Social Change* (New Delhi, Heritage Publishers, 1982), as well as an unpublished manuscript by Zelliot, also contributed to the general picture of this region. For data on the early years of the Swami Narayana Sect two articles were particularly relevant: M. J. Mehta, 'The Swami Narayana sect (a case study of Hindu religious sects in modern times)', *Quarterly Review of Historical Studies* (Calcutta, April 1978), and Vijay Singh Chavda, 'Social and religious reform movements in Gujarat in the nineteenth and twentieth centuries' in Sen, *Social and Religious Reform Movements*. This latter article also has information on other groups in Gujarat. A valuable scholarly study on the Swami Narayana sect is Raymond B. Williams, *A New Face of Hinduism: The Swaminarayanan Religion* (Cambridge, 1984). This is particularly useful for individuals interested in the post-Independence expansion of the Swami Narayana movement.

Data on the early years of the Satnamis of Chhattisgarh was derived almost totally from one government publication: A. E. Nelson (ed.), *Central Provinces District Gazetteers, Raipur, 1909, Vol. A., Descriptive*. Information on later developments is available in Lawrence A. Babb, 'The Satnamis – political involvement of a religious movement' in Michael Mahar (ed.), *The Untouchables of Contemporary India* (Tucson, 1972), and his recent volume, *The Divine Hierarchy, Popular Hinduism in Central India* (New York, 1975). The account of the Satya Mahima Dharma was drawn from three sources: K. M. Patra, 'Religious movement in modern Orissa "Satya Mahima Dharma"', *Journal of Indian History* (University of Kerala, April–Aug. 1977), Binayak Misra, 'Alekh religion in Orissa', *Modern Review* (Calcutta, 1931), and a series of articles in Daiyatri Panda (ed.), *Mahima Dharma O Darshana* (Koraput, Orissa, 1972). Data on the little-known Manav Dharma Sabha and the Paramahansa Sabha came almost solely from Vijay Singh Chavda, 'Social and religious reform movements in Gujarat in the nineteenth and twentieth centuries', and J. V. Naik, 'Early anti-caste movement in Western India: the Paramahansa Sabha', *Journal of the Asiatic Society of Bombay* (1974–6). For background information on the Parsis of India as well as on Parsi reform societies two books, Ervad Sheriarji Dadabhai Bharucha, *Zoroastrian Religion and Custom* (Bombay, 1893), and Mary Boyce, *Zoroastrians, Their Religious Beliefs and Practices* (London, 1979), and one MA thesis in Anthropology, Joan L. Erdman, 'Parsi progress and Zoroastrian preservation' (Chicago, 1975), supplied the necessary information. The discussion of the last region, the Dravidian South, was also crafted from diverse sources.

A general historical context was derived from K. A. Nilakanta Shastri, *Development of Religion in South India* (Bombay, 1963), Burton Stein, 'Circulation and the historical geography of Tamil country', *Journal of Asian Studies*

(Nov. 1977), and Susan Bayly, 'Hindu kingship and the origin of community: religion, state, and society in Kerala, 1750–1850', *Modern Asian Studies* (April 1984). For events of the nineteenth and twentieth centuries, three books proved beneficial: R. Suntharalingam, *Politics and Nationalist Awakening in South India* (Tucson, 1974), *History of Higher Education in South India: University of Madras, 1857–1957* (Associated Printers, Madras, 1957), and Eugene F. Irschick, *Politics and Social Conflict in South India: The Non-Brahman Movement and Tamil Separatism, 1916–1929* (Berkeley, 1969). The examination of the Christian Nadars and the question of Christian conversions rested on Robert L. Hargrave, *The Nadars of Tamilnad: The Political Culture of a Community in Change* (Berkeley, 1969), Sundaraj Manickam, *The Social Setting of Christian Conversion in South India, 1820–1947* (Wiesbaden, 1977), and Robert E. Frykenberg, 'The impact of conversion and social reform upon society in south India' in Philips and Wainwright, *Indian Society.*

Information on the Hindu reform movements in the South, that is on the Brahmo Samaj, Veda Samaj and Prarthana Samajes, came from one important article, R. Srinivasan, 'The Brahmo Samaj in Tamilnadu', *Journal of the University of Bombay* (1975–6), plus items from Frank F. Conlon, *A Caste in a Changing World, The Chitrapur Saraswat Brahmans, 1700–1935* (Berkeley, 1977), and Carolyn M. Elliot, 'Decline of a patrimonial regime: the Telengana rebellion in India, 1946–1951', *Journal of Asian Studies* (Nov. 1975). Even more diverse were the works that helped to construct a picture of the development of the Theosophical movement. Two volumes supplied the majority of data, Bruce F. Campbell, *Ancient Wisdom Revived, A History of the Theosophical Movement* (Berkeley, 1980), and Anonymous, *The Theosophical Movement, 1875–1925, A History and Survey* (New York, 1925). Other bits and pieces on the Theosophists came from many of the sources already mentioned in this essay. Finally, the Guru Narayana movement of Kerala was described in Valiyaveetil Thomas Samuel, 'One caste, one religion and one God for man: a study of Sree Narayana Guru (1854–1928) of Kerala, India', a doctoral dissertation submitted to Hartford Seminary Foundation, 1973, M. S. A. Rao, *Social Movements and Social Transformation: A Study of Two Backward Caste Movements in India* (Delhi, 1979), and P. M. Mammen, *Communalism Versus Communism: A Study of the Socio-Religious Communities and Political Parties in Kerala, 1892–1970* (Columbia, Missouri, 1981).

The literature utilized in preparing this study demonstrates the diverse nature of scholarship on the religions of South Asia. No single discipline dominates as the various manifestations of religion and the religious experience have been examined by scholars in history, political science, anthropology, sociology, comparative religion, and the history of religion. Yet many of the sources used here were also drawn from the writings of government officials, adherents to various movements and missionaries of different religions. More often than not individuals wrote within the limits of a particular religion in spite of the fact that each religious movement existed within the context of different and competing religions. The material, therefore, is vast and invites extended scholarly endeavour to create a coherent vision of the past. This volume is only a step in that direction.

234

INDEX

Muhammad Ahmad, 201
Muhammad Husain, Maulawi, 95, 115–17
Muhammad ibn 'Abd al-Wahhab, 8
Muhammad Ishaq, 56
Muhammad Isma'il, 53–5
Muhammad Naimuddin, 24
Muhammad Qasim Nanautawi, 58, 61
Muhammad Shafi, 95
Muhammadan Anglo-Oriental College,
   Aligarh, 67; College Fund Committee,
   68; Educational Conference, 69, 185
Muhammadi, 55, 83
muhtamin, 59
mujaddid, 72, 116, 200
mujāhidīn, 54
Mukand Das, 131
Mulji; see Mul Shankar
Mulla Firoz Madrassah, 148
Mul Rai, see Singh, Darbara Baba
Mul Shankar, 96; see Dayananda Saraswati,
   Swami
Madrassah, 148
Munro, Colonel, 158
Munshi Ram, Lala, 99–102, 113
Murad, Maulana, 19
Murli Dhar, Lala, 112
Mushin al-Din Ahmad, see Dudu Miyan
Muslim League, 184–5
Muslim Literary Society, 64
Muslims, Sunni, 118
Mustafa Khan, 69

nabī, 200
Nadans, 156
Nadars, 156–60, 166, 180, 182, 210–11,
   216; Christian, 157, 159, 210
Nadwah dar ul-'Ulum, 69, 83
Naidu, O. M. Rajavelu, 165
Naidu, Sridharalu, 164–5; death of, 165; in
   Madras, 163; take over of Veda Samaj,
   164
Naidu, Venkataroylu, 163
Nairobi, 193
Namdhari, 107, 109, 211; missionaries, 92;
   movement, 90–4
Naraini Devi, 72
Narasimalu, S. P., 165
Narayana Dharma Sangha Trust, 206
Nasīhat nāmahs, 24
Nationalism, competing, 209–10; Islamic,
   221; secular, 184
Native Bible and Tract Society, 157
Native Education Society, 136
Nava Samhitā, 38
Nava Vidhan, 37–8
Naya Miyan, 21–2

Nazir Husain, Sayyid, 56, 95, 116
nechārīs, 66
New Dispensation, newspaper, 38; see
   Nava Vidhan
Newton, J., Reverend, 106
Nigamagama Mandali Mathura, 81
Nihal Ahmad, Shaikh, 58
Nilakantha Brahmachari, see Pande,
   Ghanashyam
nirānkār, marriage ceremony, 89;
   movement, 87–90; Nirankaris, 87–90, 93,
   211; Nirankari Darbar, 88
nirguna, 13
Nirmalanda, Swami, 187
Niti Prakash Sabha, Ludhiana, 108
Nizam of Hyderabad, 197
Nrisinhacharyaji, 177
Nur ud-Din Ahmad, Mawlawi, 188,
   199–200

Olcott, Henry Steel, Colonel, 168–75,
   177–8
Order of the Star in the East, 176
Oriental Seminary, 28–9
Orientalism, 26–8, 62–3

Pachaiyappa College, 162; School, 162
Pal, Bipan Chandra, 41
Palpu, Dr, 181–2, 203, 205, 206
Panch Khalsa Diwan, 112
Panchāyat Taraqqi Hunūd, 77
Pande, Ghanashyam, 125
Pandiah, Sivasankara, 178
Pandurang, Atmaram, Dr, 141
Pandurang, Dadoba, 139–40
Panicker, Velayudha, 180
Pantalu, Ramakrishna, 178
Paramahansa, Brahmananda, 40
Paramahansa Mandali, 139–41, 144, 151;
   Poona, 140
Paramahansa, Ramakrishna, Swami, 37,
   40–3, 214; see Chatterji, Gadadhar
pardah, 119
Parmananda, Bhai, 193, 221
Parsi Panchayat, 146, 151
Parsis' Reform Society, 147; see Rahnumai
   Mazdayansnan Sabha
Pashupatas, 10
Patna School, 56
Pfander, K. G., 53
Philosophy, Advaitavād, 177
Pillai, Kumanpalli Raman, 180
Pillay, Srinivasa, 163
pīr, 8, 24, 60, 71, 83, 217
pīr-murīdī, 24
Poona, 135–7, 140, 165; Sanskrit College,
   136–7

THE NEW CAMBRIDGE HISTORY OF INDIA

I The Mughals and their contemporaries

*M. N. Pearson, *The Portuguese in India*
*Burton Stein, *Vijayanagara*
*Milo Cleveland Beach, *Mughal and Rajput painting*
*Catherine Asher, *Architecture of Mughal India*
+*John F. Richards, *The Mughal Empire*
*George Michell, *Architecture and art of Southern India*
Richard M. Eaton, *Social history of the Deccan*
Bruce R. Lawrence, *Indian Sufism and the Islamic world*
George Michell and Mark Zebrowski, *Architecture and art of the Deccan Sultanates*

II Indian states and the transition to colonialism

+*C. A. Bayly, *Indian society and the making of the British Empire*
*P. J. Marshall, *Bengal: the British bridgehead: eastern India 1740–1828*
*J. S. Grewal, *The Sikhs of the Punjab*
*Stewart Gordon, *The Marathas, 1600–1818*
Richard B. Barnett, *Muslim successor states*
Om Prakash, *The northern European trading companies and India*
David Washbrook, *South India*

III The Indian Empire and the beginnings of modern society

*Kenneth W. Jones, *Social and religious reform movements in British India*
*Sugata Bose, *Peasant labour and colonial capital: rural Bengal since 1770*
+*B. R. Tomlinson, *The economy of modern India, 1860–1970*
+*Thomas R. Metcalf, *Ideologies of the Raj*
David Arnold, *Science, technology and medicine, c. 1750–1947*
Susan Bayly, *Caste in India*
Gordon Johnson, *Government and politics in India*
David Ludden, *Agriculture in Indian history*
B. N. Ramusack, *The Indian princes and their states*

IV The evolution of contemporary South Asia

+*Paul R. Brass, *The politics of India since Independence: second edition*
*Geraldine Forbes, *Women in modern India*
Raj Chandavarkar, *The urban working classes*
Nita Kumar, *Education and the rise of a new intelligentsia*
Francis Robinson, *Islam in South Asia*
Anil Seal, *The transfer of power and the partition of India*

* Already published
+Available in paperback